"With the exception of George Marsden and Kenneth ... to find someone more knowledgeable about Jonathan Edwards than Douglas Sweeney. In focusing his book on Edwards as minister, Sweeney offers academic and clerical readers a treasure trove of insight and elegant prose. If not Luther's Ninety-Five Theses, the inclusion of seven 'theses' for discussion at the end is a stroke of genius and will certainly enhance the reading experience for church groups of all levels. For anyone interested in getting to know America's greatest theologian in greater detail, this masterful analysis is must-reading."

Harry S. Stout, Jonathan Edwards Professor of American Religious History, Yale University

"Douglas Sweeney has written an admirable 'Jonathan Edwards for Christians.' It is at once authoritative and addressed to the practical concerns of evangelicals in the pews."

George Marsden, author of *Jonathan Edwards: A Life* and *A Short Life of Jonathan Edwards*

"Strangely, it has taken nearly three centuries for us to realize the obvious: that Jonathan Edwards had a lifelong love affair with the Bible. Doug Sweeney has been at the forefront of elucidating Edwards the exegete and the biblical foundations of his theology. In this new work, Sweeney shows the vital, reflective and informed connections between Edwards' Biblicism and his calling as a 'faithful minister of the Word.' Even more, Sweeney points out the extent to which Edwards' more formal theological formulations arose directly out of his local pastoral experience. This study will be a blessing to pastors, preachers and spiritual leaders, who can learn from Edwards' faith, thought and experience."

Dr. Kenneth P. Minkema, executive director, Jonathan Edwards Center, and adjunct assistant professor of American religious history, Yale University

"A lively, intimate portrait of a man many have found distant and intimidating. Douglas Sweeney reveals Jonathan Edwards to be the flesh-and-blood Christian we should have suspected he was, in a way that neither patronizes nor idealizes him. As importantly, we have here for the first time an account of Edwards' life that rightly places the Bible at the center of his intellectual and pastoral genius."

Robert E. Brown, assistant professor, Department of Philosophy and Religion, James Madison University, and author of *Jonathan Edwards and the Bible*

"I love this book! Doug Sweeney not only demonstrates the central role of Scripture in the theology and pastoral ministry of Jonathan Edwards but also provides us with a vibrant portrayal of his life and the many brilliant insights that have rightly contributed to his global reputation. Combining clarity and ease of style with a remarkable breadth of research, Sweeney has given us a treatment of Edwards that may well prove to be the standard against which all future contributions are judged. I highly recommend it!"

Sam Storms, Ph.D., senior pastor, Bridgeway Church, Oklahoma City, Oklahoma

"Doug Sweeney gives us a nourishing and tasty introduction to the real Edwards, and focuses in this brief but substantial volume on Edwards' ministry of the Word. He provides a fascinating entrée to the life and career of Edwards, and then zeroes in on Edwards' multifaceted understanding of Scripture. Sweeney gives us enough detail to stimulate new insights into Edwards, Scripture and its Author. But his writing is not so technical that the general reader would not be abundantly rewarded by perusing this slim but informative and illuminating volume."

Gerald McDermott, professor of religion, Roanoke College, Salem, Virginia

"Doug Sweeney has written a fine introduction to Jonathan Edwards' life and theology. Accessible and accurate, this introduction is a good place to start in trying to understand Edwards as a man, a Christian, a theologian and a pastor."

Mark Dever, senior pastor, Capitol Hill Baptist Church, Washington, D.C.

A Model of Faith and Thought

Jonathan Edwards
AND THE MINISTRY OF THE WORD

Douglas A. Sweeney

IVP Academic

An imprint of InterVarsity Press
Downers Grove, Illinois

InterVarsity Press
P.O. Box 1400, Downers Grove, IL 60515-1426
World Wide Web: www.ivpress.com
E-mail: email@ivpress.com

InterVarsity Press® is the book-publishing division of InterVarsity Christian Fellowship/USA®, a student movement active on campus at hundreds of universities, colleges and schools of nursing in the United States of America, and a member movement of the International Fellowship of Evangelical Students. For information about local and regional activities, write Public Relations Dept., InterVarsity Christian Fellowship/USA, 6400 Schroeder Rd., P.O. Box 7895, Madison, WI 53707-7895, or visit the IVCF website at <www.intervarsity.org>.

All Scripture quotations, unless otherwise indicated, are taken from the Holy Bible, King James Version.

Design: Cindy Kiple

Images: North Wind Picture Archives

ISBN 978-0-8308-3851-6

Printed in the United States of America ∞

 InterVarsity Press is committed to protecting the environment and to the responsible use of natural resources. As a member of Green Press Initiative we use recycled paper whenever possible. To learn more about the Green Press Initiative, visit <www.greenpressinitiative.org>.

Library of Congress Cataloging-in-Publication Data

Sweeney, Douglas A.
Jonathan Edwards and the ministry of the Word: a model of faith and
thought / Douglas A. Sweeney.
     p. cm.
Includes bibliographical references and indexes.
ISBN 978-0-8308-3851-6 (pbk.: alk. paper)
1. Edwards, Jonathan, 1703-1758. I. Title.
BX7260.E3S94 2009
285.8092—dc22

                                                      2009011676

P   21   20   19   18   17   16   15   14   13   12   11   10   9   8   7   6   5   4   3   2

Y   27   26   25   24   23   22   21   20   19   18   17   16   15   14   13   12   11   10   09

To

Terry Breum and Bill Shields,

Ministers of the Word

Contents

TIMETABLE

Landmarks in the History of
Edwards' Development as a Minister[1]

October 5, 1703	Edwards is born in his parents' parsonage in East Windsor, Connecticut.
1709	Edwards begins to study Latin with his father, Timothy Edwards, in preparation for college (Greek and Hebrew would soon follow).
1712	Awakening occurs in East Windsor; Edwards builds a prayer booth.
September 1716	Edwards begins his studies at Yale (then the Connecticut Collegiate School), enrolling in Wethersfield under the tutelage of his cousin Elisha Williams.
May 1720	Edwards completes his bachelor's degree at Yale's (now permanent) New Haven campus.
September 1720	Edwards delivers his class's valedictory address at Yale's commencement, then begins his master's degree.
May/June 1721	Edwards' conversion experience.
August 1722	Edwards begins serving the English Presbyterian congregation in Manhattan.

---

[1]A more comprehensive "Chronology of Edwards' Life and Writings" has been compiled by Kenneth P. Minkema, executive editor of *The Works of Jonathan Edwards* at Yale University, and may be found in *The Princeton Companion to Jonathan Edwards*, ed. Sang Hyun Lee (Princeton: Princeton University Press, 2005), pp. xxiii-xxviii. I have relied on Minkema's work—and that of several other editors of *The Works of Jonathan Edwards*—in this table.

1722	Edwards begins composing his "Resolutions," spiritual "Diary" and "Miscellanies."
September 1723	Edwards delivers his master's thesis (in Latin) on justification by faith alone at Yale's commencement (and receives his master's degree).
November 1723	Edwards accepts a new pastorate at the Congregational Church in Bolton, Connecticut.
January 1724	Edwards begins composing his "Notes on Scripture."
May 1724	Edwards becomes a tutor at Yale.
August 1726	Edwards is called to serve as Solomon Stoddard's assistant in Northampton, Massachusetts.
February 15, 1727	Edwards is ordained.
July 28, 1727	Edwards marries Sarah Pierpont.
February 11, 1729	Stoddard dies, leaving Edwards the sole pastor in Northampton.
October 1730	Edwards begins composing his "Blank Bible."
July 8, 1731	Edwards (re)preaches "God Glorified in the Work of Redemption" in Boston (the sermon was published later that year).
August 1733	Edwards preaches "A Divine and Supernatural Light" in Northampton (the sermon was published in 1734).
December 1734	Revival spreads through the Connecticut River valley.
March 13, 1737	Northampton church gallery (balcony) falls during worship service.
December 25, 1737	New meetinghouse (under construction

	for over a year) dedicated.
1737	Edwards publishes first edition of *A Faithful Narrative*.
July 22, 1739	Abigail Bridgman excommunicated by the Northampton church for habitual drunkenness.
October 17–19, 1740	George Whitefield preaches in Northampton.
July 8, 1741	Edwards (re)preaches "Sinners in the Hands of an Angry God" in Enfield, Connecticut (the sermon was published later that year).
Summer 1741	Height of the Great Awakening in New England.
August 24, 1741	Hannah Pomeroy excommunicated by the Northampton church (for bearing false witness against Sarah Clap).
September 1741	Edwards delivers *Distinguishing Marks of a Work of the Spirit of God* at Yale's commencement (the discourse was published later that year).
Jan./Feb. 1742	Samuel Buell guest preaches in Northampton, and Sarah Edwards undergoes powerful spiritual ecstasies.
March 16, 1742	Northampton church renews its congregational covenant.
1743	Edwards publishes *Some Thoughts Concerning the Present Revival of Religion in New England*.
June 12, 1743	Samuel Danks excommunicated by the Northampton church (for fornication).
Spring 1744	"Bad Book" episode.
1746	Edwards publishes his *Treatise Concerning Religious Affections*.

May 1747	David Brainerd moves into Northampton parsonage.
October 9, 1747	Brainerd dies in Northampton parsonage.
Fall 1747	Edwards begins writing Brainerd's *Life*.
1747	Edwards publishes *An Humble Attempt to Promote Explicit Agreement and Visible Union of God's People in Extraordinary Prayer for the Revival of Religion and the Advancement of Christ's Kingdom on Earth, Pursuant to Scripture Promises and Prophecies Concerning the Last Time*.
February 14, 1748	Jerusha Edwards dies.
August 1748	Elisha Hawley excommunicated by the Northampton church (for fornication).
1749	Edwards publishes *An Account of the Life of the Late Reverend Mr. David Brainerd*.
1749	Edwards publishes *An Humble Inquiry into the Rules of the Word of God, Concerning the Qualifications Requisite to a Compleat Standing and Full Communion in the Visible Christian Church*.
June 22, 1750	Edwards fired by his Northampton congregation.
February 22, 1751	Edwards called to serve the Stockbridge mission.
August 8, 1751	Edwards installed at Stockbridge.
1752	Edwards publishes *Misrepresentations Corrected, and Truth Vindicated*.
February 1754	Edwards wins complete control of the Stockbridge mission after protracted battle with other white residents of the town.
1754	Edwards publishes *The Freedom of the Will*.
September 24, 1757	Aaron Burr (Edwards' son-in-law) dies.

September 29, 1757	Princeton trustees invite Edwards to assume their presidency.
February 16, 1758	Edwards installed as third president of the College of New Jersey (Princeton).
February 23, 1758	Edwards inoculated for smallpox.
March 22, 1758	Edwards dies.
1758	Edwards' treatise on *Original Sin* published posthumously.
1765	Posthumous publication of Edwards' *Two Dissertations: I. Concerning the End for Which God Created the World. II. The Nature of True Virtue.*

Edwards' Family Members[2]

EDWARDS' PARENTS

Rev. Timothy Edwards (1669–1758)

Esther Stoddard Edwards (1672–1770), daughter of Rev. Solomon Stoddard (Northampton, Massachusetts)

EDWARDS' SISTERS

Esther (1695–1766) married Rev. Samuel Hopkins (West Springfield, Massachusetts) in 1727.

Elizabeth (1697–1733) married Jabez Huntington in 1724.

Anne (1699–1790) married John Ellsworth in 1734.

Mary (1701–1776) remained single, caring for her Stoddard

---

[2]I have compiled this information from a multitude of sources. The hardest to find is that on his sisters, but see Kenneth P. Minkema, "Hannah and Her Sisters: Sisterhood, Courtship, and Marriage in the Edwards Family in the Early Eighteenth Century," *New England Historical and Genealogical Register* 146 (January 1992): 35-56. For a complete genealogy of Edwards' family tree, see Elizur Yale Smith, "The Descendants of William Edwards," in *The New York Genealogical and Biographical Record* 71 (1940): 217-24, 323-32, and vol. 72 (1941): 124-25.

grandparents in Northampton and then her parents in East Windsor as they grew old.

Eunice (1705–1788) married Rev. Simon Backus (Newington, Connecticut) in 1729.

Abigail (1707–1764) married Rev. William Metcalf (Lebanon, Connecticut) in 1737.

Jerusha (1710–1729) died as a teenager.

Hannah (1713–1773) married Seth Wetmore in 1746.

Lucy (1715–1736) died as a young adult.

Martha (1718–1794) married Rev. Moses Tuttle (Granville, Massachusetts) in 1746.

Edwards' Wife

Sarah Pierpont Edwards (1710–1758), daughter of Rev. James Pierpont (New Haven, Connecticut)

Edwards' Children

Sarah (1728–1805) married Elihu Parsons in 1750.

Jerusha (1730–1748) died as a teenager.

Esther (1732–1758) married Rev. Aaron Burr in 1752 (a pastor of various churches in Massachusetts and New Jersey who became the second president of the College of New Jersey, later Princeton University, in 1748).

Mary (1734–1807) married Timothy Dwight in 1750 (the two later had a child, also named Timothy Dwight, who served as president of Yale).

Lucy (1736–1786) married the Honorable Jahleel Woodbridge in 1764.

Timothy (1738–1813) became a merchant and a judge in Berkshire County, Massachusetts.

Susannah (1740–1803) married Eleazur Porter in 1761.

Eunice (1743–1822) married Thomas Pollock in 1764.

Jonathan Jr. (1745–1801) became a pastor in Connecticut, a theologian and the president of Union College in Schenectady, New York.

Elizabeth (1747–1762) died as a teenager.

Pierrepont (1750–1826) became a lawyer, a Revolutionary War hero, a politician, a congressman (federal and state) and a judge in New Haven, Connecticut.

EDWARDS' SLAVES

Venus: purchased in Newport, Rhode Island on June 7, 1731 (Edwards' receipt for this purchase has been published in *A Jonathan Edwards Reader*, ed. John E. Smith, Harry S. Stout and Kenneth P. Minkema [New Haven: Yale University Press, 1995], 296-97).

Leah: perhaps the same person as Venus (now given a biblical name); she was baptized in 1736.

Rose and Joab Binney: Edwards performed their wedding in 1751. The couple stayed in Stockbridge after Edwards left for Princeton; Rose joined the Stockbridge church in 1771. Joab died and Rose married another man named Salter. Rev. Stephen West (who succeeded Edwards in Stockbridge) published an essay on Rose's spiritual experiences (without revealing her name) in *The Theological Magazine, or Synopsis of Modern Religious Sentiment on a New Plan* (January–February 1797), 191-95, reprinted as the "Appendix" to Kenneth P. Minkema, "Jonathan Edwards's Defense of Slavery," *Massachusetts Historical Review* 4 (2002): 23-59.

Titus: son of Rose.

Joseph and Sue: sold in 1759.

Map of Edwards' World

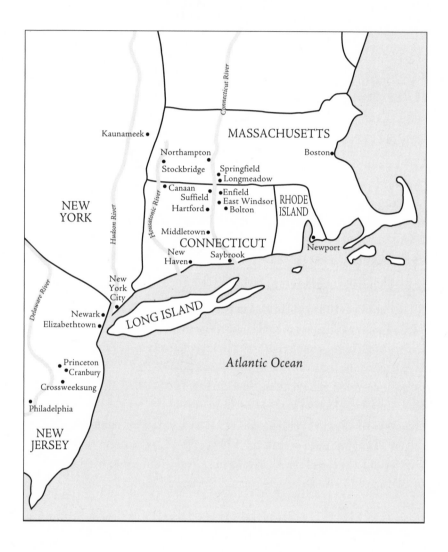

PREFACE

*J*onathan Edwards (1703–1758) is the most influential thinker in all of evangelical history. He worked as a parish pastor, missionary and college teacher. He mentored younger pastors and he published many books. By the time he had died, at the age of fifty-four, he had sparked a new movement of Reformed evangelicals who played a major role in fueling the rise of modern missions, preaching revivals far and wide, and wielding the cutting edge of American theology. Edwards' works are read today on every continent in the world (except Antarctica, of course). He has never gone out of print. Younger Christians, in particular, continue to flock to seminars and conferences on him.

Hundreds of books and articles exist on Jonathan Edwards (not to mention the many doctoral dissertations written about him).[1] He remains one of the best-studied figures in our past. But few have written books on Edwards aimed at fellow Christians, people looking for a state-of-the-art discussion of his life in order to use him as a model of Christian faith, thought and ministry.

This is such a book. I have written it with Christians at the forefront of my mind: pastors, students and everyone else who wants a brief, accessible book, full of essential information and explicitly Christian comment on this most important founder of the evangelical movement.

---

[1]See M. X. Lesser, *Reading Jonathan Edwards: An Annotated Bibliography in Three Parts, 1729–2005* (Grand Rapids: Eerdmans, 2008).

I have tried through most of the chapters to convey the rich story of Edwards' life and varied labors (chapters one, two, four, six and part of chapter seven). But I have also set up this story with a tour of Edwards' world and its profoundly biblical structure that I hope will help my readers imagine Edwards' life more vividly and think more comprehensively about its distance from theirs (the introduction). I have also devoted two chapters to the things that mattered most to Edwards himself as he pursued his ministerial vocation: his study of the Bible (chapter three) and his theological passions (chapter five). My book concludes with reflections on the legacy of Edwards and suggestions about what we can learn from him (chapter seven).

I am an academic specialist on Edwards and his times. But I have worked hard to make these pages clear, concise and compelling. I have had the help of friends who live outside of the academy and challenged me to render Edwards' life in lucid prose. Special thanks in this regard go to the following individuals whose input was invaluable: Pastor Steve Farish, Pastor Brian Farone, Pastor Steve Mathewson, Ben Peays, Lynae Peays, Dr. Greg Scharf (a former pastor, now a teacher), Pastor Greg Strand, Wilma Sweeney, and hundreds of students at Trinity.

I should also thank the churches that put up with my remarks on Edwards' ministry over the years (and thus contributed inadvertently to this volume): St. Mark Lutheran Church, Lindenhurst, Illinois; Moody Church, Chicago, Illinois; Winnetka Bible Church, Winnetka, Illinois; Arlington Heights Evangelical Free Church, Arlington Heights, Illinois; Lancaster Evangelical Free Church, Lancaster, California; Crossroads Church, Grayslake, Illinois; Lakeview Presbyterian Church, Vernon Hills, Illinois; Libertyville Evangelical Free Church, Libertyville, Illinois; New Life Church, Vernon Hills, Illinois; Village Church of Lincolnshire, Lincolnshire, Illinois; St. Paul's Lutheran Church, Waukegan, Illinois; First Church of Christ, Bethlehem, Connecticut; Bethesda Lutheran Church, New Haven, Connecticut; and First Lutheran Church, Nashville, Tennessee.

Hearty thanks go to the following academics and librarians, each of whom made major contributions to this project: Gary Deddo (my editor at InterVarsity Press), Scott Manetsch (who reads everything I write with great discernment), Ken Minkema (the most important Edwards scholar ever), Jackie Pointer (a great librarian-detective here at Trinity), Wolter Rose (a Dutch scholar who loves Edwards and the Bible, although not in that order), and Robert Yarbrough (a frequent partner in crime).

I am grateful to the Beinecke Rare Book and Manuscript Library, Yale University, for granting me its Jonathan Edwards Research Fellowship (2003–2004). I am grateful to the Jonathan Edwards Center, also at Yale, for its continual support of my research.

Last but certainly not least, eternal gratitude is due to Terry Breum and Bill Shields, my pastors at St. Mark Lutheran Church in Lindenhurst, Illinois. They exemplify the best of Edwards' ministerial legacy. I dedicate this book to them with love and appreciation.

INTRODUCTION

The Word in Edwards' World

For the word of God is quick, and powerful, and sharper than any two-edged sword, piercing even to the dividing asunder of soul and spirit, and of the joints and marrow, and is a discerner of the thoughts and intents of the heart.

HEBREWS 4:12[1]

The more I teach Jonathan Edwards to my seminary students, the more I realize it is impossible to duplicate his ministry. Not that I have tried. I have never been so foolish as to think that I could make Edwards clones of the people in my classes, sending them out in periwigs to preach demanding, lengthy sermons, loaded with biblical theology and detailed application, to congregations raised on PowerPoint and praise songs. I must admit, however, that I am so compelled by Edwards' devotion to the reality of the divine, the divinity of the Bible, and the Bible's importance for life, that I have found myself attempting to make it contagious. So many of my students, moreover, have caught the Edwards bug that they feel guilty, all too often, for failing to minister as he did.

Our world is vastly different from Edwards' eighteenth-century New England. Many Americans, at least, still go to church and read

---

[1]All Scripture quotations are taken from the King James Bible (1611), the translation used most often by Edwards himself.

the Bible. The Barna Group reports that 59 percent of the Protestants they asked in 2004 had read the Bible in the past week, while 88 percent of evangelicals surveyed in 2005 had read the Bible during the past several days. The Gallup Poll confirms that Americans take their Bibles seriously. In November 2004, 34 percent of the people whom they asked about its authority said that "the Bible is the actual word of God." Another 48 percent called it "the inspired word of God," while merely 15 percent preferred to characterize the Bible as "an ancient book of fables and legends."[2]

Still, despite our apparent esteem for the Bible's status and authority, few believers living today know as much about its contents as they do about Hollywood movies, popular music or athletics. Even within the United States, whence these survey data derive, most church members lack rudimentary biblical literacy. As anyone who teaches in our churches can attest, few today know the ten commandments (I mean all ten, in proper order), the twelve apostles, the letters of Paul or even the titles of the books included within the biblical canon. A basic grasp of Bible doctrine is also hard to find today. How many Christians do you know who can articulate what Scripture teaches about our Lord's two natures, or the ministry of the Spirit, or the nature of the church? Even first-year seminarians have trouble with these things. Indeed, our lives are so full of busyness, our world so full of distractions, that sustained attention to God and his Word requires a rare sort of countercultural tenacity.[3]

Edwards' world was far from perfect, as will be seen in the chapters that follow. Our own is much more equitable, resourceful, ecumenical. But Edwards dwelled in a preindustrial, "Protestant" civili-

---

[2]See the Barna Group's topical link on "The Bible," viewed March 30, 2006, at http://www .barna.org; and Albert L. Winseman, "Teens' Stance on the Word of God: Protestant, Catholic Teens Disagree About Bible's Origins," posted March 22, 2005, http://poll.gallup.com. Significantly, Winseman notes that in another survey taken at the beginning of 2005, American teens reported even higher views of the Bible's authority.
[3]For more on these realities, see Stephen Prothero, *Religious Literacy: What Every American Needs to Know—and Doesn't* (San Francisco: HarperSanFrancisco, 2007).

zation, one that, on the surface at least, proved more conducive to the ministry of words—and of the Word.

Edwards lived his entire life in small-town, Puritan New England, which had been settled a century before mainly by Christians who were dissatisfied with the progress of the Reformation in England. These so-called Puritan[4] predecessors sought to purify their national church by means of biblical teaching, bold liturgical reforms, as well as an emphasis on genuine conversion. Suffering persecution at home, many fled to the "new world," where they established "Bible commonwealths" to carry out their plan. They hoped to set an attractive example for their loved ones back in Britain that would lead to the purification of the Church of England everywhere. They often spoke of themselves in terms of the Sermon on the Mount (Mt 5–7), as "a city set on a hill," a shining "light" for all to see. And while they failed, ultimately, to win control of the Church of England, their New England colonists developed a host of new congregations and a "New England Way" of life that served to embody, however imperfectly, their religious aspirations.

Let me invite you to travel with me into the thick of Edwards' world, using your mind's eye (and nose and ear) to imagine its major features and their bearing on the ministry of the Word. First of all, some demographics: In the year of Edwards' birth (1703), New England was populated by fewer than 100,000 English subjects. By

---

[4]Roman Catholic critics first labeled these ardent Protestants "Puritans" amid the struggles for control of the English Church in the 1570s. During the 1580s and 1590s, many others adopted the term. Some of the Puritans themselves claimed it as a badge of honor beginning in roughly 1605. On the vagaries of the term and its varied uses in church history, see the pithy summary in David Daniell, *The Bible in English: Its History and Influence* (New Haven: Yale University Press, 2003), pp. xvii-xix. Cf. Patrick Collinson, *The Elizabethan Puritan Movement* (Oxford: Clarendon, 1967), pp. 60-61, who suggests that the term may have been coined during the mid-1560s as the Church of England's ministers debated the wearing of vestments (special liturgical clothes). I employ the term here not to suggest that all Puritans were the same, or easy to spot, but as a convenient way of referring to Edwards' nearest spiritual forebears: those who worked to purify the Church of England from within by calling its members to personal faith based on a detailed knowledge of Scripture, to genuine conversion by the power of the Spirit, and to rid their Church's liturgy of most of its Catholic remnants—thereby paving the way for modern evangelicalism.

the time of his death (1758) this number had surged, but the region still boasted only 450,000. At the height of Edwards' ministry, or the time of the Great Awakening (c. 1740), America's three largest cities—Boston, New York and Philadelphia—each contained about 10,000-15,000 inhabitants; England's North American colonies held over 900,000 people; Edwards' Northampton had about 1,400 residents. To put these numbers in perspective, it is useful to remember that there are more people today living in Naperville, Illinois, than there were in all New England at the time of Edwards' birth. The combined populations of Boston, New York and Philadelphia during the height of the Great Awakening could fit with ease inside our largest sporting arenas. And the total population of British America at the time was less than that of San Jose, California, today.

Perhaps the first thing you would notice as you entered one of the small towns that structured Edwards' world is the quietness of the daily lives of its residents. To be sure, you would hear noises—people talking and working with tools, the rhythmic clopping of horses' hooves, the lowing of cows and bleating of sheep. But you would not hear any engines, whether of cars or heavy machinery. You might well hear a town crier making announcements to the community with the help of a hand bell, a conch shell or even a drum. But you would not hear any planes, trains, automobiles or trucks. Nor would you hear the steady humming, beeping, honking and general wailing of industrial equipment. In fact, the loudest sound to be heard in many early New England towns was the ringing, by the sexton, of the church bell.[5]

As you traversed the town green, you would notice the smell of dung. (In early New England these spaces were often used for grazing.) But once you became inured to it, and learned to watch your step, your gaze would likely be fixed on the most important building on the green, the local church, or "meeting house," as the Puri-

---

[5]For more on the sound of Edwards' world, see Richard Cullen Rath, *How Early America Sounded* (Ithaca, N.Y.: Cornell University Press, 2003).

tans usually called it. You would not find it impressive. England's neogothic churches were aesthetically far more pleasing. From cavernous, cross-shaped naves, they attracted attention heavenward with their massive, vaulted ceilings, then to the altar, richly adorned and set in the center of the chancel. Worshipers walked forward reverently at the height of the liturgy to kneel at the rail (which divided nave and chancel very clearly), meet the priest, and then receive the body of Christ.

Walking into a meeting house in Puritan New England, by comparison, was like walking into a barn. In Edwards' day, many churches sought to improve their meeting houses, adding pew cushions, arched windows, bell towers and spires. But the whitewashed, neoclassical, picture-perfect churches featured in regional tourist guides are the results of nineteenth-century nostalgia.[6] In colonial New England, churches were plain and sided with clapboard that was often left unpainted. As members entered them for worship, their gaze was not drawn toward the heavens or toward the Lord's table. Ceilings were low. Most of the time members went without the Eucharist, and when they did commune, they usually sat at portable tables.

The center of attention in the Puritan meeting house was the pulpit, or "the desk," as New Englanders commonly dubbed it for its importance as the locus of biblical scholarship in their midst. As discussed in chapter two, from start to finish Puritan worship services centered on the Scriptures. Most of the liturgy was abandoned, as were visual and musical arts. Puritans called their churches meeting houses in order to mark this change.[7] They ruled out crosses, stained glass windows, indeed all manner of "graven images"—everything they thought would distract attention from the Word. They sang the Psalms a cappella, banning the use of musical instruments and

---

[6]On this theme, see Joseph A. Conforti, *Imagining New England: Explorations of Regional Identity from the Pilgrims to the Mid-Twentieth Century* (Chapel Hill: University of North Carolina Press, 2001).

[7]Their opponents called them meeting houses because they would not stoop to call the Puritan buildings churches.

resisting the use of hymnody in worship.[8] (As we will see later, Edwards and others would come to favor the use of hymns, causing a stir among traditionalists in the region.) Their clergy shed their vestments (ornate liturgical clothes), preaching instead in academic gowns that symbolized their calling to learned, biblical ministry (rather than sacramental priesthood). In short, they organized their towns, built their churches and planned their services to fix people's attention on the Word.[9]

Though the Puritans in New England eschewed the Catholic church calendar, they also kept time in a manner conducive to biblical thought. In fact, they left behind the hundreds of holy days of the church year in order to organize their schedules much more simply around the Lord's Day. Sunday, for the Puritans, was observed as a Christian sabbath, a day of worship, rest and meditation on Scripture. As the day of the resurrection, it outshone the numerous red-letter days that cluttered the Anglican calendar. Indeed, its sacredness was eternal, tied to God's decision to rest upon the seventh day of creation and to the sabbatarian practices of ancient Israel. The Christian sabbath, in fact, was to culminate, according to most Puritans, in the saints' everlasting rest in the New Jerusalem.[10]

---

[8]The Puritans did at times perform songs from other parts of Scripture. On this underappreciated fact, see especially Rowland Ward's discussion in Richard A. Muller and Rowland S. Ward, *Scripture and Worship: Biblical Interpretation and the Directory for Public Worship*, The Westminster Assembly and the Reformed Faith (Phillipsburg, N.J.: P & R Publishing, 2007), p. 136.

[9]The most accessible introduction to Puritan worship is Horton Davies, *The Worship of the American Puritans, 1629–1730* (New York: P. Lang, 1990), which is built upon Horton Davies, *The Worship of the English Puritans* (Westminster [London]: Dacre Press, 1948). On early Reformed worship generally, see James Hastings Nichols, *Corporate Worship in the Reformed Tradition* (Philadelphia: Westminster Press, 1968); and Frank C. Senn, *Christian Liturgy: Catholic and Evangelical* (Minneapolis: Fortress, 1997). The most accessible introductions to the Puritans written for Christians are Leland Ryken, *Worldly Saints: The Puritans as They Really Were* (Grand Rapids: Academie Books, 1986); and J. I. Packer, *A Quest for Godliness: The Puritan Vision of the Christian Life* (Wheaton, Ill.: Crossway, 1990).

[10]For more on Puritan sabbatarianism, see Winton U. Solberg, *Redeem the Time: The Puritan Sabbath in Early America* (Cambridge, Mass.: Harvard University Press, 1977); Kenneth L. Parker, *The English Sabbath: A Study of Doctrine and Discipline from the Reformation to the Civil War* (Cambridge: Cambridge University Press, 1988); and John H. Primus, *Holy Time: Moderate Puritanism and the Sabbath* (Macon, Ga.: Mercer University Press, 1989). On British Protestants and the church calendar generally in this period, see David Cressy, *Bonfires and Bells: National*

Until 1752, New England also shared in the use of the ancient Julian calendar, which had been introduced by Julius Caesar in 46 B.C. and later Christianized in the early Middle Ages. Its new year began on March 25, Annunciation Day, the day when the angel Gabriel appeared to the Virgin Mary in Nazareth and Jesus was conceived by the Holy Spirit in her womb.[11] In Christian tradition, this event was dated nine months prior to Christmas. Many believed (for symbolic reasons) that it should also be known as the first day of creation (so that the first day of each year would be associated both with God's creation and redemption of the world). Beginning in roughly 525, a Russian monk named Dionysius Exiguus ("the small") began to modify the church's use of the Julian calendar by distinguishing the years that had transpired since Jesus' birth, or the years of the "Christian era," with the prefix *anno Domini* (A.D., "the year of the Lord")—never mind that he miscalculated the year of the Savior's birth. Not until 1752 did England correct the astronomical errors of Julius Caesar's men, adopt our current, Gregorian calendar and push the first day of the new year back to January 1. Even then, New England retained the use of A.D., B.C. ("before Christ") and their sabbath day traditions, marking time—now much more accurately—with biblical concerns.[12]

Memory and the Protestant Calendar in Elizabethan and Stuart England (Berkeley: University of California Press, 1989).

[11]Despite the fact that Edwards lived for most of his life with the ancient calendar, marking time in the "old style," I have rendered the dates in this book in the Gregorian "new style" (for the convenience of the reader), as if the new year had always begun on January 1.

[12]Significantly, our current calendar is named for Pope Gregory XIII, who introduced its reforms in 1582. (Gregory's astronomers determined that the solar year is 11 minutes and 14 seconds shorter than Julius Caesar's men had calculated in 46 B.C., and thus that ten days must be added to their previous calendar if it was to track the solar/seasonal cycles accurately.) Anti-Catholic sentiment slowed the adoption of the new calendar in England. As explained by Jennifer Powell McNutt, "Protestant rejection of the Gregorian calendar is best understood as a reaction to the reform or counter-reform agenda of the Council of Trent and to a perceived papal plot for religious and political domination. The belief that the pope was seeking to dictate even time itself was spurred on when the decree for calendar reform was pronounced through a papal bull, a medium that asserted the authority of the pope and rendered the reform of the calendar an issue of Roman Catholic ecclesiastical rule." Jennifer Powell McNutt, "Hesitant Steps: Acceptance of the Gregorian Calendar in Eighteenth-Century Geneva," *Church History* 75 (Sep-

The Puritans also organized their laws according to Scripture, building their civic life on the teachings of the Bible. The laws of the Bible commonwealths were liberalized somewhat by the time of Edwards' ministry. Still, in most of early New England, no one could vote or hold office who was not a church member, and no one could join the church without a public testimony (that is, regarding conversion). Legislators and magistrates were viewed as God's servants, making and executing laws on the basis of the Bible. Sins against the ten commandments proved to be punishable offenses, as did related acts like fornication and cross-dressing. Church attendance was mandatory (though exceptions were often made for nursing mothers, men at war, the aged, ailing and infirm). So was the payment of local taxes in support of the churches' ministries. In early Massachusetts children had to be taught to read (most were taught to read the Bible). Towns with more than fifty households had to hire a reading teacher. Towns with more than a hundred families had to found a grammar school—that is, a school where boys learned Latin in order to ready themselves for college.[13] Parents could be fined for failing to teach their children English. Fathers could be punished for failing to catechize their families.

In sum, Puritan New England may have been the most biblically oriented and literate society in the world before the time of Edwards' ministry. Its inhabitants owned no televisions, went without the Internet, and had no access to cell phones or video games. Their skies were dark at night, pitch-dark on cloudy nights. They had no light

---

tember 2006): 547-48. Cf. Robert Poole, *Time's Alteration: Calendar Reform in Early Modern England* (London: UCL Press, 1998); and G. V. Coyne, M. S. Hoskin and O. Pedersen, *Gregorian Reform of the Calendar: Proceedings of the Vatican Conference to Commemorate its 400th Anniversary, 1582–1982* (Vatican City: Specola Vaticana, 1983).

[13]The General Court of Massachusetts included these rules as part of its famous Ould Deluder Satan law, passed in 1647. Most of New England's other colonies followed Massachusetts' lead. Similar laws were passed in Connecticut (1650), Plymouth Colony (1658) and New Haven (1657). On the teaching of basic literacy in colonial America, see especially E. Jennifer Monaghan, *Learning to Read and Write in Colonial America*, Studies in Print Culture and the History of the Book (Amherst: University of Massachusetts Press, 2005).

bulbs, gas lights or even the means to power them.[14] Most would spend their evenings reading or socializing by candlelight, or huddling round the fire, ruminating about the things that mattered most. Moreover, even during the day, while working hard to make ends meet, Puritans thought about the Bible and the challenges of faith. In the words of Harriet Beecher Stowe, the daughter of one of New England's best known nineteenth-century ministers, "it is impossible to write a story of New England life and manners for superficial thought or shallow feeling. They who would fully understand the springs which moved the characters [there] must go down with us to the very depths."[15]

Other testimonies survive regarding the spiritual characteristics of New England's early Protestants, but Stowe's historical novels—such as *The Minister's Wooing* (1859), *Oldtown Folks* (1869) and *Poganuc People* (1878)—offer the most vivid depictions. The region's sermons, Stowe attested in the first and best of these novels, were

> discussed by every farmer, in intervals of plough and hoe, by every woman and girl, at loom, spinning-wheel, or wash-tub. New England was one vast sea, surging from depths to heights with thought and discussion on the most insoluble of mysteries. And it is to be added, that no man or woman accepted any theory or speculation simply as theory or speculation; all was profoundly real and vital,—a foundation on which actual life was based with intensest earnestness.[16]

Stowe drove this point home in a piece she wrote for *Atlantic Monthly:* "nowhere in the world, unless perhaps in Scotland, have merely speculative questions excited the strong and engrossing interest among the common people that they have in New England. Every man, woman, and child was more or less a theologian."[17]

---

[14]A fascinating discussion of nighttime during the early modern period may be found in A. Roger Ekirch, *At Day's Close: Night in Times Past* (New York: W. W. Norton, 2005).

[15]Harriet Beecher Stowe, *The Minister's Wooing*, in *Harriet Beecher Stowe: Three Novels* (New York: The Library of America, 1982), p. 727.

[16]Ibid., p. 728.

[17]Harriet Beecher Stowe, "New England Ministers," *Atlantic Monthly* 1 (February 1858): 486-87.

Clearly then, Edwards' world was strikingly different from ours. Its pastors worked as theologians. Its theologians worked as pastors. People expected ordained clergy to spend the bulk of their time in study, preparing to minister the Word to them in depth and rich detail. They wanted their pastors to be learned more than flashy, therapeutic, businesslike or even approachable. They paid attention to words, biblical words most of all. Many knew their Bibles well, believing their lives depended upon it.

No wonder it is impossible to duplicate Edwards' ministry. No wonder many are tempted to despair in failing to do so. His world had much to commend it, as did its Christian ministries. But let's not kid ourselves. It was not much better than ours. It had both strengths and glaring weaknesses, much as our own world does. It seethed with violence, fear and grief. Its leaders were often publicly frustrated, like us, by spiritual lethargy. They, too, assumed that the grass was greener somewhere else in time. They, too, looked for resources that would give them needed perspective on the challenges of their day.

As Edwards fretted to one of his Scottish friends, the Rev. John Erskine, in a letter he wrote on July 7, 1752, "It now appears to be a remarkable time in the Christian world; perhaps such an one as never has been before. Things are going downhill so fast; truth and religion, both of heart and practice, are departing by such swift steps that I think it must needs be, that a crisis is not very far off."[18] Where have we heard that before? In literally thousands of times and places through the history of the church, on the lips of countless Christians longing for Christ's kingdom to come. Edwards certainly never thought that his was a golden age of faith. He worried that Britain's state-church system fostered spiritual apathy, a merely nominal

---

[18]Jonathan Edwards to the Rev. John Erskine, July 7, 1752, in *Letters and Personal Writings*, ed. George S. Claghorn, *The Works of Jonathan Edwards*, vol. 16 (New Haven: Yale University Press, 1998), p. 491. The Yale edition of Edwards' *Works* is cited frequently below. For the sake of efficiency, I refer to it hereafter as *WJE*, and do not repeat the publisher's name or place of publication (though I do provide all volume numbers and years of publication).

Christianity, and rampant hypocrisy. He dreaded the rise of "infidelity" throughout Enlightenment Europe.[19] Indeed, he could spread gloom and doom just as dreadfully as the most excitable, chicken-little Christian leaders today.

The task that faces those who would look to Edwards for help today is not to search for a time machine that we can use to live in his world, but to live in our own world thoughtfully, appreciatively and lovingly, and to ask ourselves how we can apply his insights in our time. What can we do *in our own world* to draw attention to the Word, enhance the ministries of the church and deepen faith in the things of God? What can be done to encourage Christians to pay attention to the divine, thinking biblically, theologically, about their daily lives? We will return to these questions later, after the summary that follows of Edwards' life and ministry. This book will end with seven theses I have crafted for discussion by those who want to apply Edwardsian examples to their lives. But even as we survey his biography below, I hope that you will be thinking about what God would have us learn from it today.[20]

As Edwards wrote in his bestselling book, *The Life of David Brainerd* (1749), about a student and friend well-known for his short-lived work in Indian missions,

> There are two ways of representing and recommending true religion and virtue to the world, which God hath made use of: the one is by doctrine and precept; the other is by instance and example: Both are abundantly used in the holy Scriptures. . . . God also in his Providence has been wont to make use of both these methods to hold forth light to mankind, and inducement to their duty, in all ages: He has

---

[19]See my "Editor's Introduction" to Jonathan Edwards, *The "Miscellanies" (Entry Nos. 1153–1360)*, ed. Douglas A. Sweeney, *WJE*, vol. 23 (2004), pp. 23-29.

[20]A helpful sourcebook was published recently for those in pastoral ministry trying faithfully to make good on the church's historic emphases on biblical knowledge, doctrine and piety. See Paul Ballard and Stephen R. Holmes, eds., *The Bible in Pastoral Practice: Readings in the Place and Function of Scripture in the Church*, Using the Bible in Pastoral Practice (2005; Grand Rapids: Eerdmans, 2006). My thanks to Professor Greg Scharf of Trinity's Pastoral Theology department for recommending this book to me.

from time to time raised up eminent teachers, to exhibit and bear testimony to the truth in their doctrine, and oppose the errors, darkness
and wickedness of the world; and also has from age to age, raised up
some eminent persons that have set bright examples of that religion
that is taught and prescribed in the Word of God; whole examples
have in divine providence been set forth to public view. These have
a great tendency to engage the attention of men to the doctrines and
rules that are taught, and greatly to confirm and enforce them.[21]

Won't you pray with me that God will use this book on Jonathan
Edwards, as he has used the life of Brainerd, to "engage the attention" of Christians, advancing the ministry of the Word around the
world?

---

[21]Jonathan Edwards, *The Life of David Brainerd*, ed. Norman Pettit, *WJE*, vol. 7 (1985), pp. 89-
90.

Chapter 1

STUDY TO SHEW
THYSELF APPROVED

Study to shew thyself approved unto God, a workman that needeth not
to be ashamed, rightly dividing the word of truth. But shun profane
and vain babblings: for they will increase unto more ungodliness.

2 TIMOTHY 2:15-16

*J*onathan Edwards was born on October 5, 1703, the fifth child
and only son of the Rev. Timothy Edwards and Esther Stoddard Edwards, a pastor's daughter. He had four older sisters, Esther, Elizabeth, Anne and Mary, and would eventually have six younger sisters
as well (Eunice, Abigail, Jerusha, Hannah, Lucy and little Martha,
who was born when brother Jonathan was in college). The Edwardses
were tall, at least by eighteenth-century standards. Father Timothy
would boast that he had sixty feet of daughters. The older girls doted
on Jonathan, as did many in the town. Nearly everyone expected him
to become a pastor himself.[1]

Indeed, Edwards had the privilege and weighty responsibility of

---

[1]On Edwards' sisters and their advanced intellectual attainments, see Kenneth P. Minkema,
"Hannah and Her Sisters: Sisterhood, Courtship, and Marriage in the Edwards Family in the
Early Eighteenth Century," *New England Historical and Genealogical Register* 146 (January 1992):
35-56.

growing up in a well-known clerical family. Both his father and his grandfather were powerful clergymen. His mother's father, Solomon Stoddard, was especially influential. He served as pastor of Northampton, Massachusetts, most of his life (1670–1729). Local wags called him the "pope." A major power broker in towns throughout the western part of New England, most of which dotted the valley running along the Connecticut River, Stoddard was also known regionally as one of the "river gods." As we will see in chapter four, he cast a mighty long shadow over Edwards' ministry.

Edwards grew up in a crowded parsonage in East Windsor, Connecticut (now South Windsor, Connecticut), a house in which his parents lived for over sixty years. His father, Timothy, was known as a fine Puritan-style preacher. He was also highly regarded for the role he played in training students for college. In fact, Timothy used the parlor of the parsonage as a school. He had it fitted with school benches local boys could use for study. (One can hardly imagine what Mrs. Edwards thought of this.)[2] In colonial New England only boys could enter college—mainly privileged, teenage boys, most of whom would become pastors.[3] The entrance exams at Harvard and Yale tested proficiency in Latin, Koine Greek and biblical Hebrew, the classical languages on which the college curriculum was based. Grammar schools were founded to help young boys prepare for these

---

[2]Lest this sound hopelessly sexist, it is important to remember that the Edwardses also educated their daughters in this parsonage. As Minkema explains: "Timothy, with Esther's assistance, put all of his children through the same preparatory tutorship that he gave the local boys." All of their children "were taught their 'tongues' (all of the sisters learned Latin, and some of them Greek), worked mathematical and logic problems, and were immersed in both the old and the current learning. The older daughters, who were farther along in their lessons, assisted the younger; even the young Jonathan was tutored by his sisters. . . . Indeed, all of the Edwards daughters, save one, attended finishing schools in Boston, which set them apart . . . from the majority of young women of the colonial gentry." Minkema, "Hannah and Her Sisters," p. 41.

[3]In colonial America, bachelor's degrees from legally incorporated colleges were rare. Though many young men received training at the dozens of tiny academies that sprouted temporarily (modeled after the Dissenting academies in England and among Scots-Irish Presbyterians in Ireland), specialists estimate that even as late as the 1760s, only one in a thousand males had college degrees. See Elizabeth Nybakken, "In the Irish Tradition: Pre-Revolutionary Academies in America," *History of Education Quarterly* 37 (Summer 1997): 163-83.

exams. They were run by college graduates, often pastors helping to fortify the churches of the future.

Jonathan began to study Latin at age six. By the age of twelve, he was also reading Greek and a little Hebrew. He proved unusually sensitive spiritually from a very young age. In fact, at the tender age of nine, he became a local spiritual leader. As he recounted many years later to future son-in-law Aaron Burr, in a letter commonly known as Edwards' "Personal Narrative," a local awakening in East Windsor in 1712–1713 stirred in his soul a deep concern about "religion" and "salvation."

> I used to pray five times a day in secret, and to spend much time in religious talk with other boys; and used to meet with them to pray together. I experienced I know not what kind of delight in religion. My mind was much engaged in it, and had much self-righteous pleasure; and it was my delight to abound in religious duties. I, with some of my schoolmates joined together, and built a booth in a swamp, in a very secret and retired place, for a place of prayer. And besides, I had particular secret places of my own in the woods, where I used to retire by myself; and used to be from time to time much affected. My affections seemed to be lively and easily moved, and I seemed to be in my element, when engaged in religious duties.

Looking back at these events, Edwards did not find them salvific. As he went on to tell Burr, a recent Presbyterian minister and future college president, "in process of time, my convictions and affections wore off; and I entirely lost all those affections and delights, and left off secret prayer, at least as to any constant performance of it; and returned like a dog to his vomit, and went on in ways of sin."[4]

---

[4]Jonathan Edwards, "Personal Narrative," in *Letters and Personal Writings*, ed. George S. Claghorn, *WJE*, vol. 16 (1998), pp. 790-91. Specialists date the "Personal Narrative" to December 1740. Burr would marry Edwards' daughter Esther in 1752. Their son Aaron Burr Jr. would become vice president of the United States under Thomas Jefferson, earning scorn from many Christians, particularly in New England, for abandoning his faith and slaying Alexander Hamilton in a duel (on July 11, 1804, in Weehawken, New Jersey). When Edwards wrote his "Personal Narrative," Burr served as the pastor of the First Presbyterian Church of Newark, New Jersey. In 1748, Burr was elected to the presidency of the

Throughout his youth, Edwards was thought to be on a pre-ministerial track. He was brilliant, studied hard and seemed to be a spiritual prodigy. Most importantly, perhaps, he came from a strong clerical family. In the early eighteenth century, parents did not assure their children that they could choose their own careers. Most apples fell close to the tree. Children's options were much more limited than they are in the West today. Still, Jonathan guarded his heart. He knew that while many people expected him to assume the family business, he must be sure that he was qualified for the job. And the number-one qualification of a minister of the Word, according to Edwards, was a life truly converted by the Spirit.

EDWARDS GOES TO YALE

Edwards enrolled at Yale when he was only twelve years old, in September 1716, one month prior to his birthday. The college was in flux when he left home to matriculate. Founded in 1701 as the Connecticut Collegiate School, in 1716 classes were still meeting in three separate locations (New Haven, Saybrook and Wethersfield). Jonathan joined with nearly a dozen other boys at Wethersfield, which is today a suburb of Hartford, under the tutelage of his cousin Elisha Williams. Williams was a Harvard man, still in his early twenties. Young men, more often than not, served as tutors in the colleges of colonial New England, working their way up the ladder to pastoral ministry. Collegiate study consisted primarily of reading, memorization, written work and recitations. The task of tutors was to supervise, to run boys through the paces, rather than hold forth in lengthy, lively, extemporaneous lectures. Williams soon became a pastor in nearby Newington, Connecticut, returning to Yale in 1726 as president (or rector). He played an important role in Jonathan's life for many years to come, ending his own days as a civic leader and military hero.

College of New Jersey (today's Princeton University).

By the fall of 1718, school officials determined to locate the college permanently in New Haven. They erected a stately building there, named the school Yale (after Elihu Yale, a leading English benefactor), and required that all their students board together. The Wethersfield party complied, though not without a protest. They moved south, submitting themselves to the tuition of Samuel Johnson, senior tutor in New Haven at the age of twenty-one. Very quickly, though, they balked at his Arminian doctrinal views. (Sturdy scions of the Puritans, Edwards and his compatriots proved staunchly Calvinistic.)[5] They returned to Williams in Wethersfield, upsetting Yale's trustees. Tutor Johnson was investigated, fired and quickly replaced by a much older, ordained clergyman who was named the college president—a thirty-five-year-old man named Timothy Cutler, who had been serving a local Congregational church for nearly a decade. Samuel Johnson stayed nearby, becoming a pastor in West Haven. As we will see more fully below, he later converted to Anglicanism and, by 1754, founded the Anglican King's College (today's Columbia University).[6] But now that he was gone from Yale, the Wethersfield boys returned (in June 1719). For a time, the school was stable. In September 1720, Edwards re-

---

[5]The differences between Calvinists and Arminians will be referred to several times in the pages that follow. For the sake of the uninitiated, I offer a brief description of them here. Calvinists are followers of the French Reformed pastor and theologian Jean Cauvin (1509–1564), spelled in English John Calvin, who emphasized the depravity of unconverted sinners and the sovereignty of God in choosing some (and not others) for salvation—regardless of merit. Arminians are followers of the Dutch theologian Jakob Hermans (1560–1609), that is, Jacob Arminius, who opposed Calvin's doctrine of divine predestination and emphasized the role that sinners play in their own conversions. The differences between Calvinists and Arminians came to a head at the Dutch Reformed Synod of Dordt (1618–1619), from whose proceedings English Calvinists derived the famous "five points of Calvinism." Of course, there is far more to Calvinism than five simple points. Nonetheless, the five letters of the TULIP acronym (inspired by the floral passions of the Dutch Reformed) have summarized for many (not least the Arminian "remonstrants") the essential doctrinal tenets of the Calvinists: Total depravity (of unregenerate sinners); Unconditional election (of those redeemed by God from sin); Limited atonement (Christ's saving work on the cross atoned for only the sins of the elect); Irresistible grace (saving grace never fails to effect conversion); Perseverance of the saints (once converted the elect will never fall from saving grace).

[6]Technically speaking, "Anglicanism" is a nineteenth-century term. I use it here for the sake of expediency to refer to the ways and means of the Church of England.

---

ceived his bachelor's degree. He graduated first in his class, delivering a valedictory speech (in Latin) in Yale's new building.[7]

Edwards' bachelor of arts degree represented a broad education. Still, theology ruled the roost at Yale. It remained the queen of the sciences. Undergraduates spent two days a week investigating the Scriptures, learning Calvinist dogmatics and familiarizing themselves with both scholastic and more modern theological methodology—in addition to their devotions, chapel attendance and church commitments. Two theology texts prevailed: Puritan William Ames' masterpiece, *Medulla Theologiae* (*The Marrow of Theology*, 1627), and a handbook by the Swiss Reformed pastor and professor Johann Wolleb, *Compendium Theologiae Christianae* (*Compendium of Christian Theology*, 1626).[8] But many additional theological works circulated widely. Forty of them belonged to the school's original collection. In September 1714, several hundred more arrived as London's Jeremiah Dummer, a former colonist who was working now as an agent for the colonies (of Massachusetts and Connecticut), collected and shipped over eight hundred books to Yale's Saybrook campus. The Dummer Collection included famous works by leading Enlightenment thinkers, from Isaac Newton and John Locke to Daniel Defoe, Pierre Bayle, Henry More and John Tillotson. In 1718–1719, it was transferred to New Haven, where Edwards himself enjoyed poring over its contents.[9]

---

[7]For a transcription of the speech, which survives in manuscript at Yale, see the printed catalogue of the Edwards tercentennial exhibit at Jonathan Edwards College, Yale University: *Jonathan Edwards Tercentennial Exhibition: Selected Objects from the Yale Collections, 1703–2003, with Essays by Kenneth P. Minkema and George G. Levesque* (New Haven: Jonathan Edwards College, Yale University, 2003), pp. 39-41, where Levesque has also offered an English translation of the speech.

[8]Both of these works are available in English translation. See William Ames, *The Marrow of Theology*, ed. John D. Eusden (1968; Grand Rapids: Baker, 1997); and Johannes Wollebius, *The Abridgement of Christian Divinitie*, trans. Alexander Ross (London: T. Mab and A. Coles, 1650). Cf. Johannes Wollebius, *Compendium Theologiae Christianae*, in *Reformed Dogmatics*, ed. and trans. John W. Beardslee III, A Library of Protestant Thought (New York: Oxford University Press, 1965), pp. 27-262.

[9]Sadly, 260 books were stolen/lost from the collection during the struggle over the college's location. On the contents of the collection, see Anne Stokely Pratt, "The Books Sent from England by Jeremiah Dummer to Yale College," and Louise May Bryant and Mary Patterson, "The List of Books Sent by Jeremiah Dummer," both in *Papers in Honor of Andrew Keogh, Librarian of Yale*

In fact, these bibliographical resources kept Edwards in New Haven for nearly two additional years after he graduated from college, during which time he read for a master of arts degree. The colonies contained no modern, postbaccalaureate seminaries. The most thoughtful boys with a calling to ecclesiastical ministry took time for further, independent study after college. Their congregations expected them to lead theologically. Ministers were supposed to be the smartest people in town, local sources of practical wisdom on the events and cultural trends beyond New England's narrow borders. Parishioners relied on their intelligence, perspective and profound biblical worldview. Only sixteen years of age when he received his bachelor's degree, Edwards knew better than to rush right into ministry.

Edwards' extra time at Yale also enabled him to deepen his relationship with God. Undergraduate life was hectic, full of mandatory assignments and prescribed religious duties. Graduate school was more flexible. It gave one time to breathe. Edwards needed this flexibility. He needed space to grow. Up to that time, his life had been laden with expectations and obligations. He had always been a good boy. He had honored his father and mother. But he had not possessed sufficient time to pursue God personally, to commit himself (or not) to the Christian life he had inherited. He had never rebelled against the cardinal doctrines of Christianity.[10] Baptized into a state church, raised in a godly home, Edwards had always gone along with the religion he was given. But he knew that there was more to Christianity

---

University, *by the Staff of the Library, 30 June 1938* (New Haven: privately printed, 1938), pp. 7-44, 423-92; and Thomas Clap, *A Catalogue of the Library of Yale-College in New-Haven* (New London, Conn.: T. Green, 1743).

[10]Like many Christian leaders before him (including John Calvin), Edwards did resist the doctrine of divine predestination. As he wrote in his "Personal Narrative," his "mind had been wont to be full of objections against the doctrine of God's sovereignty, in choosing whom he would to eternal life, and rejecting whom he pleased; leaving them eternally to perish, and be everlastingly tormented in hell. It used to appear like a horrible doctrine to me." By the time of his conversion, though, Edwards' mind had changed. He became convinced of this doctrine's truthfulness and delighted in its promise of God's power over history. "I have often since, not only had a conviction, but a *delightful* conviction. The doctrine of God's sovereignty has very often appeared, an exceeding pleasant, bright and sweet doctrine to me: and absolute sovereignty is what I love to ascribe to God." In *Letters and Personal Writings*, pp. 791-92.

than religion. And he longed for what the Puritans called experimental divinity, experiential faith, true religion or what we might call authentic Christianity. As he would preach years later,

> there is a difference between having an opinion that God is holy and gracious, and having a sense of the loveliness and beauty of that holiness and grace. There is a difference between having a rational judgment that honey is sweet, and having a sense of its sweetness. A man may have the former, that knows not how honey tastes; but a man can't have the latter, unless he has an idea of the taste of honey in his mind. So there is a difference between believing that a person is beautiful, and having a sense of his beauty. The former may be obtained by hearsay, but the latter only by seeing the countenance. There is a wide difference between mere speculative, rational judging anything to be excellent, and having a sense of its sweetness, and beauty. The former rests only in the head, speculation only is concerned in it; but the heart is concerned in the latter.[11]

Edwards desired, with King David, to "taste and see that the LORD is good" (Ps 34:8). He wanted an existential acquaintance with the God he was to serve.

CONVERSION, SPIRITUAL GROWTH AND EDWARDS' EARLY PASTORAL MINISTRY

In the spring of 1721, he got what he desired. As he recounted famously in the "Personal Narrative" cited above, something happened in May or June of that year that changed his life forever. He would never specify a point in time when this occurred. As we will see in chapter four, he never felt a need to do so—and could probably not have done so anyway. Nevertheless, he did believe that this experience changed his life. He reckoned it divine, a supernatural event. It gave him a new,

---

[11]Jonathan Edwards, "A Divine and Supernatural Light, Immediately Imparted to the Soul By the Spirit of God, Shown to Be both a Scriptural, and Rational Doctrine (1734)," in *The Sermons of Jonathan Edwards: A Reader*, ed. Wilson H. Kimnach, Kenneth P. Minkema and Douglas A. Sweeney (New Haven: Yale University Press, 1999), pp. 127-28.

spiritual sense of the reality of God. His account of it is so telling that I quote it here at length. It happened as Edwards meditated on 1 Timothy 1:17, "Now unto the King eternal, immortal, invisible, the only wise God, be honor and glory for ever and ever. Amen."

> As I read the words, there came into my soul, and was as it were diffused through it, a sense of the glory of the divine being; a new sense, quite different from anything I ever experienced before. Never any words of Scripture seemed to me as these words did. I thought with myself, how excellent a Being that was; and how happy I should be, if I might enjoy that God, and be wrapt up to God in heaven, and be as it were swallowed up in him. I kept saying, and as it were singing over these words of Scripture to myself; and went to prayer, to pray to God that I might enjoy him; and prayed in a manner quite different from what I used to do; with a new sort of affection. But it never came into my thought [i.e., at the time], that there was anything spiritual, or of a saving nature in this.
>
> From about that time, I began to have a new kind of apprehensions and ideas of Christ, and the work of redemption, and the glorious way of salvation by him. I had an inward, sweet sense of these things, that at times came into my heart; and my soul was led away in pleasant views and contemplations of them. And my mind was greatly engaged, to spend my time in reading and meditating on Christ; and the beauty and excellency of his person, and the lovely way of salvation, by free grace in him. . . . [I] found . . . an inward sweetness, that used . . . to carry me away in my contemplations; in what I know not how to express otherwise, than by a calm, sweet abstraction of soul from all the concerns o[f] this world; and a kind of vision, or fixed ideas and imaginations, of being alone in the mountains, or some solitary wilderness, far from all mankind, sweetly conversing with Christ, and wrapt and swallowed up in God. The sense I had of divine things, would often of a sudden . . . kindle up a sweet burning in my heart; an ardor of my soul, that I know not how to express.[12]

Edwards had finally *tasted* divinity. He knew the sweetness of

---

[12]Edwards, "Personal Narrative," in *Letters and Personal Writings*, pp. 792-93.

God. And though he would later harbor doubts about the form of his conversion and the degree of his spirituality, he would always view this time as one of spiritual rebirth.[13]

In August 1722, Edwards took his first church, a Presbyterian congregation in the heart of New York City. It met in a building on William Street between Liberty and Wall, an easy walk today from Ground Zero.[14] It was a tiny congregation, the result of a church split. Its parent church, First Presbyterian, was founded three years earlier by a small group of Scottish and English dissenters. (New York was officially Anglican in the early eighteenth century.) By 1722, the English members, now dissatisfied with their pastor James Anderson, decided to leave and form a church of their own. They called Edwards, still a teenager, to minister to their needs. Within a year, their schism was healed, thanks in part to Edwards' ministry. Anderson resigned the pulpit at First Presbyterian and Edwards' flock returned to its former pasture.[15] Despite the brief and rocky history of this wayward congregation, though, its people treated Edwards well and gave him room to grow. By all accounts, his first pastorate proved a blessing to all concerned.

When Edwards moved to New York City, it contained roughly 7,100 people,[16] mostly on Manhattan, living and working in about 2,000

---

[13]For evidence of Edwards' ongoing spiritual anxiety, see the entries in his "Diary" for December 18, 1722, January 2, 1722/23, and August 12, 1723, in the last of which he wrote: "The chief thing, that now makes me in any measure to question my good estate, is my not having experienced conversion in those particular steps, wherein the people of New England, and anciently the Dissenters of Old England, used to experience it. Wherefore, now resolved, never to leave searching, till I have satisfyingly found out the very bottom and foundation, the real reason, why they used to be converted in those steps." Jonathan Edwards, "Diary," in *Letters and Personal Writings*, pp. 759-60, 779 (quotation from p. 779). The relationship between Edwards' own conversion and those of his predecessors will be covered much more fully in chapter four.

[14]This building no longer exists. Its successor church, First Presbyterian of New York, is found today on Fifth Avenue between Eleventh and Twelfth Streets in Manhattan's Greenwich Village.

[15]It took them a while, but the reunited members of New York's First Presbyterian Church eventually settled a permanent pastor, Ebenezer Pemberton, who served them from 1727 to 1753.

[16]Approximately 81% of the city's population was white. Roughly 19% was black. Of the whites, by 1730, nearly 50% were British, nearly 40% were Dutch, 8% were French, 2% were Jewish and 1% was German. This information is based on the census data in Evarts B. Greene and Virginia D.

---

buildings.[17] It boasted nearly twenty churches, two established Anglican parishes, two Dutch Reformed churches and a smattering of others—German Lutheran, Moravian, even a Quaker meeting house.[18] New York was nowhere near as great as it would be a century later. It was not the "Big Apple" till the early twentieth century. It was big, however, a busy, bustling, bumptious seaport town, with people of all kinds coming and going to places skirting most of the Atlantic.

Edwards boarded in New York with Mrs. Susanna Smith and her son John Smith, a leather worker, recent immigrants from England who also worshiped at his church. He enjoyed "abundance of sweet religious conversation" with them both. But he grew closest to John Smith. The two were about the same age. (Smith was twenty at the time. Edwards himself was nineteen.) The two would often "[walk] together, to converse of the things of God; and our conversation used much to turn on the advancement of Christ's kingdom in the world, and the glorious things that God would accomplish for his church in the latter days." Edwards also knew John's older brother, William, who had finished a year ahead of him at college in New Haven.[19]

Edwards' pastorate permitted time for study and spiritual growth. Still single and charged with a small, understanding congregation, he went on long walks in the woods for prayer and spiritual meditation. He liked to sit by the Hudson River, contemplating the things of God. As he remembered to Aaron Burr,

Harrington, *American Population Before the Federal Census of 1790* (New York: Columbia University Press, 1932), pp. 97-98, and fleshed out helpfully in Jill Lepore, *New York Burning: Liberty, Slavery, and Conspiracy in Eighteenth-Century Manhattan* (2005; New York: Vintage Books, 2006), pp. 21-22, 233-46.

[17]As to the number of New York's buildings, I have followed Philip F. Gura, *Jonathan Edwards: America's Evangelical* (New York: Hill and Wang, 2005), p. 29, who bases his estimate on William Smith Jr., *The History of the Province of New-York*, ed. Michael Kammen, 2 vols. (1752; Cambridge, Mass.: Harvard University Press, 1972), 1:202-27. Jill Lepore offers a lower estimate, based on I. N. Phelps Stokes, *Iconography of Manhattan Island, 1498–1909*, 6 vols. (1915–1928; New York: Arno Press, 1967), 6:23-24. See Lepore, *New York Burning*, 284 n. 13.

[18]The city's Jews still met in homes, founding the first American synagogue in 1729, Congregation Shearith Israel.

[19]Edwards, "Personal Narrative," in *Letters and Personal Writings*, p. 797.

> While I was there, . . . [m]y longings after God and holiness, were much increased. Pure and humble, holy and heavenly Christianity, appeared exceeding amiable to me. I felt in me a burning desire to be in everything a complete Christian; and conformed to the blessed image of Christ: and that I might live in all things, according to the pure, sweet and blessed rules of the gospel. I had an eager thirsting after progress in these things.[20]

It was also in New York that Edwards began his spiritual "Diary" and drafted more than half of his now-famous "Resolutions." Edwards' "Diary" recounts his growth in grace as a young Christian. Comprised of 148 entries, it commences on December 18, 1722 and ends on June 11, 1735 (though only six of its entries date from after 1725). Edwards used it to record his ardent struggle with sanctification, confiding to its pages an "abundance of listlessness" and "abominable corruption," his "want of dependence on God," even his failure in "not allowing time enough for conversation." Edwards did appear to progress during the time he kept the "Diary." But even toward the end he bemoans his chronic sinfulness, confessing spiritual atrophy since finishing his master's degree: "'Tis just about three years, that I have been for the most part in a low, sunk estate and condition, miserably senseless to what I used to be, about spiritual things." Like nearly every other Christian, Edwards would know both highs and lows over the course of his Christian life. But unlike most, he felt them keenly, faced them squarely, and took them seriously as indicators of his spiritual health.[21]

Edwards' "Resolutions" have long been used to characterize his intensity, especially as a young man. They are comprised of seventy vows made before God while in his teens, between the time of his conversion and the completion of his master's degree. Edwards would later come to believe that in this period of his life he grew too cocky spiritually, "which afterwards," he wrote, "proved a great damage

---

[20]Ibid., p. 795.

[21]Edwards, "Diary," in *Letters and Personal Writings*, pp. 760, 761, 780, 781, 788 (final quotation from an entry dated September 26, 1726).

to me." He came to regret that his "experience had not then taught me, as it has done since, my extreme feebleness and impotence, every manner of way; and the innumerable and bottomless depths of secret corruption and deceit, that there was in my heart."[22]

Still, the "Resolutions" impress with their sincerity and earnestness. They illuminate not only Edwards' zealous personality but also his new life in the Holy Spirit.

1. Resolved, that I will do whatsoever I think to be most to God's glory, and my own good, profit and pleasure, in the whole of my duration, without any consideration of the time, whether now, or never so many myriads of ages hence. Resolved to do whatever I think to be my duty, and most for the good and advantage of mankind in general. Resolved to do this, whatever difficulties I meet with, how many and how great soever. . . .

3. Resolved, if ever I shall fall and grow dull, so as to neglect to keep any part of these Resolutions, to repent of all I can remember, when I come to myself again.

4. Resolved, never to do any manner of thing, whether in soul or body, less or more, but what tends to the glory of God; nor be, nor suffer it, if I can avoid it.

5. Resolved, never to lose one moment of time; but improve it the most profitable way I possibly can.

6. Resolved, to live with all my might, while I do live.

These "Resolutions" tend to weary middle-aged and older Christians, but they thrill the young at heart, the most extreme disciples of Christ.

7. Resolved, never to do anything, which I should be afraid to do, if it were the last hour of my life.

8. Resolved, to act, in all respects, both speaking and doing, as if nobody had been so vile as I, and as if I had committed the same sins, or had the same infirmities or failings as others; and that I will let the knowledge of their failing promote nothing but shame

---

[22]Edwards, "Personal Narrative," in *Letters and Personal Writings*, p. 795.

in myself, and prove only an occasion of my confessing my own sins and misery to God. . . .

9. Resolved, to think much on all occasion of my own dying, and of the common circumstances which attend death. . . .

11. Resolved, when I think of any theorem in divinity to be solved, immediately to do what I can towards solving it, if circumstances don't hinder.

12. Resolved, if I take delight in it as a gratification of pride, or vanity, or on any such account, immediately to throw it by.[23]

Perhaps by now the point is clear. From the time of his conversion through his ministry in New York, Edwards searched his soul and devoted himself to a life of divine service.

He also cultivated important scholarly disciplines. Edwards' earliest biographer, his student Samuel Hopkins, said that Edwards thought "with his pen in his hand," resembling "the busy bee, collecting from every opening flower, and storing up a stock of knowledge, which was indeed sweet to him, as the honey and the honey-comb."[24] This turn of phrase is apt, for it depicts the kind of aggressive study Edwards began in New York, study that laid a solid foundation for his future writing projects.

Long before computers, Edwards stored information in an extensive system of notebooks, which he carefully cross-referenced and arranged in his desk drawers.[25] The best known are nine books of

---

[23]Jonathan Edwards, "Resolutions," in *Letters and Personal Writings*, pp. 753-54.

[24]Samuel Hopkins, *The Life and Character of the Late Reverend Mr. Jonathan Edwards* (Boston: S. Kneeland, 1765), p. 41.

[25]This practice was inculcated by older pastors like Boston's Cotton Mather (1663–1728), who published advice for younger pastors such as the following: "One thing that I advise you to, is this. Keep your quotidiana. I mean have your blank books, in which note with your pen, for the most part every day . . . some notable thing, which in reading you have newly met withal. By this action you will fix the valuable notion in your mind: and in a few years, you will have a treasure, from whence as a scribe instructed for the kingdom of heaven, you may bring out things new and old [Mt 13:52], and have agreeable grains of salt for all your discourses." See Cotton Mather, *Manuductio ad Ministerium: Directions for a Candidate of the Ministry*, reproduced from the original edition, Boston, 1726, with a bibliographical note by Thomas J. Holmes and Kenneth B. Murdock (New York: Published for the Facsimile Text Society by Columbia University Press, 1938), p. 72.

theological "Miscellanies," begun while in New York, containing over 1,400 miscellaneous reflections—some brief, others prolix— a running manuscript record of the issues that he faced. But there were other notebooks too: a "Blank Bible," "Notes on Scripture," a "Catalogue" of readings, "The Mind," typological books, "Notes on the Apocalypse." Smaller booklets treated Christian doctrines, natural science, metaphysics and aesthetics. Some are discussed below. All were initiated well before he reached the age of thirty. I mention them here to make clear Edwards' early determination to redeem the time he was given and prepare for a long life of theological ministry.

In April 1723, Edwards left New York by boat. His congregation was returning to the fold at First Presbyterian and he now felt compelled to return to his own home in Connecticut. He had left Yale without completing his master's *quaestio*, the capstone project for the master of arts degree. So he parted from the Smiths, traveled by water to East Windsor, and moved back into his parents' home for the summer. "My heart seemed to sink," he wrote, "at leaving the family and city, where I had enjoyed so many sweet and pleasant days. . . . As I sailed away, I kept sight of the city as long as I could; and when I was out of sight of it, it would affect me much to look that way, with a kind of melancholy mixed with sweetness."[26] Edwards hated to leave his friends, but he was aware that life moves on. In fact, in the brief period of time since he had left to work in New York, things at Yale had moved on quickly and considerably. President Cutler had been fired for leaving the Congregational Church and plaguing New England with what would soon be called "the great apostasy."

At commencement in September, Cutler had stunned those in attendance by concluding with words from the Church of England's *Book of Common Prayer*, "and let all the people say, Amen." Today these words seem inoffensive. Many Christian leaders use them.

---

[26]Edwards, "Personal Narrative," in *Letters and Personal Writings*, pp. 797-98.

They are found throughout the Bible.[27] But in 1722 they were fighting words. Though the Puritan movement had coalesced to reform the Church of England, and New England's early Puritans had belonged to the national Church, after the English Civil War and Restoration of the monarchy the Puritans were outlawed and New England's Congregationalists took on a new identity—one defined in terms of dissent, or opposition, to Anglicanism and its increasingly broad, catholic and Arminian proclivities. Now the Anglicans were suspect, both doctrinally and liturgically. New Englanders resisted their encroachments in the colonies. So when the president of Yale, senior tutor Daniel Browne, former tutor Samuel Johnson, and four other regional clergymen (Jared Eliot, John Hart, James Wetmore and Samuel Whittelsey) all left for the Church of England, making their exit ostentatious and attributing it in part to the books in Yale's Dummer Collection, they incited a great alarm over the future of the churches.[28]

Yale's presidents usually posed the master's *quaestio* for their students (the Latin proposition debated at commencement). In 1723, however, Yale still had no president. We no longer know who posed the *quaestio* for Edwards' exercise. But we do know the *quaestio*, as well as Edwards' response to it. Scholars speculate that Edwards posed it himself in order to counteract what happened the year before with Cutler and company. Yale's commencement was a time for regional ministers to gather. Graduates displayed their learning in Latin disputations, much like bucks butting heads, and all who understood

---

[27]See, for example, Ps 106:48, "Blessed be the LORD God of Israel from everlasting to everlasting: and let all the people say, Amen. Praise ye the LORD."

[28]On the basis of their reading and conversation with Church officials, such as the Anglican missionary George Pigot of nearby Stratford (the site of Cutler's former church), the so-called Yale rebels came to believe that episcopal ordination (i.e., at the hands of Anglican bishops) was superior to their own congregational ordination (at the hands of local laymen). President Cutler, for his part, went on to serve as the founding rector of Boston's (Anglican) Old North Church, known technically as Christ Church, in 1723, a congregation that made history in 1775 when its sexton, Robert Newman, ascended its steeple and held two lanterns as a sign from Paul Revere that the British were moving by sea—and not by land—toward Lexington and Concord.

the language enjoyed the show. Edwards knew that this was the case. He saw potential for scoring public points against the Church of England. It is surely not a coincidence that his thesis sounded a strong note of Calvinist commitment: *Peccator Non Iustificatur Coram Deo Nisi per Iustitiam Christi Fide Apprehensam* ("A Sinner Is Not Justified in the Sight of God Except through the Righteousness of Christ Obtained by Faith").[29]

Edwards' *quaestio* shows little of his theological genius. It reads too much like a stodgy, academic disputation. But its defense of a Calvinist view of justification by faith alone established his scholarly credentials as a Reformed theologian. "The task which concerns us today," he declaimed, "is of the very highest importance, . . . that is, to defend the truth of the Reformed religion to Protestants and of the Christian religion to Christians." He argued, "a sinner is justified in the sight of God neither totally nor in part because of . . . any works at all, but only on account of what Christ did and suffered, received by faith." He went on to contend, moreover, "that Christ is the complete Savior and not merely the partial author of our eternal salvation. . . . we deny that a sinner is his own redeemer and mediator." In short, Edwards fought valiantly for "the purity of Reformed Christianity," doing battle throughout his speech against all who say "that the sinner is justified by repentance and reformation," by trying to be good without trusting in the Lord's vicarious righteousness. He concluded "fearlessly" for "the truth" of "Reformed" Protestantism, assuring his elders in the ministry that all was not lost at Yale.[30]

Shortly after this exercise, Edwards began to preach in Bolton, fifteen miles east of Hartford, an assignment that his father had helped to arrange (because it was nice and close to home). The Bol-

---

[29]Jonathan Edwards, "Quaestio: Peccator Non Iustificatur Coram Deo Nisi per Iustitiam Christi Fide Apprehensam," in *Sermons and Discourses, 1723–1729*, ed. Kenneth P. Minkema, *WJE*, vol. 14 (1997), p. 55.

[30]I have followed the translation provided by George G. Levesque in Edwards, *Sermons and Discourses, 1723–29*, pp. 60-66.

ton church was Congregational. It was also very new. The town of Bolton had been incorporated only three years earlier (1720). Nearly twenty years of age, Edwards served as its first pastor. He stayed there several months, even agreeing to settle permanently in response to the church's offer on November 11, 1723. However, for reasons no longer known, the Bolton church did not ordain him. It likely failed to muster sufficient financial support to keep him there. Though it had built a meeting house, the town had not yet built a parsonage. Whatever the case, Edwards moved again the following May, accepting a call from Yale to serve as its senior tutor. He later arranged to have a former classmate take his place in Bolton. Thomas White would become the Bolton church's first *ordained* pastor. He was installed October 25, 1725, the time from which the church has usually dated its founding.

A TUTORSHIP AT YALE

When Edwards returned to New Haven, Yale had roughly forty students. A younger scholar named Robert Treat would join him as a junior tutor. But the college had no president. Its future was up for grabs. President Cutler had not been replaced, and Yale's trustees now looked to Edwards both to stabilize the school and to bear the bulk of its volatile administrative load.

Always a conscientious Christian, Edwards worked with all his might to fulfill this set of expectations. He labored so diligently, in fact, with such ascetic devotion to duty, that in September 1725 he fell seriously ill. New England's eighteenth-century scholars suffered from numerous physical ailments. They led sedentary lives and worked extremely long hours, often by candlelight, on starchy, meaty, heavily salted diets in the days before the rise of modern medicine. Many damaged their eyes and met with a host of aches and pains, including migraines and what colonists called "the ague" (i.e., recurrent fever chills). Edwards suffered all his life from these and other such infirmities. We will see that his spindly body broke down frequently under stress. As he explained years later in response to a job offer, "I have a constitution in many respects peculiar unhappy, attended with flaccid solids, vapid, sizy and scarce fluids, and a low tide of spirits; often occasioning a kind of childish weakness and contemptibleness of speech, presence, and demeanor."[31] Here and elsewhere, Edwards employed medieval physiological language. But he was not exaggerating. His constitution failed him shortly after returning to Yale. It would fail him again and again throughout the rest of his ministry.[32]

"In September 1725, was taken ill at New Haven; and endeavoring to go home to Windsor, was so ill at the North Village, that I could go no further: where I lay sick for about a quarter of a year."[33] Edwards had tried, in other words, to make it home to the care of his mother. He grew so sick, however, that he could travel only as far as North Haven, just a few miles north of Yale. He crashed violently in the house of a local friend, Isaac Stiles.[34] His mother rushed to his side. Only as Edwards' pain subsided was he able to make it home, staying briefly in East Windsor before returning to Yale to work the winter term. Still ailing as late as the spring of 1726, however, Edwards went back home again, convalescing there at length and not resuming his full round of responsibilities at Yale until sometime in the early days of summer.

Throughout the spring and early summer, Edwards preached in Glastonbury (another town quite close to Hartford), reigniting his passion for congregational ministry. He continued as senior tutor at Yale until that year's commencement, fighting the summer heat in

---

[31]Jonathan Edwards to the Trustees of the College of New Jersey, October 19, 1757, in *Letters and Personal Writings*, p. 726.

[32]On Edwards' lifelong personal struggles, both physical and emotional, see also Kenneth P. Minkema, "Personal Writings," in *The Cambridge Companion to Jonathan Edwards*, ed. Stephen J. Stein (New York: Cambridge University Press, 2007), pp. 39-60.

[33]Edwards, "Personal Narrative," in *Letters and Personal Writings*, p. 798.

[34]Stiles hailed from East Windsor. He had graduated from Yale College in 1722. Late in 1724, he settled as pastor in North Haven. Late in 1727, he became the father of Ezra Stiles, a future president of Yale (1778-1795).

New Haven while preparing students to graduate. By the end of that year, Elisha Williams was elected to serve as Yale's new president. Edwards had more freedom now to consider other options. And on August 29, when Solomon Stoddard's church in Northampton asked him to help his aging grandfather as pastoral assistant, he was ready and rearing to go. His time as tutor had been a trial—both physically and spiritually. His first "Diary" entry as a tutor says it all: "This week has been a remarkable week with me with respect to despondencies, fears, perplexities, multitudes of cares and distraction of mind; being the week I came hither to New Haven, in order to entrance upon the office of Tutor of the College. I have now abundant reason to be convinced of the troublesomeness and vexation of the world, and that it never will be another kind of world."[35] Two years of such despair proved overwhelming.

Stoddard was nearly eighty-three. He had been ministering in Northampton by himself for half a century. Finally in 1725, the town had voted to hire him help. And after a brief junior pastorate by a well-born Harvard graduate (Israel Chauncy, who seems to have suffered from a severe mental depression),[36] nearly everyone in town was eager to hear from Stoddard's grandson. Edwards' reputation preceded him. He had probably preached in Northampton at some point the previous spring. He would surely have done so earlier if not for his lengthy illness. He was the brightest junior prospect in New England's clerical ranks. All Northampton hoped that he would carry on his family legacy.

Edwards trotted into town in October 1726. In November of that

---

[35]Edwards, "Diary," entry for June 6, 1724, in *Letters and Personal Writings*, p. 786.

[36]As recorded by Northampton's local historian, James Trumbull, "After his services in this town, [Chauncy] preached at Housatonnuck, but becoming delirious he returned to his father at Hadley. On account of his infirmity he was confined in a small house near the parsonage. This building caught fire in the night, and he was burned to death. He was accustomed to cry fire during the night, and consequently no notice was taken of his cries at this time. He had been invited to settle at Norwalk and Glastonbury, Ct., but declined." James Russell Trumbull, *History of Northampton, Massachusetts, from Its Settlement in 1654*, vol. 2 (Northampton: Press of Gazette Printing Co., 1902), p. 43 n. 1.

year the congregation "settled" him formally. Ordained on February 15, 1727, he spent the next twenty-three years serving the people of Northampton. Edwards was well prepared for this. Although but twenty-three years of age when he began his work with Stoddard, he had preached by then for six years, pastored two other churches, and become the best young theological mind in all of America. He worked very hard. He loved the Lord with all his might. He would soon learn to love his congregation.

Chapter 2

PREACH THE WORD

I charge thee . . . before God, and the Lord Jesus Christ, who shall judge the quick and the dead. . . . Preach the word; be instant in season, out of season; reprove, rebuke, exhort with all long-suffering and doctrine. For the time will come when they will not endure sound doctrine; but after their own lusts shall they heap to themselves teachers, having itching ears; And they shall turn away their ears from the truth, and shall be turned unto fables. But watch thou in all things, endure afflictions, do the work of an evangelist, make full proof of thy ministry.

2 TIMOTHY 4:1-5

*J*t is more than likely that Edwards lived with his grandparents Esther and Solomon Stoddard as he settled in Northampton. He was still young and single, insufficiently acquainted with the members of his parish, and in constant need of help with the material side of life. The Stoddard home on Round Hill stood a stone's throw from the church, at the center of Northampton's social network. The town's farms meandered outwards from this geo-cultural eminence, most importantly to the east, sloping toward the Connecticut River. But its houses huddled close, within earshot of the meeting house, for spiritual, commercial, even military purposes. As Edwards noted astutely about a decade after settling, the people of Northampton "mostly dwell more compactly together than any town of such a bigness in these parts of the country; which probably has been an occasion that both our corruptions and reformations have been, from time to time, the more swiftly propagated from one to another through the town."[1]

In 1726, Northampton probably housed fewer than 1,100 people. By the mid 1730s it would grow to 1,300 and have 620 communicant members in its church. By the time of the Great Awakening in the early 1740s, nearly 700 people worshiped regularly with Edwards. Upwards of 1,000 people crowded in to hear George Whitefield. Church attendance was required, but not for mothers nursing infants, soldiers traveling on assignment, the sick, disabled or infirm (as we noted in the preface). The town had grown unusually large by the standards of its day. Still, Edwards' congregation was smaller than many expect today. It is amazing what God can do in seemingly out-of-the-way places.[2]

Edwards Aids His Ailing Grandfather

Edwards ascended to the pulpit in Northampton twice a week, wearing an academic gown and sporting a powdered periwig. "Mr. Stoddard," we are told, "though so much advanced in years, had a good degree of strength, both of body and mind; and, for a considerable period after the settlement of his grandson, he was able to offici-

---

[1] Jonathan Edwards, A Faithful Narrative of the Surprizing Work of God in the Conversion of Many Hundred Souls in Northampton, in The Great Awakening, ed. C. C. Goen, WJE, vol. 4 (1972), p. 145.

[2] Most of these numbers are estimates based on Edwards' A Faithful Narrative (1737), pp. 145, 157, which reports that by 1737 Northampton had "about 200 families" and "about six hundred and twenty communicants, which include almost all our adult persons." We know that in 1764, Northampton had 203 families living in 186 houses for a total population of nearly 1,300 people. It is probably safe to assume that a similar ratio of families to general population obtained in Edwards' day. For more such estimations, see Iain H. Murray, Jonathan Edwards: A New Biography (Edinburgh: Banner of Truth Trust, 1987), p. 89; Kenneth P. Minkema, "Old Age and Religion in the Writings and Life of Jonathan Edwards," Church History 70 (December 2001): 674-704 (esp. 699); and George M. Marsden, Jonathan Edwards: A Life (New Haven: Yale University Press, 2003), p. 127.

ate in the desk the half of every Sabbath."[3] Northamptonites convened for corporate worship thrice a week, twice for regular sabbath services and once on a weekday afternoon for a service called the "lecture" (held more often than not on Wednesday). Thus from late in 1726 till late in 1728 (when Stoddard's health declined), Edwards preached once every Lord's Day and "lectured" once a week, adding a third sermon per week to his already busy schedule as he turned twenty-five.

Typical Sunday morning services began with a call to worship (usually based on a Bible passage), then a corporate "prayer of approach," before the people stood to hear the public reading of the Word. New Englanders cited Nehemiah 8 as biblical precedent for the seriousness with which they handled public Bible reading. Just as the Jews had stood for hours of solemn Scripture reading shortly after they finished rebuilding the outer walls of Jerusalem after the exile, New Englanders stood for the reading and singing of several chapters of Scripture every service in their Bible commonwealths. As recounted in Nehemiah,

> And all the people gathered themselves together as one man into the street that was before the water gate; and they spake unto Ezra the scribe to bring the book of the law of Moses, which the LORD had commanded to Israel. And Ezra the priest brought the law before the congregation. . . . And he read therein . . . from the morning until midday . . . and the ears of all the people were attentive unto the book of the law. And Ezra the scribe stood upon a pulpit of wood, which they had made for the purpose. . . . And Ezra opened the book in the sight of all the people . . . and when he opened it, all the people stood

---

[3]Sereno E. Dwight, "Memoirs of Jonathan Edwards, A.M.," most widely available in *The Works of Jonathan Edwards*, ed. Edward Hickman (1834; Edinburgh: Banner of Truth Trust, 1974), p. xxxviii. (Dwight's "Memoirs" were published originally in the less accessible Sereno E. Dwight, ed., *The Works of President Edwards . . . in Ten Volumes* [New York: S Converse, 1829–1830].) Significantly, Stoddard thought that wearing (showy) periwigs was sinful, except in cases of baldness. Far more clergy wore them in Edwards' day than in seventeenth-century America. See Joseph A. Conforti, *Imagining New England: Explorations of Regional Identity from the Pilgrims to the Mid-Twentieth Century* (Chapel Hill: University of North Carolina Press, 2001), p. 71.

up: And Ezra blessed the LORD, the great God. And all the people answered, Amen, Amen, with lifting up their hands: and they bowed their heads, and worshipped the Lord with their faces to the ground. . . . So they read in the book in the law of God distinctly, and gave the sense, and caused them to understand the reading.

And Nehemiah . . . and Ezra the priest the scribe, and the Levites that taught the people, said unto all the people, This day is holy unto the LORD your God; mourn not, nor weep. For all the people wept, when they heard the words of the law. (Neh 8:1-9)

After an Old Testament reading (usually at least a chapter in length), the minister "gave the sense" of the text, offered a New Testament lesson (typically *lectio continua*, continuous reading, week by week, of major sections of Scripture) and then explained that text as well. The people sang a metrical psalm. The pastor led a corporate prayer of public confession and intercession. Then he preached a massive, exegetical sermon (usually one to two hours in length).[4] After another corporate prayer, often lasting half an hour, the congregation sang another psalm and heard the benediction (which was usually from the Bible). Worship services in New England centered attention on the Scriptures![5]

---

[4]Richard Bernard, the author of one of the standard Puritan preaching manuals, told ministers to conclude their sermons "within the compasse of the houre, or immediately after, except upon extraordinarie occasion: Neither is this to binde Gods spirit to an houre: but to follow the order of the Church, and thereupon the expectation of the hearers, and their infirmitie; which who so regardeth not, knoweth not well how to keepe measure in speaking: neither hath discretion to see what is convenient. Manie for want of observing time, and commonly going beyond the customarie space allotted thereunto, doe make their labour to their daily hearers tedious, themselves to be condemned of pride, loving to heare themselves talke; or of follie, without wit to keepe a meane, or to know that as much may be uttered in an houre, as can be of any almost rightlie understood and well carried away." See Richard Bernard, *The Faithfull Shepheard: Or the Shepheards Faithfulnesse* (London: Printed by Arnold Hatfield for John Bill, 1607), p. 80. Not all Puritan clergy followed Bernard's sage advice.

[5]New England clergy followed the guidance of the Westminster Assembly with regard to worship services, especially its *Directory for the Public Worship of God* (1644/45). See *The Westminster Directory, being A Directory for the Publique Worship of God in the Three Kingdomes*, with an introduction by Ian Breward, Grove Liturgical Study No. 21 (Bramcote, U.K.: Grove Books, 1980). With regard to the "publique reading of the holy Scriptures," the Assemblymen advised: "How large a portion shall be read at once, is left to the wisdome of the Minister: but it is convenient, that ordinarily one Chapter of each Testament bee read at every meeting; and sometimes

Edwards was used to this routine well before his work with Stoddard. But during his first winter serving as Northampton's junior pastor, he grew confident that its rhythm would set the pace for the rest of his life. On February 15, he finally received his ordination, at the age of twenty-three, in a sacred service led by Stoddard and other regional ministers. His uncle William Williams, then the sixty-two-year-old shepherd of the flock in nearby Hatfield (Stoddard's son-in-law and the father of Edwards' cousin Elisha Williams), preached the ordination sermon. It has been lost. We know that its text was 2 Corinthians 4:7 ("But we have this treasure in earthen vessels, that the excellency of the power may be of God, and not of us"). Williams was widely known as a powerful public speaker.

Edwards also preached a sermon at his ordination service, only a fragment of which survives. He cannibalized a manuscript he had already preached in New York on the theme of seeking God, for it contained material helpful in setting the tempo for his ministry. "Let us now," he boldly intoned, "earnestly set ourselves to seek the favor, presence, and blessing [of God] in that affair which is before us. The success of his means and ordinances, and the ministry of the Word, depends on his blessing." Edwards developed this theme with characteristic artistry and passion, concluding in language that would become a standard refrain in later sermons:

> Let us all therefore earnestly seek to God, that he would now lift up the light of his countenance and shine forth, that he would appear and manifest his approbation and favor, that he would come

---

more, where the Chapters be short, or the coherence of matter requireth it. It is requisite that all the Canonical Books be read over in order, that the people may be better acquainted with the whole Body of the Scriptures: And ordinarily, where the Reading in either Testament endeth on one Lords Day, it is to begin the next. Wee commend also the more frequent reading of such Scriptures, as hee that readeth shall thinke best for edification of his Hearers; as the Book of Psalmes, and such like" (p. 11). For more on Puritan worship services, see Richard A. Muller and Rowland S. Ward, *Scripture and Worship: Biblical Interpretation and the Directory for Public Worship*, The Westminster Assembly and the Reformed Faith (Phillipsburg, N.J.: P & R Publishing, 2007), pp. 111-40. A version of the *Directory* offering modernized spelling, punctuation, and word forms is found in Muller and Ward, *Scripture and Worship*, pp. 141-75.

---

down and dwell in the midst of us: dwell here in his house, as he hath done in times past, and give us to see his goings in his sanctuary; and would hereafter, from time to time, make the ministration of the gospel successful for the converting of many souls, and the edifying of saints. And let us not keep away, or drive away, God's Spirit by our carelessness and negligence, or by our sins, but seek him till he come and command his blessing upon us, even life forever more.[6]

After his ordination service Edwards carried on as before. He joined the Hampshire County Association of Congregational clergy, making new friends, swapping books with other pastors in the area, and enjoying opportunities for ministerial dialogue.[7] He worked on new sermons, got to know his growing parish, prayed fervently for help with the daunting task now set before him, and made progress on his steep, ministerial learning curve. Lest he appear a one-track man, though, it is necessary to note that in the spring of 1727 Edwards was in love—with a girl for whom he had fallen while at Yale.

LOVE, MARRIAGE AND FAMILY

Sarah Pierpont was a pastor's daughter seven years his junior. Edwards probably saw her first when she was too young to view romantically. Her father, James, who died young (1714), had served for thirty years as the minister of the First Congregational Church in New Haven. He was also a founder of Yale. We no longer know when Jonathan first approached his daughter for conversation. But we do know he was smitten, probably sometime during his service as the senior tutor at Yale. As he wrote of her in a long-famous tribute to her soul:

They say there is a young lady in [New Haven] who is beloved of that

---

[6]Jonathan Edwards, "Fragment: From an Application on Seeking God," in *Sermons and Discourses, 1720–1723*, ed. Wilson H. Kimnach, *WJE*, vol. 10 (1992), p. 387.

[7]For information on the books in the Hampshire Association library (started in 1732), see *Catalogues of Books*, ed. Peter J. Theusen, *WJE*, vol. 26 (2008), pp. 357-60.

almighty Being, who made and rules the world, and that there are certain seasons in which this great Being, in some way or other invisible, comes to her and fills her mind with exceeding sweet delight, and that she hardly cares for anything, except to meditate on him— that she expects after a while to be received up where he is, to be raised up out of the world and caught up into heaven; being assured that he loves her too well to let her remain at a distance from him always. There she is to dwell with him, and to be ravished with his love and delight forever. Therefore, if you present all the world before her, with the richest of its treasures, she disregards it and cares not for it, and is unmindful of any pain or affliction. She has a strange sweetness in her mind, and singular purity in her affection; is most just and conscientious in all her actions; and you could not persuade her to do anything wrong or sinful, if you would give her all the world, lest she should offend this great Being. She is of a wonderful sweetness, calmness and universal benevolence of mind; especially after those seasons in which this great God has manifested himself to her mind. She will sometimes go about from place to place, singing sweetly; and seems to be always full of joy and pleasure; and no one knows for what. She loves to be alone, and to wander in the fields and on the mountains, and seems to have someone invisible always conversing with her.[8]

These pastors' kids were kindred spirits. Jonathan loved Sarah's beauty, but attributed her attractiveness to the fullness of God in her soul. To call theirs love at first sight would be to mislead most modern readers. These two fell in love with the image and glory of God they saw in each other.

They were married in New Haven on July 28, which fell on a Friday in the year 1727. After saying goodbye to family, Sarah journeyed north with Jonathan and made her home in Northampton, in a new parsonage on (what later became) King Street. Jonathan's settlement provided them with one hundred pounds per year, regular cost-of-

---

[8]Jonathan Edwards, "On Sarah Pierpont," in *Letters and Personal Writings*, ed. George S. Claghorn, WJE, vol. 16 (1998), pp. 789-90.

living raises, fifty acres of arable land (ten of them in town, "Against Slow Bridge Next by John Alexanders Land," the other forty "Up Munhan River above Pumrys Meadow," nearly five miles away), and an additional three hundred pounds for the purchase of "a Homestead, or building: or both as Their shall be ocation" (with more funds pledged if this was not enough "to Commodate Mr Edwards with a Sutable Habitation"). In March 1728, the Edwardses asked for an extra eighty pounds to pay for the parsonage. In summer 1729, Northampton built them a large barn. After Rev. Stoddard died, Edwards' salary was doubled. All in all, the Edwards family was well furnished.[9]

By all accounts, the Edwards home was full of love and conviviality. Many have made too much of Samuel Hopkins' striking statement that Edwards "commonly spent thirteen Hours every Day in his Study."[10] They conclude from this too hastily that Edwards was an egghead, a recluse, who could not have been a sensitive family man. But this is not what people thought who knew the Edwards family best. Concerning Jonathan and Sarah, George Whitefield wrote in his journal, "A sweeter couple I have not yet seen."[11] The Edwards marriage proved much stronger than those of many of their peers (such as the Whitefields and the Wesleys).[12] And their

---

[9]Quotations taken from Northampton town records, as provided by James Russell Trumbull, *History of Northampton, Massachusetts, from Its Settlement in 1654*, vol. 2 (Northampton: Press of Gazette Printing Co., 1902), pp. 44-45.

[10]Samuel Hopkins, *The Life and Character of the Late Reverend Mr. Jonathan Edwards* (Boston: S. Kneeland, 1765), p. 40.

[11]*George Whitefield's Journals*, ed. Iain Murray (Edinburgh: Banner of Truth Trust, 1960), p. 476 (entry for Sunday, October 19, 1740). Whitefield went on to note that the Edwards marriage rekindled his own desire to find a suitable wife: "Mrs. Edwards is adorned with a meek and quiet spirit; she talked solidly of the things of God, and seemed to be such a helpmeet for her husband, that she caused me to renew those prayers, which, for some months, I have put up to God, that He would be pleased to send me a daughter of Abraham to be my wife" (p. 477). For further, personal testimony to Edwards' strong marriage, see Kenneth P. Minkema, "Personal Writings," in *The Cambridge Companion to Jonathan Edwards*, ed. Stephen J. Stein (New York: Cambridge University Press, 2007), pp. 47-48.

[12]For a brief, depressing summary and psychological interpretation of the love lives and marital problems of Whitefield, Wesley and Howell Harris, a popular Welsh revivalist, see Michael Watts, *The Dissenters: From the Reformation to the French Revolution* (Oxford: Clarendon, 1978), pp. 419-21.

home appears to have been much warmer too.

The fact is that Edwards met with family and friends within his study. He was clearly an intellectual who spent much time alone. He was not known for making frequent calls in others' homes.[13] But he did spend many hours every week with other people, investing time in the lives of family, friends and numerous other visitors to his bustling parsonage. The family hosted scores of guests—visiting dignitaries, relatives and eager pastoral interns (such as Samuel Hopkins himself), some for several months at a time, all with selfless hospitality. In the words of Leonard Sweet, a pastor-scholar in his own right, "A constant stream of visitors inundated the manse . . . turning it into more a spiritual retreat center than a private home."[14]

In the midst of all this traffic, Edwards managed to find time for private romance with his wife. The couple conceived eleven children.[15] To the day on which he died, moreover, Edwards proved a thoughtful spouse, a tender lover of Sarah. We will cover his death below. But Hopkins' account of his dying words, spoken miles away from Sarah through their grown daughter Lucy, ought to be quoted briefly here: "give my kindest love to [Sarah], and tell her, that the uncommon union, which has so long subsisted between us, has been

---

[13]"He did not make it his Custom to visit his People in their own Houses, unless he was sent for by the Sick; or he heard that they were under some special Affliction; in stead of visiting from House to House, he used to preach frequently at private Meetings in particular Neighbourhoods; and often call the young People and Children to his own House: when he used to pray with them & treat with them in a manner suited to their Years & Circumstances." It "appeared to him, that he could do the greatest good to Souls, and most promote the interest of Christ by preaching and writing, and conversing with Persons under religious Impressions in his Study; where he encouraged all such to repair." Indeed, in times "of the out-pouring of God's Spirit, and the revival of Religion among his People, his Study was throng'd with Persons to lay open their spiritual Concerns to him, and seek his Advice and Direction. . . . He was a skilful Guide to Souls under spiritual Difficulties, And was therefore sought unto not only by his own People, but by many who lived scores of Miles off." Hopkins, *The Life and Character of the Late Reverend Mr. Jonathan Edwards*, pp. 49-51.

[14]Leonard I. Sweet, "The Laughter of One: Sweetness and Light in Franklin and Edwards," in *Benjamin Franklin, Jonathan Edwards, and the Representation of American Culture*, ed. Barbara B. Oberg and Harry S. Stout (New York: Oxford University Press, 1993), p. 120.

[15]Sarah (born in 1728), Jerusha (1730), Esther (1732), Mary (1734), Lucy (1736), Timothy (1738), Susannah (1740), Eunice (1743), Jonathan Jr. (1745), Elizabeth (1747) and Pierrepont (1750).

of such a nature, as I trust is spiritual, and therefore will continue for ever."[16] The Edwards marriage was "uncommon," as these dying words attest: uncommon in its intimacy, uncommon in its affection, uncommonly well grounded in God's grace, mercy and love.[17]

Hopkins left a vivid account of Edwards' "general manner of life," one worth quoting in detail for the way it fills out our picture of Edwards and the Edwards family home. Edwards usually rose "by four," or "between four and five in the Morning." He was "wont to have his Family up in season in the Morning; after which, before the Family entered on the Business of the Day, he attended on Family Prayers." He read "a Chapter in the Bible . . . commonly by Candle-light in the Winter; upon which he asked his Children Questions according to their Age and Capacity." He explained the Scriptures to them "as he thought most proper." Throughout the day, more-over, "[h]e was careful and thorough in the Government of his Chil-dren," in response to which "they reverenced, esteemed and loved him." Edwards "took Opportunities to treat with them in his Study, singly and particularly about their . . . Soul's Concerns." He spent most Saturday evenings teaching them the catechism (the *Westminster Shorter Catechism* of 1647), "not merely by taking care that they learned it by Heart; but by leading them into an understanding of the Doctrines therein taught, by asking them Questions on each An-swer, and explaining it to them." On such nights, he also prepared

---

[16]See Hopkins, *The Life and Character of the Late Reverend Mr. Jonathan Edwards*, p. 81. As Hopkins tells the story, "a little before his death, [Edwards] call'd his daughter to him . . . and address'd her in a few words, which were immediately taken down in writing, as near as could be recol-lected" (p. 80). The words were taken down by Edwards' physician and friend, William Ship-pen, and are available in an unpublished manuscript letter: William Shippen to Sarah Pierpont Edwards, March 22, 1758, folder 1756-59C, #1-2, Franklin Trask Library, Andover-Newton Theological School.

[17]Edwards' views of familial love are handled well by Stuart Piggin, "Domestic Spirituality: Jona-than Edwards on Love, Marriage and Family Life," in *The Bible and the Business of Life: Essays in Honour of Robert J. Banks's Sixty-fifth Birthday*, ed. Simon Carey Holt and Gordon Preece, ATF Series (Adelaide: ATF Press, 2004), pp. 149-63. For insightful commentary on the ways in which Edwards' marriage illuminates his well-known theological projects, see James Wm. McClendon Jr., *Systematic Theology*, vol. 1, *Ethics* (Nashville: Abingdon Press, 1986), pp. 110-31, 148-50.

his family well for the coming sabbath, directing them in the singing of psalms and prayer.[18]

Edwards "was thought by some, who had but a slight Acquaintance with him to be stiff & unsociable." However, Hopkins claimed that "this was owing to want of better Acquaintance." He "was not a Man of many Words . . . and was somewhat reserved among Strangers." But "how groundless the imputation of *stiff* and *unsociable* was, his known and tried Friends best knew." These men "always found him easy of access, kind and condescending; and tho' not talkative, yet affable and free." Indeed, among his closest friends, Edwards "threw off the Reserve, and was most open and free. . . . And indeed, he was on all Occasions, quite sociable and free with all, who had any special Business with him."[19]

When not at work in his study, or socializing with others, Edwards liked to ride his horse and go on long country walks. "He would commonly, unless diverted by Company, ride two or three Miles after Dinner to some lonely Grove, where he would dismount and walk a while. At which times he generally carried his Pen and Ink with him, to note any Thought that should be suggested, which he chose to retain and pursue." During the winter, when such exercise was thwarted by the weather, "he was wont almost daily to take an Ax and chop Wood . . . for the space of half an Hour or more."[20]

Edwards never made a show of it, but he loved to help the poor. Indeed, his "great Benevolence" proved itself in "the uncommon regard he shewed to . . . the Poor and Distressed." He "was much in recommending this," in "publick" and in "private." He often said "that professed Christians . . . are greatly deficient in this Duty." In fact, he taught that "every . . . Church ought by frequent and liberal Contributions, to maintain a publick Stock, that might be ready for" its "poor and necessitous Members." He refused, furthermore,

---

[18]Hopkins, *The Life and Character of the Late Reverend Mr. Jonathan Edwards*, pp. 39-40, 43-44.
[19]Ibid., pp. 41-42.
[20]Ibid., p. 40.

to "content himself" with preaching this, "but practis'd it" as well—
"Tho'," his student was quick to add, "he took great Care to conceal"
his deeds. "[D]oubtless most of his Alms-deeds will be unknown till
the Resurrection, which if known, would prove him to be as great an
Instance of Charity as any that can be produced in this Age."[21]

Edwards was not a handy man. In fact, he "left the particular Over
sight and Direction of the temporal Concerns of his Family, almost
entirely to Mrs. Edwards." He "seldom knew when and by whom his
Forrage for Winter was gathered in, or how many milk Kine [cows]
he had; whence his Table was furnished," or much of anything else
pertaining mainly to the keeping of his house.[22]

This latter piece of information raises a painful, shameful subject.
The Edwardses were able to manage a home such as this, raising
eleven children well, farming fifty acres of land, and entertaining in
high style because they owned several slaves. Beginning in June 1731,
Edwards joined the slave trade, buying "a Negro Girle named Venus ages Fourteen years or thereabout" in Newport, at an auction,
for "the Sum of Eighty pounds."[23] By 1736, he owned a slave named
Leah (perhaps a biblical name for Venus). And over the years, he and
Sarah acquired at least five more: Joab and Rose Binney (whom Edwards married in 1751); Titus, Rose's son (described as a "negro boy"
in the family estate); and another African couple, Joseph and Sue
(who were sold soon after the Edwardses died, in 1759). We know
Rose Binney best, later Rose Binney Salter, for she later earned her
freedom, became a member of the Stockbridge church in 1771, and
was the subject of a spiritual narrative penned by Stephen West, her
minister in Stockbridge and a devotee of Edwards.[24]

---

[21]Ibid., pp. 45-46.

[22]Ibid., p. 49.

[23]See "Receipt for Slave Venus (1731)," in *A Jonathan Edwards Reader*, ed. John E. Smith, Harry S.
Stout and Kenneth P. Minkema (New Haven: Yale University Press, 1995), pp. 296-97.

[24]On Edwards' slaves and his roles in the transatlantic slave trade, see Kenneth P. Minkema,
"Jonathan Edwards on Slavery and the Slave Trade," *William and Mary Quarterly* 54 (October
1997): 823-34; Kenneth P. Minkema, "Jonathan Edwards's Defense of Slavery," *Massachusetts
Historical Review* 4 (2002): 23-59; Charles E. Hambrick-Stowe, "All Things Were New and As-

Edwardsians like West played a role in ending the slave trade—and did so, as they claimed, on Edwardsian grounds. Edwards himself owned a slave or two at a time for most of his life, even defending his right to do so in a famous letter draft.[25] But his doctrine of the regenerate will's "disinterested benevolence" (discussed in chapter five) paved the way for Christian antislavery activism. Samuel Hopkins preached regularly for African manumission long before it became a popular thing to do (especially in Newport, Rhode Island, a center of the slave trade, where he ministered at the time). And Edwards' son Jonathan Jr. joined the antislavery movement, providing the cause a strong, genetic link to Edwards.[26]

Still, Edwards owned slaves, as did many of his colleagues in colonial Christian ministry (most notably, George Whitefield). This needs to be confessed with utter clarity. He was complicit in this country's most notorious national sin. Christians today should not excuse this. Nor should we gloss it over glibly. Edwards' slave owning stands as a stark reminder of the sinfulness of our greatest Christian heroes. It should keep us from thinking too highly of them. It should also keep us humble. For if Edwards proved this sinful, woe is me, and woe are most of us whose piety frankly pales in comparison to his. We can only hope and pray that our humility will make us able to learn from other sinners. If we cannot, we are the losers. Life is

---

tonishing: Edwardsian Piety, the New Divinity, and Race," in *Jonathan Edwards at Home and Abroad: Historical Memories, Cultural Movements, Global Horizons*, ed. David W. Kling and Douglas A. Sweeney (Columbia: University of South Carolina Press, 2003), pp. 121-36; Kenneth P. Minkema and Harry S. Stout, "The Edwardsean Tradition and the Antislavery Debate, 1740–1865," *The Journal of American History* 92 (June 2005): 47-74; and Richard A. Bailey, "From Goddess of Love to Unloved Wife: Naming Slaves and Redeeming Masters in Eighteenth-Century New England," in *Slavery/Antislavery in New England*, The Dublin Seminar for New England Folklife Annual Proceedings 2003, ed. Peter Benes (Boston: Boston University, 2005), pp. 44-55.

[25]Jonathan Edwards, "Draft Letter on Slavery," in *Letters and Personal Writings*, pp. 71-76.

[26]They did so most famously in strident publications, such as Samuel Hopkins, *A Dialogue concerning the Slavery of the Africans, Showing It To Be the Duty and Interest of the American States to Emancipate All Their African Slaves* (1776); and Jonathan Edwards Jr., *The Injustice and Impolicy of the Slave Trade, and of Slavery* (1791). Selections of these works may be found in Douglas A. Sweeney and Allen C. Guelzo, eds., *The New England Theology: From Jonathan Edwards to Edwards Amasa Park* (Grand Rapids: Baker Academic, 2006).

poor, the view is bad, and self-righteousness abounds atop the moral high ground.[27]

It is difficult to say this, but slaves helped the Edwardses accomplish all they did, including their Christian ministries. Slave labor helped Jonathan to focus on his calling, freeing him up to spend the bulk of his time in prayer, reading and writing. Slaves also helped Sarah run the Edwards home efficiently, giving her time to cultivate her well-known Christian spirituality.

Sarah stood out clearly among the Christians of her day as an evangelical role model, a woman of vital faith. Despite her sins as a slave mistress—even because of these very sins—she took more time than most to work on her love for God. Edwards often used females as examples of genuine piety, most prominently in his well-known *Faithful Narrative* (1737).[28] But none of the women whom he heralded for the beauty of their faith proved to him as emblematic of earnest, evangelical holiness, or nearly as influential on the evangelical movement, as his own wife Sarah.

Edwards featured her anonymously in another major treatise, *Some Thoughts Concerning the Present Revival of Religion in New-England* (1743). He described her spiritual raptures, commended them to his readers and defended her ecstatic evangelical religion. Sarah usually demonstrated deep devotion to God. But during the time of the Great Awakening (discussed at length below), she underwent such a powerful experience of the Spirit that her husband asked her to write about it privately. He used her account right away in one of his books, *Some Thoughts*. Ever since, others have used it to hail her evangelical faith.

---

[27]I deal with evangelical complicity in the sins of the slave trade at greater length in Douglas A. Sweeney, *The American Evangelical Story: A History of the Movement* (Grand Rapids: Baker Academic, 2005), pp. 107-31. The most helpful Christian analysis of learning from a slave owner is that of Sherard Burns, a black pastor and Edwards scholar, "Trusting the Theology of a Slave Owner," in *A God Entranced Vision of All Things: The Legacy of Jonathan Edwards*, ed. John Piper and Justin Taylor (Wheaton, Ill.: Crossway, 2004), pp. 145-71.

[28]Abigail Hutchinson and little Phebe Bartlet, both residents of Northampton, are depicted in that treatise as examples of true religion that resulted from the revival in the Connecticut River valley (1734–1735). See Edwards, *A Faithful Narrative*, in *The Great Awakening*, pp. 191-205.

Edwards recounted avidly his wife's "frequent dwelling . . . in such views of the glory of the divine perfections" that her soul was "perfectly overwhelmed, and swallowed up with light and love and a sweet solace, rest and joy of soul, that was altogether unspeakable." On more than one occasion, this continued

> five or six hours . . . without any interruption . . . so that . . . the soul remained in a kind of heavenly Elysium, and did as it were swim in the rays of Christ's love, like a little mote swimming in the beams of the sun, or streams of his light that come in at a window; and the heart was swallowed up in a kind of glow of Christ's love, coming down from Christ's heart in heaven, as a constant stream of sweet light, at the same time the soul all flowing out in love to him; so that there seemed to be a constant flowing and reflowing from heart to heart.

He extended this account with many more such breathless sentences, attempting to make a sensory impression on his readers. After several pages of this, toward the end of his report on Sarah's own great awakening, he brings his readers up for air, assuring them of his quasi-mystical spouse's spiritual sanity.

> These things have been attended [in Sarah] with a constant sweet peace and calm and serenity of soul, without any cloud to interrupt it. . . . These things have been accompanied with an exceeding concern and zeal for moral duties . . . and an uncommon care to perform relative and social duties . . . a great inoffensiveness of life and conversation in the sight of others; a great meekness, gentleness and benevolence of spirit and behavior; and a great alteration in those things that formerly used to be the person's failings; seeming to be much overcome and swallowed up by the late great increase of grace, to the observation of those that are most conversant and most intimately acquainted.

Edwards finished with a flourish meant to disarm the wary reader, "Now if such things are enthusiasm, and the fruits of a distempered brain, let my brain be evermore possessed of that happy distemper!"[29]

---

[29]Jonathan Edwards, *Some Thoughts Concerning the Present Revival of Religion in New-England, and*

At least parts of Sarah's own account of this have been preserved, not in original manuscript, but through the work of a later editor, Sereno Edwards Dwight, a great-grandson of hers. In her fuller account we learn that Sarah's ecstasies occurred under the preaching of a young, prospective student of her husband, the Rev. Samuel Buell, who had supplied Edwards' pulpit at the height of the revival.[30] At first, Sarah worried about young Buell's prodigiousness. She feared he might surpass her husband in evangelistic usefulness. But after she resigned these reservations to the Lord, numerous friends were slain in the Spirit[31]—and Sarah seemed to drift through "the sweetest night I ever had in my life."

---

the Way in Which It Ought To Be Acknowledged and Promoted, Humbly Offered to the Publick . . . , in The Great Awakening, pp. 331-41.

[30]As Edwards himself wrote in a letter to his friend Thomas Prince, Buell's preaching caused a stir throughout Northampton. "About the beginning of February 1741/2, Mr. Samuel Buell came to this town, I being then absent from home, and continued so till about a fortnight after. Mr. Buell preached from day to day, almost every day, in the meetinghouse (I having left to him the free liberty of my pulpit, hearing of his designed visit before I went from home) and spent almost the whole time in religious exercises with the people, either in public or private, the people continually thronging him. . . . There were very extraordinary effects of Mr. Buell's labors; the people were exceedingly moved, crying out in great numbers in the meetinghouse, and great part of the congregation commonly staying in the house of God for hours after the public service, many of them in uncommon circumstances. . . . almost the whole town seemed to be in a great and continual commotion, day and night; and there was indeed a very great revival of religion. But it was principally among professors [i.e., previously converted Christians]; the appearances of a work of conversion were in no measure equal to what had been the summer before. When I came home I found the town in very extraordinary circumstances, such in some respects as I never saw it in before. Mr. Buell continued here a fortnight or three weeks after I returned: there being still great appearances attending his labors; many in their religious affections being raised far beyond what they ever had been before: and there were some instances of persons lying in a sort of trance, remaining for perhaps a whole twenty-four hours motionless, and with their senses locked up; but in the meantime under strong imaginations, as though they went to heaven, and had there a vision of glorious and delightful objects. But when the people were raised to this height, Satan took the advantage, and his interposition in many instances soon became very apparent: and a great deal of caution and pains were found necessary to keep the people, many of them, from running wild." See Jonathan Edwards to the Rev. Thomas Prince, December 12, 1743, in Letters and Personal Writings, pp. 120-21.

[31]The phrase "slain in the spirit" is usually associated with the Pentecostal and charismatic movements. It refers to the experience of unusual spiritual ecstasy. Surprisingly, perhaps, many eighteenth-century Calvinists also underwent such ecstasies, albeit in a controlled and less sensational environment than those that often characterize the charismatic movement (and usually without an emphasis on special gifts of the Spirit such as healing and speaking in tongues).

I never before, for so long a time together, enjoyed so much of the light, and rest, and sweetness of heaven in my soul, but without the least agitation of body during the whole time. The great part of the night I lay awake, sometimes asleep, and sometimes between sleeping and waking. But all night I continued in a constant, clear, and lively sense of the heavenly sweetness of Christ's excellent and transcendent love, of his nearness to me, and of my dearness to him; with an inexpressibly sweet calmness of soul in an entire rest in him. . . . So far as I am capable of making a comparison, I think that what I felt each minute, during the continuance of the whole time, was worth more than all the outward comfort and pleasure, which I had enjoyed in my whole life put together. It was a pure delight, which fed and satisfied the soul. It was pleasure, without the least sting, or any interruption. It was a sweetness, which my soul was lost in. It seemed to be all that my feeble frame could sustain, of that fullness of joy, which is felt by those, who behold the face of Christ, and share his love in the heavenly world.[32]

Well supported by such a singular wife, in such a loving Christian home, with slave labor to care for his family's numerous temporal needs, Edwards had everything he wanted, save perhaps a strong body, to carry out his ministry.

THE CHURCH BECOMES HIS OWN

It is a good thing too, for two years after he commenced his junior pastorate in Northampton, on a cold day in February (February 11, 1729), Stoddard died at home, leaving Edwards, who was now twenty-five, to serve as the only pastor of the most prominent church in all

---

[32]Dwight, "Memoirs of Jonathan Edwards, A.M.," pp. lxii-lxx (quotation on p. lxv). After the Great Awakening, Buell settled down at the Presbyterian church in East Hampton, Long Island, where he served from 1746 to 1798. Edwards preached his installation sermon (September 19, 1746), quickly published in Boston as *The Church's Marriage to her Sons, and to her God* (1746). See Jonathan Edwards, "The Church's Marriage to Her Sons, and to Her God," in *Sermons and Discourses, 1743–1758*, ed. Wilson H. Kimnach, *WJE*, vol. 25 (2006), pp. 164-96. On Buell's subsequent career, see also Thomas S. Kidd, *The Great Awakening: The Roots of Evangelical Christianity in Colonial America* (New Haven: Yale University Press, 2007), esp. 274-81.

of western New England.[33] William Williams preached the sermon at Stoddard's burial two days later.[34] Shortly thereafter, Edwards himself preached a sermon honoring Stoddard, titled "Living Unconverted Under an Eminent Means of Grace." He warned Northampton's nominal Christians of the "danger of being finally left of God, when sinners have lived long . . . under eminent means of conversion." Rev. Stoddard had served them well, he said, preaching the gospel faithfully and giving all a chance to turn their hearts over to God. "[I]t looks darkly upon you that are left," he chided, "especially you that have lived unconverted a long while under his ministry." Edwards cautioned the congregation that "God sometimes takes away his Spirit from a people when he takes away eminent means of grace." He concluded the sermon alarmingly, attempting to honor Stoddard by scaring his wayward sheep from the road that leads to perdition: "Woe to them that go to hell out of Northampton and that lived under Mr. Stoddard's ministry! . . . The many powerful awakening sermons that you have heard won't be forgotten. . . . They'll all be remembered, and you must hear 'em rehearsed again. Though you was so quiet under 'em when you heard 'em, yet when you hear 'em again, you will not be so quiet; they'll be thunder to you. Every word will pierce your heart through and through with torments."[35]

Edwards had obviously begun to assume control of his inheritance. He took his new role seriously—so seriously, in fact, that he soon plummeted physically. He grew ill and had to absent himself from church in April and May. He collapsed sometime in June. Sarah's brother, Benjamin Pierpont, had to travel in to preach for him. Again, Edwards' body failed to hold up beneath the weight of his

---

[33]Because Edwards himself was now married and had established a home of his own, his sister Mary moved to Northampton to care for their widowed grandmother, Esther Stoddard, who lived until 1736.

[34]It was published as William Williams, *The Death of a Prophet Lamented and Improved . . .* (Boston: B. Green, 1729).

[35]Jonathan Edwards, "Living Unconverted under an Eminent Means of Grace," in *Sermons and Discourses, 1723–1729*, ed. Kenneth P. Minkema, WJE, vol. 14 (1997), pp. 357-70. On Edwards' later tributes to Stoddard, see p. 357 n. 1.

own, heavy sense of calling. This would not be the last time that it buckled under pressure.

By the early days of summer, though, he was on the mend again. He rose eagerly to meet the demands of solo parish ministry, becoming the bright, young star of the region's ministerial ranks. In late July, he celebrated his second wedding anniversary. In August, he celebrated his daughter Sarah's first birthday. He had preached for seven years now on a fairly regular basis. He continued to inscribe his deepest thoughts in private notebooks, preparing himself for a long life of theological ministry. The thing he wanted most, though, was to be a faithful shepherd. He longed to be a wise steward of the gifts that he received, to hear "well done" from the lips of Christ on judgment day (Mt 25).

EDWARDS AS A PREACHER

The first public confirmation of his giftedness in ministry—at least the first one to make the papers back in Boston—came in July 1731, when Edwards was asked to preach there to a meeting of regional clergy during the week of Harvard's commencement. At this renowned public event, Edwards chose to deliver a sermon he had preached the previous fall to the people of Northampton. His text was 1 Corinthians 1:29-31, "That no flesh should glory in his presence. But of him are ye in Christ Jesus, who of God is made unto us wisdom, and righteousness, and sanctification, and redemption: That, according as it is written, He that glorieth, let him glory in the Lord." Edwards phrased his doctrine simply, making clear his Protestant orthodoxy: "God is glorified in the wisdom of redemption in this, that there appears in it so absolute and universal a dependence of the redeemed on him."[36]

---

[36]Jonathan Edwards, *God Glorified in the Work of Redemption, By the Greatness of Man's Dependence upon Him, in the Whole of it. Preached on the Public Lecture in Boston, July 8, 1731* (Boston: Samuel Kneeland and Timothy Green, 1731). Available in *Sermons and Discourses, 1730–1733*, ed. Mark Valeri, *WJE*, vol. 17 (1999), pp. 196-216.

Like the Puritans before him, Edwards organized his sermons into three main parts: (1) the *text*, a brief section in which he described the historical setting of his chosen Scripture passage; (2) the *doctrine*, a longer section in which he identified and developed a thesis statement for his sermon, one that he took from the text itself but supported with other Scriptures; (3) the *application*, or *use*, the longest section of the sermon, in which he applied his Scripture doctrine to his listeners' daily lives. The *Westminster Directory* (1644/45) commended such a format. Virtually all Reformed authorities had emphasized the *use*, moreover, stressing the importance of a practical application of the principles of Scripture to the everyday experience of the parish. William Ames called the failure to apply one's text a "sin," exhorting preachers to "sharpen" their doctrine by making "specially relevant some general truth with such effect that it may pierce the minds of those present with the stirring up of godly affections. Men are to be pricked," he wrote, "to the quick so that they feel individually what the Apostle said, namely, that the word of the Lord is a two-edged sword, piercing to the inward thoughts and affections and going through to the joining of bones and marrow [Heb 4:12]." The Westminster Assemblymen corroborated Ames, instructing the preacher "not to rest in generall Doctrine although never so much cleared and confirmed, but to bring it home to speciall Use, by application to his hearers."[37]

To the ministers in Boston, no ordinary hearers, some of whom he suspected of doctrinal heterodoxy—Harvard prided itself by then on being more open and "catholic" than Yale—Edwards applied his Scripture doctrine in a brief, old-fashioned way: "Let us be exhorted to exalt God alone, and ascribe to him all the glory of redemption." This nod to orthodoxy, though, helped him score his main point. Indeed, it *was* his main point, with which he hoped to prick this learned

---

[37]William Ames, *The Marrow of Theology*, ed. John D. Eusden (1968; Grand Rapids: Baker, 1997), 1.35.30, 45-46 (pp. 192-94); and *The Westminster Directory*, pp. 15-18 (quotation taken from p. 16).

group of clergy to the quick. Edwards sharpened his doctrine swiftly, but no less effectively, as he pled for orthodoxy in a rapidly changing climate, for Calvinist commitment among a people he suspected of harboring dangerous doctrinal views. "Those doctrines and schemes of divinity that are in any respects opposite to such an absolute and universal dependence on God," he declared, "do derogate from God's glory, and thwart the design of the contrivance for our redemption."

> Those schemes that put the creature in God's stead, . . . that exalt man into the place of either Father, Son, or Holy Ghost, in anything pertaining to our redemption; that however they may allow of a dependence of the redeemed on God, yet deny a dependence that is so absolute and universal; that own an entire dependence on God for some things, but not for others; [etc.]. . . . and whatever other way any scheme is inconsistent with our entire dependence on God for all, and in each of those ways, of having all *of* him, *through* him, and *in* him, it is repugnant to the design and tenor of the gospel, and robs it of that which God accounts its luster and glory.[38]

Whatever Boston's clergy thought of this up-and-coming Calvinist, whatever Harvard's men thought of this delegate of Yale, they paid him homage by inviting the publication of his sermon. Before the calendar year ended, it was circulating widely under the title that has endured more than a score of reprintings, *God Glorified in the Work of Redemption, By the Greatness of Man's Dependence.*[39]

As in the case of his personality, so in reference to his preaching, Edwards' reputation has suffered through years of negative publicity. Many assume the common caricature of Edwards is correct: he read his sermons in monotone, rarely looking up from his notes, putting parishioners to sleep with dry, academic droning. One late

---

[38]Edwards, "God Glorified in Man's Dependence," in *Sermons and Discourses, 1730–1733*, pp. 212-14.

[39]On the publication history of Edwards' writings, including this sermon, see Thomas H. Johnson, *The Printed Writings of Jonathan Edwards, 1703–1758: A Bibliography*, rev. ed. by M. X. Lesser, An Occasional Publication of Studies in Reformed Theology and History (Princeton: Princeton Theological Seminary, 2003).

nineteenth-century source went so far as to claim that, when Edwards did look up from his manuscript, he usually fixed his eyes on the bell rope at the entrance to the church, avoiding eye-contact with those who had come to hear him.[40]

But again, the Edwards of history does not conform to the stereotype. He wrote his sermons out in full until the early 1740s. He read parts of them to his people, as did many of his peers. But textual evidence in his manuscripts, as well as from those who heard him, shows that Edwards was a more lively preacher than many have assumed. After the early 1740s, Edwards preached from sketchy notes.[41] (Whitefield showed him how the Spirit could use extemporaneous speech.) Both his father and his grandfather had taught him to preach from memory.[42] He had always marked his sermons with cues for winsome oral delivery. We know that hundreds were

---

[40]William Edwards Park, "Edwardean," p. 202, folder 1668, box 37, Jonathan Edwards Collection, Beinecke Rare Book and Manuscript Library, Yale University (referred to as Beinecke hereafter).

[41]Even in the 1740s and 1750s, though, Edwards drafted complete sermons when making important public statements, as when he preached his farewell sermon to the people of Northampton, "A Farewell Sermon Preached at the First Precinct in Northampton, After the People's Public Rejection of Their Minister . . . on June 22, 1750," in *Sermons and Discourses, 1743–1758,* pp. 457-93.

[42]In fact, Stoddard publicly criticized the clergy who read their sermons. He and Timothy Edwards drafted lengthy sermons and preached them from memory. See Solomon Stoddard, *The Defects of Preachers Reproved, in a Sermon Preached at Northampton, May 19th, 1723* (New London, Conn.: T. Green, 1724); and Timothy Edwards, *All the Living Must Surely Die: Election Sermon* (New London, Conn.: T. Green, 1732), which also testifies clearly to the importance of good delivery: "Let us labour in a very particular, convincing and awakening manner to dispense the Word of God; so to speak as tends most to reach and pierce the Hearts and Consciences, and humble the Souls of them that hear us" (p. 25). As Cotton Mather taught young preachers at about the same time, "If you must have your notes before you in your preaching, . . . yet let there be with you a distinction between the neat using of notes, and the dull reading of them. Keep up the air and life of speaking, and put not off your hearers with an heavy reading to them. How can you demand of them to remember much of what you bring to them; when you remember nothing of it yourself? . . . Let your notes be little other than a quiver, on which you may cast your eye now and then, to see what arrow is to be next fetch'd from thence; and then, with your eye as much as may be on them whom you speak to, let it be shot away, with a vivacity becoming one in earnest, for to have the truths well entertained with the auditory." See Cotton Mather, *Manuductio ad Ministerium: Directions for a Candidate of the Ministry,* reproduced from the original edition, Boston, 1726, with a bibliographical note by Thomas J. Holmes and Kenneth B. Murdock (New York: Published for the Facsimile Text Society by Columbia University Press, 1938), pp. 105-6.

---

converted under his biblical exposition. We know that many cried aloud when Edwards preached during revival. In fact, when Edwards preached in Enfield, Massachusetts (now Connecticut), for revival, using his famous hellfire sermon, "Sinners in the Hands of an Angry God" (1741),

> There was a great moaning and crying out through [the] whole House—What Shall I do to be sav[ed]—oh I am going to Hell—Oh what shall I do for Christ [etc.] So [that the] minister was obliged to desist—[the] shrieks & crys were piercing & Amazing—after Some time of waiting the Congregation were Still so [that] a prayer was made . . . & after that we descen[ded] from the pulpitt and discourse[ed] with the people . . . and Amazing and Astonishing [the] power [of] God was seen.[43]

There was something in his preaching that grabbed his listeners by the heart, wrapped their attention around the Word, and sent them away with food for thought. In our own day of light and insubstantial mini-sermons, when many ignore preachers who fail to entertain or make them laugh, perhaps we can learn a thing or two from the so-called "fiery Puritan."[44]

As Samuel Hopkins testified, "Mr. Edwards had the most universal Character of a *good Preacher* of almost any Minister in this Age." Indeed, "There were but few that heard him, who did not call him a good Preacher, however they might dislike his religious Principles, and be much offended at the same Truths when delivered by others: And most admired him above all that ever they heard." Hopkins thought that Edwards' effectiveness derived from three qualities: "*First*, The great Pains he took in composing his Sermons, especially in the first Part of his Life. . . . *Secondly*, His great acquaintance with

---

[43]This quotation comes from the diary of Edwards' cousin Stephen Williams, a pastor in Longmeadow, Massachusetts, and eye-witness of these events. It is most readily available in Murray, *Jonathan Edwards*, p. 169.

[44]Henry Bamford Parkes, *Jonathan Edwards: The Fiery Puritan* (New York: Minton, Balch & Co., 1930).

Divinity, his study and knowledge of the Bible. . . . *Thirdly*, His . . . great Acquaintance with his own Heart, his inward Sense and high Relish of divine Truths, and the high Exercise of true, experimental Religion."[45]

His "Appearance in the Desk," we are told, "was with a good Grace, and his delivery easy, natural and very solemn." He "had not a strong, loud Voice; but appear'd with such gravity and solemnity, and spake with such distinctness, clearness and precision; his Words were so full of Ideas, set in such a plain and striking Light, that few Speakers have been so able to demand the Attention of an Audience." Edwards' preaching often revealed "a great degree of inward fervor." He preached with little "external Emotion," yet his words often "fell with great weight on the Minds of his Hearers." He stood still behind the pulpit, "but spake so as to discover [i.e., reveal] the Motion of his own Heart, which tended in the most natural and effectual manner to move . . . others."[46]

As to the matter of Edwards' dependence on his notes during delivery, "he was not so confined to his Notes . . . but that, if some Thoughts were suggested while he was speaking, which did not occur when writing, and appeared to him pertinent and striking, he would deliver them; and that with as great propriety and fluency, and oftner with greater pathos, and attended with a more sensible good affect on his Hearers, than all he had wrote." To be sure, he was "wont to read" a "considerable . . . part" of his sermons. But "he was far from thinking this the best way of preaching in general; and look'd upon his using his Notes so much as he did, a Deficiency and Infirmity." Toward the end of his life, in fact, he "was inclined to think it had been better, if he had never accustomed himself to use his Notes at all. It appeared to him that preaching wholly without Notes . . . was by far the most natural way." Like his father and grandfather, then, he eventually encouraged the student preacher to

---

[45]Hopkins, *The Life and Character of the Late Reverend Mr. Jonathan Edwards*, pp. 46-47.
[46]Ibid., p. 48.

"write all his Sermons . . . out at large; and instead of reading them to his Hearers, take pains to commit them to Memory."[47]

In the spirit of the Puritans, Edwards labored over his preaching. He took comfort in the well-worn words of the Westminster Shorter Catechism, "The Spirit of God maketh the reading, but especially the preaching of the Word, an effectual means of convincing and converting sinners, and of building them up in holiness and comfort, through faith, unto salvation." He even shared the little-known sentiment of the Second Helvetic Confession (1566) that "when this Word of God is now preached in the church by preachers lawfully called, we believe that the very Word of God is preached, and received of the faithful" (*ipsum Dei verbum annunciari et a fidelibus recipi*).[48] With these weighty truths in mind, and with advice from the tradition of the Puritan preaching manuals,[49] Edwards expended most of his energy in efforts to help others confront the Word of God in all its existential truth and power.

Several homiletical handbooks circulated among the Puritans and their eighteenth-century heirs.[50] None received as much attention,

---

[47]Ibid., pp. 48-49.

[48]Westminster *Shorter Catechism*, Q. 89, laid out helpfully in *Reformed Confessions Harmonized*, ed. Joel R. Beeke and Sinclair B. Ferguson (Grand Rapids: Baker, 1999), pp. 211; and *Second Helvetic Confession*, available most readily in *The Creeds of Christendom*, ed. Philip Schaff, rev. by David S. Schaff, 3 vols., 6th ed. (Grand Rapids: Baker, 1983), 3:237 (Latin), 3:832 (English). For helpful commentary on this sentiment from the second Swiss confession, see Greg R. Scharf, "Was Bullinger Right about the Preached Word?" *Trinity Journal* 26 (2005): 3-10. See also Chad B. Van Dixhoorn, *A Puritan Theology of Preaching*, St. Antholin's Lectureship Charity Lecture 2005 (London: Pentecost Printing & Design, 2005), pp. 31-35, which discusses this sentiment amidst a fine summary of the homiletical teachings of the Westminster divines.

[49]One of the classics, by Richard Bernard, confirmed the *Second Helvetic Confession*: "When a minister speakes truly Gods Word, he may speake freely to all: And all must heare him, as if God spake, with reverence: els[e], it will be easier for Sodome and Gomorrha in the day of judgement than for that person or people." Bernard, *The Faithfull Shepheard*, p. 4.

[50]The most popular among them were William Perkins, *The Art of Prophesying* (Latin, 1592; English, 1607), and Bernard, *The Faithfull Shepheard* (1607). We know that Edwards read the Englishman John Edwards' *The Preacher* (1705), and the New Englander Cotton Mather's *Manuductio ad Ministerium* (1726). Other important works on preaching included William Chappell, *The Preacher* (English, 1656); John Wilkins, *Ecclesiastes, or, A Discourse concerning the Gift of Preaching as It Falls under the Rules of Art* (2nd ed., 1646); and Stoddard, *The Defects of Preachers Reproved* (1724). William Dugard's bestseller, *Rhetorices Elementa* (30th ed., 1705), was used as a text at Harvard (and possibly at Yale). For more on Edwards and the manuals, see Wilson H.

though, as *The Art of Prophesying* (1592), the leading summary of the Puritan "plain style" of biblical preaching. It was written by a Cambridge theologian, William Perkins. It remains in print today. It is the best source available for understanding the Puritans' aspirations in the pulpit and the ways in which they differed from those of high church opponents. "In the promulgation" of sermons, Perkins advised, "two things are required: the hiding of human wisdom and the demonstration or showing of the Spirit."[51] Edwards' sermons often revealed a fair amount of human wisdom, leading some to believe that he was not a typical Puritan preacher. In the main, however, he tried to emulate his Puritan forebears. He was so concerned that people understand the Word of God that he did everything he could to make it clear and "show the Spirit."

In contrast to the ornate performances characteristic of England's so-called metaphysical preachers (sophisticated speakers with a flair for learned drama, such as John Donne, George Herbert and Bishop Lancelot Andrewes),[52] Puritan plain-style preachers tried to "open" the Bible simply, "preach Christ crucified" (1 Cor 1:23), and then get out of the Spirit's way—letting God drive the text home in the hearts of their parishioners. Calvin had taught them long ago that Scripture is "self-authenticated; hence, it is not right to subject it to proof and reasoning. And the certainty it deserves with us, it attains by the testimony of the Spirit," not the preacher.[53] Thus the

---

Kimnach, "General Introduction to the Sermons: Jonathan Edwards' Art of Prophesying," in Edwards, *Sermons and Discourses, 1720–1723*, pp. 3-21.

[51]William Perkins, *The Art of Prophesying*, in *The Work of William Perkins*, ed. Ian Breward (Abingdon, U.K.: Sutton Courtenay Press, 1970), p. 345.

[52]Although "metaphysical preachers" is mainly a nineteenth-century label, anachronistically applied to seventeenth-century clergymen, Horton Davies' summary treatment of the preaching of Donne et al. remains a useful place to begin to see their differences from the Puritans. Horton Davies, *Like Angels from a Cloud: The English Metaphysical Preachers, 1588–1645* (San Marino, Calif.: Huntington Library, 1986).

[53]John Calvin, *Institutio Christianae religionis* (1559), 1.7.5. I have used the English translation of Ford Lewis Battles, found in John Calvin, *Institutes of the Christian Religion*, ed. John T. McNeill, 2 vols., The Library of Christian Classics (Louisville: Westminster John Knox, 1960), 1:80. Significantly, Calvin provided a general defense of biblical authority in book 1 of his *Institutes*, complementing his emphasis on the witness of the Spirit.

Puritans preferred that "Human wisdom . . . be concealed, whether it be in the matter of the sermon or in the setting forth of the words, because the preaching of the word is the testimony of God and the profession of the knowledge of Christ and not of human skill: and . . . because the hearers ought not to ascribe their faith to the gifts of man, but to the power of God's word" (1 Cor 2:1-2, 5). What is more, explained Perkins,

> If any man think that by this means barbarism should be brought into pulpits, he must understand that the minister may, yea and must, privately use at his liberty the arts, philosophy and variety of reading while he is framing his sermon, but he ought in public to conceal all these from the people and not to make the least ostentation. *Artis etiam celare artem:* It is also a point of art to conceal art.[54]

Puritan clergy spent the bulk of their time in study, planning and prayer. They struggled valiantly to make the Bible real for their parishioners. They believed with William Ames, who was himself a student of Perkins, that "no one is fit for the ministry who is not greatly concerned with the Holy Scripture, even beyond ordinary believers, so that he might be said, with Apollos, to be mighty in the Scriptures, Acts 18:24."[55] However, they sought to hide their might before the simple in their flocks, reminding themselves, as William Williams had preached at Edwards' ordination, that "we have this treasure in earthen vessels, that the excellency of the power may be of God, and not of us" (2 Cor 4:7).

Clearly, Edwards and the Puritans were not dry preachers. They resented clerical showiness and theological snobbery. They exhorted one another to avoid upstaging God. But in their own flat-footed way, they also strove consistently to make the preached Word a sacrament, a special means of grace, which deepened faith, hope and love in all who listened. As in the *Westminster Directory,* so in his

---

[54]Perkins, *The Art of Prophesying,* p. 345.
[55]Ames, *The Marrow of Theology,* p. 191.

weekly pastoral practice, Edwards sought to preach the Word,

> 1. Painfully, not doing the work of the Lord negligently. 2. Plainly, that the meanest may understand, delivering the truth not in the entising words of mans wisdom, but in demonstration of the Spirit and of power, least the Crosse of Christ should be made of none effect. . . . 3. Faithfully, looking at the honour of Christ, the conversion, edification and salvation of the people, not at his own gaine or glory. . . . 4. Wisely. . . . 5. Gravely. . . . 6. With loving affection. . . . 7. As taught of God, and perswaded in his own heart, that all that he teacheth, is the truth of Christ; and walking before his flock, as an example to them in it.[56]

Edwards' diligent, plain, faithful, wise, grave and loving example still has much to teach us all.[57]

---

[56]*The Westminster Directory*, pp. 17-18.

[57]For more on the lessons to be learned today from Edwards' delivery of sermons, see the recent commentary of the seasoned veteran preacher, John Carrick, *The Preaching of Jonathan Edwards* (Edinburgh: Banner of Truth Trust, 2008), pp. 409-30.

— Chapter 3 —

SEARCH THE SCRIPTURES

Search the scriptures; for in them ye think ye have eternal life: and
they are they which testify of me. . . . had ye believed Moses, ye would
have believed me: for he wrote of me. But if ye believe not his writings,
how shall ye believe my words?

JOHN 5:39, 46-47

To support this kind of preaching, Edwards devoted most of his
waking life to meditating on Scripture, delving deeply into its contents, reading biblical commentaries and praying fervently for the
Spirit's help interpreting and applying the Bible faithfully to life.
Notwithstanding his reputation as a literary artist, natural scientist,
philosopher and psychologist of religion, he was chiefly a biblical
thinker, a minister of the Word. As Hopkins noted of his methods,
"he studied the Bible more than all other Books, and more than most
other Divines do. . . . He took his religious Principles from the Bible,
and not from any human System or Body of Divinity."[1]

---

[1]Samuel Hopkins, *The Life and Character of the Late Reverend Mr. Jonathan Edwards* (Boston:
S. Kneeland, 1765), pp. 40-41. This chapter has been adapted from a lecture first delivered at
"Jonathan Edwards in Europe," a conference cosponsored by the Bishop of the Dunamellék
(Danube) District in the Reformed Church of Hungary and the Jonathan Edwards Center of
Yale University, convened at Karoli Gaspar University, Budapest, Hungary, May 8-9, 2007. My
thanks to conference organizer Gerald R. McDermott for encouraging me to develop it for in-
clusion in this book. A different version is available in Gerald R. McDermott, ed., *Understanding*

A Love Affair with Scripture

Edwards loved to study Scripture. As he vowed in his "Resolutions" while a boy in his late teens, he sought "to study the Scriptures so steadily, constantly and frequently, as that I may find, and plainly perceive myself to grow in the knowledge of the same." And as he wrote in his "Personal Narrative" of his early spiritual life, he took "the greatest delight in the holy Scriptures, of any book whatsoever."

> Oftentimes in reading it, every word seemed to touch my heart. I felt an harmony between something in my heart, and those sweet and powerful words. I seemed often to see so much light, exhibited by every sentence, and such a refreshing ravishing food communicated, that I could not get along in reading. Used oftentimes to dwell long on one sentence, to see the wonders contained in it; and yet almost every sentence seemed to be full of wonders.[2]

Edwards shared this fascination with parishioners frequently, inculcating a passion for the wonders of the Word. In one beloved Edwards sermon, preached in 1739, he promised his flock that "things of divinity," or things revealed in the Bible, "are things of superlative excellency." Nothing is "so worthy to be known as these things." They "are as much above those things which are treated of in other sciences, as heaven is above . . . earth." They have preoccupied the attention of the "patriarchs, prophets, and apostles, and the most excellent men that ever were in the world." And if such mundane testimony were not enough to compel investment by his people in the Word, Edwards reminded them that the Bible is also "the subject of

---

Jonathan Edwards: An Introduction to America's Theologian (New York: Oxford University Press, 2009).

[2] Jonathan Edwards, "Resolutions" No. 28, in *Letters and Personal Writings*, ed. George S. Claghorn, *WJE*, vol. 16 (1998), p. 755; and Edwards, "Personal Narrative," in *Letters and Personal Writings*, p. 797. As confirmed by Sereno Edwards Dwight in a moment of family pride, "no other divine has as yet appeared, who has studied the Scriptures more thoroughly. . . . His knowledge of the Bible . . . is probably unrivalled." Sereno E. Dwight, "Memoirs of Jonathan Edwards, A.M.," most widely available in *The Works of Jonathan Edwards*, ed. Edward Hickman (1834; Edinburgh: Banner of Truth Trust, 1974), pp. clxxxvii-clxxxix.

the study of the angels in heaven [1 Pet 1:10-12]."[3]

Edwards emphasized that lifelong biblical learning was for all—not just clergy and "men of learning, but . . . persons of every character." God calls everyone to hunt the treasure hid in holy writ, both the "learned and unlearned, young and old, men and women." Not even the brightest Bible scholar will ever begin to find it all. In fact, the ones who "studied the longest, and have made the greatest attainments . . . know but little of what is to be known." The Bible's "subject is inexhaustible," for God "is infinite, and there is no end to the glory of his perfections." In Edwards' estimation, this reality leveled the playing field somewhat for simple readers while inspiring nobler efforts from sophisticated scholars. No matter how gifted the student, Scripture "contains enough" within it "to employ us to the end," indeed "to employ the . . . saints and angels to all eternity." Consequently, all of us should apply our hearts and minds to Holy Scripture, making the study of its books "a great part of the business of our lives." Edwards drove this point home by recommending that his people devote as much of their time to seeking the things of God as seeking Mammon.

> Content not yourselves with having so much knowledge as is thrown in your way, and as you receive in some sense unavoidably by the frequent . . . preaching of the word, of which you are obliged to be hearers, or as you accidentally gain in conversation; but let it be very much your business to search for it, and that with the same diligence and labor with which men are wont to dig in mines of . . . gold.[4]

EDWARDS' EXEGETICAL WRITINGS

Edwards' manuscripts attest to his great reverence for the Bible. His more than 1,200 sermons, of course, confirm his love for Scripture,

---

[3]Jonathan Edwards, "The Importance and Advantage of a Thorough Knowledge of Divine Truth (1739)," in *The Sermons of Jonathan Edwards: A Reader,* ed. Wilson H. Kimnach, Kenneth P. Minkema and Douglas A. Sweeney (New Haven: Yale University Press, 1999), pp. 35-36.
[4]Ibid., pp. 35, 38, 40, 43.

full as they are of meaty, biblical exposition. But many of Edwards' private notebooks also feature exegesis, revealing the vast extent of his Scriptural portfolio.

Edwards' best-known biblical manuscripts are called his "Notes on Scripture," four volumes of miscellaneous remarks on Scripture texts. Begun in 1724, they were kept throughout his life and cross-referenced with his other private notebooks. His most bulky biblical manuscript is called the "Blank Bible," technically known as "Miscellaneous Observations on the Holy Scriptures." It is a large, blank book, given to Edwards by his brother-in-law, the Rev. Benjamin Pierpont, interleaved with the pages of a smaller King James Bible. Beginning late in 1730, Edwards filled the ample margins that surrounded its biblical leaves with a commentary, or gloss, on the whole of sacred Scripture. Thus from Genesis to Malachi and Matthew to Revelation, he left a record of his engagement with the Word. There are other manuscripts, too, in which he wrote about the Bible. Edwards' "Notes on the Apocalypse" comprise a large volume on the book of Revelation. "Images of Divine Things" and "Types" contain remarks on much of the imagery—or types—of Christ, the church and human redemption Edwards found in Scripture and nature (especially in the Old Testament—more on this below). He kept a booklet on "Hebrew Idioms," even a notebook in "Defense of the Authenticity of the Pentateuch as a Work of Moses and the Historicity of the Old Testament Narratives." He drafted hundreds of sheets on sundry doctrines of the Bible. Altogether, this material fills thousands of manuscript pages. It is an under-studied treasure trove of biblical exegesis.[5]

---

[5]"Notes on Scripture," the "Blank Bible," "Notes on the Apocaplypse," and the typological writings are included in The Works of Jonathan Edwards. See Jonathan Edwards, Notes on Scripture, ed. Stephen J. Stein, WJE, vol. 15 (1998); Jonathan Edwards, The Blank Bible, ed. Stephen J. Stein, WJE, vol. 24 (2006); Jonathan Edwards, "Notes on the Apocalypse," in Apocalyptic Writings, ed. Stephen J. Stein, WJE, vol. 5 (1977); and Jonathan Edwards, Typological Writings, ed. Wallace E. Anderson and Mason I. Lowance Jr., with David Watters, WJE, vol. 11 (1993). "Hebrew Idioms" is located in manuscript form in folder 1211, box 16, Jonathan Edwards Collection, Beinecke. "Defense of the Authenticity of the Pentateuch as a Work of Moses and the Historicity of the

Edwards died before he could publish two enormous biblical projects, both of which had engrossed his mind for years. As explained in a letter written late in 1757 in response to an invitation to become the next president of the College of New Jersey (later Princeton University), he was loathe to take the job, for he was hoping to complete them and suspected that a presidency would only get in the way.

The first of these two works was to be built upon the longest sermon series he ever preached, a thirty-sermon exposition of the history of redemption (preached in 1739). It would be

> a great [i.e. large] work, which I call *A History of the Work of Redemption*, a body of divinity in an entire new method, being thrown into the form of an history, considering the affair of Christian theology, as the whole of it, in each part, stands in reference to the great work of redemption by Jesus Christ; which I suppose is to be the grand design of all God's designs, and the *summum* and *ultimum* of all the divine operations and decrees; particularly considering all parts of the grand scheme in their historical order.[6]

By the time he wrote this letter, Edwards had filled three notebooks with ideas on how to expand his sermon series into a book. If completed, this *magnum opus* would have secured his reputation as the world's leading biblical theologian.[7]

The second of these two works was even more exegetical. Edwards

---

Old Testament Narratives" is located in folder 1204, box 15, Jonathan Edwards Collection, Beinecke. The best example of Edwards' manuscript reflections on assorted Bible doctrines is found in Jonathan Edwards, *Writings on the Trinity, Grace, and Faith*, ed. Sang Hyun Lee, *WJE*, vol. 21 (2003). On the extent and significance of Edwards' exegesis, cf. Douglas A. Sweeney, "Edwards, Jonathan (1703–1758)," in *Dictionary of Major Biblical Interpreters*, ed. Donald K. McKim (Downers Grove: InterVarsity Press, 2007), pp. 397-400.

[6]Jonathan Edwards to the Trustees of the College of New Jersey, 19 October 1757, in *Letters and Personal Writings*, 725-30 (quotation from pp. 727-28).

[7]Sixteen years after he died, Edwards' sermon series was published with the help of his son, Jonathan Edwards Jr., as *A History of the Work of Redemption. Containing, The Outlines of a Body of Divinity, in a Method Entirely New* (Edinburgh: W. Gray, J. Buckland, and G. Keith, 1774). Frequently reprinted, it is available today in *The Works of Jonathan Edwards*. See Jonathan Edwards, *A History of the Work of Redemption*, ed. John F. Wilson, *WJE*, vol. 9 (1989). For Edwards' notes toward the turning of these sermons into a treatise, see the books in folders 1212-1214, box 16, Jonathan Edwards Collection, Beinecke.

---

titled it *The Harmony of the Old and New Testament.*

> The first [part] considering the prophecies of the Messiah, his re-
> demption and kingdom; the evidences of their references to the Mes-
> siah, etc. comparing them all one with another, demonstrating their
> agreement and true scope and sense; also considering all the various
> particulars wherein these prophecies have their exact fulfillment;
> showing the universal, precise, and admirable correspondence be-
> tween predictions and events. The second part: considering the types
> of the Old Testament, showing the evidence of their being intended
> as representations of the great things of the gospel of Christ: and the
> agreement of the type with the antitype. The third and great [larg-
> est] part, considering the harmony of the Old and New Testament,
> as to doctrine and precept.

Edwards hoped that this work would offer "occasion for an explanation of a very great part of the holy Scripture . . . in a method,
which to me seems the most entertaining and profitable, best tend-
ing to lead the mind to a view of the true spirit, design, life and soul
of the Scriptures, as well as to their proper use and improvement."[8]
He drafted hundreds of manuscript pages for inclusion in this
book. For part one, on biblical prophecy, he penned four entries in his
"Miscellanies" notebooks, all treating what he labeled either "Prophecies of the Messiah" (mainly in the Old Testament) or "Fulfillment
of the Prophecies of the Messiah" (in the New). Two of these entries
proved so large that they consumed a whole book.[9] For part two,
on the wealth of biblical types of the Messiah, Edwards drafted an-

---

[8]Jonathan Edwards to the Trustees of the College of New Jersey, October 19, 1757, in *Letters and Personal Writings*, pp. 728-29. For more on this second, unfinished work, see Kenneth P. Minkema, "The Other Unfinished 'Great Work': Jonathan Edwards, Messianic Prophecy, and 'The Harmony of the Old and New Testament,'" in *Jonathan Edwards's Writings: Text, Context, Interpretation*, ed. Stephen J. Stein (Bloomington: Indiana University Press, 1996), pp. 52-65.

[9]Sadly, these entries, Nos. 891, 922, 1067 and 1068, are the only "Miscellanies" not included in *The Works of Jonathan Edwards*. It should be noted here that Edwards also kept a very sketchy notebook on "Scripture Prophecies of the Old Testament," which treated prophecies "besides the prophecies of the Messiah and his kingdom and the prophecies of Daniel which have had an evident fulfillment." See folder 1248, box 21, Jonathan Edwards Collection, Beinecke (quota-tion from inside cover).

other entry in a "Miscellanies" notebook: "That the Things of the Old Testament Are Types of Things Appertaining to the Messiah and His Kingdom and Salvation, Made Manifest from the Old Testament Itself." In published form, this miscellany exceeds a hundred pages in length. Edwards wrote it in addition to his "Images of Divine Things" and "Types" mentioned above.[10] For part three, on the theological harmony of Scripture, Edwards kept a separate notebook on "The Harmony of the Genius, Spirit, Doctrines, & Rules of the Old Testament & the New." Most of this book is ordered canonically (Edwards made it through the Psalms). Several entries appear topically. All attest to his interest in the doctrinal integrity, or "harmony," of the Bible.[11]

EDWARDS' VIEW OF REVELATION

Edwards worked so hard on Scripture because he thought it was from God, a supernatural revelation of the mind of the Creator that unfolded his intentions for the redemption of the world. He considered it "divine." He thought it "full of wondrous things." He said its contents were "unerring," the "most excellent things in the world." He routinely extolled the privileges of those who owned a Bible, employing language such as this, preached on the eve of the Awakening:

> What a precious treasure God has committed into our hands in that he has given us the Bible. How little do most persons consider how much they enjoy in that they have the possession of that holy book. . . . What an excellent book is this, and how far exceeding all human writings. . . . He that has a Bible, and don't observe what is contained [in] it, is like a man that has a box full of silver and gold, and don't know it.

---

[10]See "Types of the Messiah," in *Typological Writings*, pp. 191-324.

[11]The "Harmony" notebook, nearly 200 pages in manuscript, did not find its way into the letterpress edition of *The Works of Jonathan Edwards*. See "The Harmony of the Genius, Spirit, Doctrines, & Rules of the Old Testament & the New," folder 1210, box 15, Jonathan Edwards Collection, Beinecke.

Edwards taught that "most . . . are to blame" for their "inattentive, unobservant way of reading" this gift of heaven. "The word of God contains the most noble, and worthy, and entertaining objects, . . . the most excellent things that man can exercise his thoughts about." Those who had truly "tasted the sweetness" of God's Scriptural divinity ought to live out their days, he said, in "longing for more and more of it."[12]

Edwards often spoke of Scripture as the very "Word of God." He also called it "the word of Christ" or, as he described it in Manhattan, "the epistle of Christ that he has written to us." The Bible functioned, then, for Edwards as a vital "word of life; as the light of life; a sweet, . . . life-giving word." He called it "a perfect rule," a reliable "guide to true happiness." And he held an exceptionally high view of its method of inspiration. He taught that God "indited" the Scriptures (i.e., proclaimed, pronounced or composed them) through the Bible's human authors, thus imbuing the biblical narratives with "a strange and unaccountable kind of enchantment." Not surprisingly, then, he thought the Bible to be "an infallible guide, a sure rule which if we follow we cannot err."[13]

---

[12]Jonathan Edwards, sermon on Matthew 24:35, L. 2r., folder 502, box 7, Beinecke; Edwards, *A History of the Work of Redemption*, pp. 290-91; Jonathan Edwards, *Freedom of the Will*, ed. Paul Ramsey, *WJE*, vol. 1 (1957), p. 438; Jonathan Edwards, "Heeding the Word, and Losing It," in *Sermons and Discourses, 1734-1738*, ed. M. X. Lesser, *WJE*, vol. 19 (2001), p. 46; and Jonathan Edwards, sermon on 1 Peter 2:2-3, L. 5r., L. 2v., folder 855, box 11, Beinecke. I have adapted some material in the following five paragraphs from Douglas A. Sweeney, "'Longing for More and More of It'? The Strange Career of Jonathan Edwards's Exegetical Exertions," in *Jonathan Edwards at 300: Essays on the Tercentenary of His Birth*, ed. Harry S. Stout, Kenneth P. Minkema and Caleb J. D. Maskell (Lanham, Md.: University Press of America, 2005), pp. 25-37.

[13]Edwards, "Personal Narrative," in *Letters and Personal Writings*, p. 801; Jonathan Edwards, "Life Through Christ Alone," in Edwards, *Sermons and Discourses, 1720-1723*, ed. Wilson H. Kimnach, *WJE*, vol. 10 (1992), p. 526; Edwards, "The Way of Holiness," in *Sermons and Discourses, 1720-1723*, p. 477; Jonathan Edwards, "Divine Love Alone Lasts Eternally," in *Ethical Writings*, ed. Paul Ramsey, *WJE*, vol. 8 (1989), p. 363; Jonathan Edwards, sermon on Psalm 119:162, L. 1r., folder 189, box 3, Beinecke; Edwards, "The Importance and Advantage of a Thorough Knowledge of Divine Truth," pp. 38, 35; Jonathan Edwards, "Profitable Hearers of the Word," in *Sermons and Discourses, 1723-1729*, ed. Kenneth P. Minkema, *WJE*, vol. 14 (1997), pp. 265-66; Jonathan Edwards, sermon on 1 Corinthians 2:11-13, L. 3v., folder 719, box 10, Beinecke; Jonathan Edwards, sermon on Matthew 13:23, L. 22r., folder 473, box 6, Beinecke; Jonathan Edwards, *Religious Affections*, ed. John E. Smith, *WJE*, vol. 2 (1959), p. 438; Jonathan Edwards,

---

According to Edwards, the best posture for those who would understand the divine was "to sit at Jesus' feet and hear his word." We must "go to him whose Word it is and beg of him to teach," for "he has reserved to himself this work of enlightening the mind with spiritual knowledge, and there is no other can do it; there is none teaches like God." Like Mary of Bethany in the Gospels, the sister of Lazarus and Martha—who took "a pound of ointment of spikenard, very costly, and anointed the feet of Jesus, and wiped his feet with her hair" (Jn 12:3)—we should know better than to busy ourselves with "[trouble] about many things." Rather, as Jesus said to Martha, only "one thing is needful; and Mary hath chosen that good part" (Lk 10:41-42), for she had clung to Christ and hung on his every word. Similarly, *we* should cling to every word that comes from the mouth of God, for "the word of God is the great means of our eternal good. . . . 'tis the most necessary means, and without which our souls must famish." It is like "MILK," Edwards proposed, flowing "from the breasts of the church." It is like "rain" for which God's people have "a great and earnest thirsting."[14]

Edwards spoke often of the need to study "what reason *and* Scripture declare." He echoed the common, Calvinist dictum that those who would understand the world and its relationship to God need the "book of nature" *and* the "book of Scripture."[15] But he emphasized consistently the priority of the Bible. As he wrote in *Distinguish-*

"Stupid as Stones," in *Sermons and Discourses, 1730–1733*, ed. Mark Valeri, *WJE*, vol. 17 (1999), p. 180; Jonathan Edwards, sermon on Luke 10:38-42, L. 6v., folder 560, box 7, Beinecke; and Jonathan Edwards, *The "Miscellanies," a-500*, ed. Thomas A. Schafer, *WJE*, vol. 13 (1994), p. 202.

[14]Edwards, sermon on Luke 10:38-42, L. 3r.; Edwards, ""Profitable Hearers of the Word," p. 266; Edwards, "Heeding the Word, and Losing It," p. 47; Jonathan Edwards, "Images of Divine Things," in *Typological Writings*, p. 93; and Jonathan Edwards, sermon on Hebrews 6:7, L. 17r., folder 820, box 11, Beinecke.

[15]Perhaps the best known example of this to be found in the Edwards corpus is Jonathan Edwards, *Concerning the End for Which God Created the World*, in *Ethical Writings*, pp. 419-20 (emphasis mine). Many medieval Christians (at least from the twelfth century) also spoke of the need to study both the "book of nature" and Scripture and, like Edwards, interpreted both books theologically. On this, see especially Peter Harrison, *The Bible, Protestantism, and the Rise of Natural Science* (Cambridge: Cambridge University Press, 1998).

---

ing Marks of a Work of the Spirit of God (1741), "all that is visible to the eye is unintelligible and vain, without the Word of God to instruct and guide the mind."[16] And as he had preached in a crucial sermon on this theme a few years earlier,

> We make a distinction between the things that we know by reason, and things we know by revelation. But alas we scarce know what we say: we know not what we should have known . . . had it not been for revelation. . . . Many of the principles of morality and religion that we have always been brought up in the knowledge of, appear so rational that we are ready to think we could have found 'em out by our own natural reason. . . . [But] all the learning, yea, all the common civility that there is in the world, seems to be either directly or indirectly from revelation, whether men are sensible of it or no. . . . Everything that is good and useful in this fallen world, is from supernatural help.[17]

This became a central theme in his response to the English deists. In opposition to their call for a modern religion of nature and reason, Edwards insisted late in his life on the necessity of transcendent, supernatural revelation—even for the maintenance of a healthy civic virtue. This was also a major theme in Edwards' early preaching and writing. As he drafted in his "Miscellanies" in 1728, "were it not for divine revelation, I am persuaded that there is no one doctrine of that which we call natural religion [but] would, notwithstanding all philosophy and learning, forever be involved in darkness, doubts, endless disputes and dreadful confusion." And as he preached to his congregation near the end of the 1730s, human reason can tell us a lot about the works of God in nature, but "there is nothing else that informs us what [the] scheme and design of God in his works is but only the holy Scriptures."[18]

---

[16]Jonathan Edwards, *The Distinguishing Marks of a Work of the Spirit of God*, in *The Great Awakening*, ed. C. C. Goen, *WJE*, vol. 4 (1972), p. 240.

[17]Jonathan Edwards, "Light in a Dark World, a Dark Heart," in *Sermons and Discourses, 1734-1738*, p. 720.

[18]Edwards, *The "Miscellanies," a-500*, p. 421 (cf. pp. 422-26, 537; Jonathan Edwards, *The "Miscel-*

Supernatural revelation and the spiritual light it provides were, for Edwards, essential for clarifying the nature of reality. It was not that the world could not be known at all without the Bible, or that the Bible served as a textbook in natural history, science or reason. Rather, for Edwards, God's Word and Spirit illuminate our worldly wisdom, rendering our knowledge more clear, beautiful and real than ever before. In a remarkable notebook entry dating from 1729, Edwards depicted this point vividly:

> A mind not spiritually enlightened [by means of the Bible and God's Spirit] beholds spiritual things faintly, like fainting, fading shadows that make no lively impression on his mind, like a man that beholds the trees and things abroad in the night: the ideas ben't strong and lively, and [are] very faint; and therefore he has but a little notion of the beauty of the face of the earth. But when the light comes to shine upon them, then the ideas appear with strength and distinctness; and he has that sense of the beauty of the trees and fields given him in a moment, which he would not have obtained by going about amongst them in the dark in a long time. A man that sets himself to reason without divine light is like a man that goes into the dark into a garden full of the most beautiful plants, and most artfully ordered, and compares things together by going from one thing to another, to feel of them and to measure the distances; but he that sees by divine light is like a man that views the garden when the sun shines upon it. There is . . . a light cast upon the ideas of spiritual things in the mind of the believer, which makes them appear clear and real, which before were but faint, obscure representations.[19]

---

lanies," *501-832*, ed. Ava Chamberlain, *WJE*, vol. 18 [2000], p. 140; and Jonathan Edwards, *The "Miscellanies," 833-1152*, ed. Amy Plantinga Pauw, *WJE*, vol. 20 [2002], pp. 52-53); and Edwards, *A History of the Work of Redemption*, p. 520. On Edwards' understanding of the relationship between reason and revelation as it was developed near the end of his life, see the "Editor's Introduction" to Jonathan Edwards, *The "Miscellanies," 1153-1360*, ed. Douglas A. Sweeney, *WJE*, vol. 23 (2003), pp. 19-29. On his response to the deists, see esp. Gerald R. McDermott, *Jonathan Edwards Confronts the Gods: Christian Theology, Enlightenment Religion, and Non-Christian Faiths* (New York: Oxford University Press, 2000).
[19]Edwards, *The "Miscellanies," a-500*, pp. 469-70.

Edwards wrote scores of pages about this "divine and supernatural light," as well as its role in the production of a "spiritual understanding" (1 Cor 2). He taught that revelation elucidates the harmony of the cosmos, grants a teleological glimpse of the world's relationship to God, that spiritual knowledge of its contents constitutes a greater blessing "than any other privilege that ever God bestowed." He went so far, in fact, as to say that those who "hear the Word . . . and keep it . . . bring forth Christ" himself in their hearts; that Christ is truly "formed in them"; that spiritual knowledge of the Bible intensifies our vital union with the living Word of God, the one through whom the world was created and for whom it is preserved; and that this union is "more blessed" than "to have Christ" within one's "arms, or at the breast, as the virgin Mary had." Spiritual knowledge even grants what Edwards referred to in one sermon as "an earnest" or "the dawnings" of the beatific vision. It enables the people of God to share in the very life of God (2 Pet 1:4). For the new principle in the souls of those who enjoy this special blessing "is not only from the Spirit, but it also partakes of the nature of that Spirit."[20]

---

[20]Jonathan Edwards, sermon on Luke 11:27-28, L. 1v., L. 6v.-7r., folder 1065, box 14, Beinecke; Jonathan Edwards, "The Pure in Heart Blessed," in *Sermons and Discourses, 1730–1733*, pp. 65-66; and Jonathan Edwards, "Treatise on Grace," in *Writings on the Trinity, Grace, and Faith*, pp. 178-80. For Edwards on spiritual understanding, see especially *Religious Affections*, pp. 205-6, 225, 266-91, 296-97, 301; Edwards, *The "Miscellanies," a-500*, pp. 286-87, 297-98, 462-63; Edwards, *The "Miscellanies," 501-832*, pp. 156-57, 245-48, 452-66; and numerous Edwards sermons, especially "A Divine and Supernatural Light"; "A Spiritual Understanding of Divine Things Denied to the Unregenerate," in *Sermons and Discourses, 1723–1729*, pp. 70-96; "False Light and True," in *Sermons and Discourses, 1734–1738*, pp. 122-42; "Light in a Dark World, a Dark Heart"; "Profitable Hearers of the Word"; and "The Importance and Advantage of a Thorough Knowledge of Divine Truth." For Edwards' notion of biblical power, see also his statement in *The Blank Bible*, at Psalm 29:3 (p. 490), that "Lightning and thunder is a very lively image of the word of God upon many accounts. 'Tis exceeding quick, and exceeding piercing, and powerful to break in pieces, and scorch, and dissolve, and is full of majesty"; and also at Hebrews 4:12 (p. 1143), where he makes reference to God's giving of the Law on Mt. Sinai "with thunders, and lightnings, and a voice so piercing, awful, and tremendous that the people could not endure it," and compares the Hebrews text, which teaches similarly that "The word in its powerful efficacy . . . does . . . cut the soul asunder."

EDWARDS AS AN INTERPRETER

In keeping with this view of supernatural revelation, Edwards interpreted the Bible with a reverence for its character, faith in its coherence and conviction that the Spirit continues to use it powerfully. In an era characterized by the rapid spread of biblical criticism, theological skepticism and religious minimalism, Edwards demonstrated a robust faith in Scripture's credibility, expounding it with confidence in traditional Christian methods.

During the age of the Enlightenment, to an extent unprecedented earlier in history, experts on the Bible focused attention on the diversity of its ancient life settings (*Sitzen im Leben*) and thus the *differences* in context, purpose, style and even meaning across its roughly 1,500 years of human composition. These "higher" biblical critics often thought of themselves as historians.[21] The leading question they asked of any text within the Bible was how it would have been understood by its original recipients. They investigated the Bible much as any other compilation of classical materials. They did not presume its unity. They bracketed, or denied, older views of its inspiration. They disassembled the canon, examined its contents separately, and used them principally to reconstruct the life of ancient Israel.

Edwards devoured their writings. He cherished biblical history and labored over the findings of the biblical avant-garde. Despite his reputation as a "pre-critical" reader, or "pre-modern" thinker, he was fully apprised of recent trends in modern critical thought.[22] He disliked the trends that seemed to hinder the progress of the gospel. He spent a lot of time defending Protestant orthodoxy in the face of new attacks against its moral viability (on this see chapter five). But this

---

[21]Scholars distinguish "higher" biblical criticism (historical criticism) from "lower" biblical criticism (textual criticism). The former deals with the history behind the biblical texts, interpreting the Bible in its sociocultural contexts. The latter deals with the history of biblical texts themselves, comparing surviving manuscripts for the sake of determining the most reliable variants (those that best resemble what must have been the "original autographs").

[22]On Edwards' learned engagement with biblical higher criticism, see Robert E. Brown, *Jonathan Edwards and the Bible* (Bloomington: Indiana University Press, 2002).

involved him deeply in the problems of historicism. It guaranteed that he would engage the critics on their turf.

Still, Edwards tried to interpret the Bible theologically. He handled it not as a collection of antiquarian artifacts, but as the living Word of One who calls himself "I Am." Thus he studied it both as scholars study sets of primary sources (to understand the lives of those for whom they were first put to writing) *and*—in a manner more important to his daily pastoral ministry—as priestly theologians study the oracles of God (to understand his will for those who still have ears to hear). This sets him apart from many other modern Western biblical scholars, whether Christian or non-Christian. For higher criticism has ruled the roost in modern biblical studies, shaping the ways that even pastors think of preaching Sunday sermons.

For several generations, learned preachers have been taught to think primarily as historians, explaining sermon texts by reference to their ancient, social contexts. Only later, if at all, have they been taught to expound their sermon texts in light of the whole canon, or the history of redemption, no matter how far apart the Bible's human authors stood. There are notable exceptions to this homiletical rule. But most of the time, when modern preachers have made theological moves they have become rather nervous. Scholars caution them to scrutinize the structural viability of the bridges that they build between the ancient worlds of Scripture and the worlds of their parishioners. Historians know better than to make great leaps of faith without sufficient natural evidence that one can survive the fall. Better to keep one's sermon fixed upon the lessons of the past than attempt to unite—awkwardly—such patently different worlds.

But Edwards rarely worried about the bridges that he built. He spent a great deal of time doing historical exegesis. He knew the Bible's contents better than most, past or present. He knew the bulk of them by heart, in fact, as evidenced by the constant use of Scripture in his speech as well as the blanks pervading his sermon notes where Bible verses should be. (Rather than take the time to copy Bible verses into his manuscripts, Edwards frequently substituted long, squiggly lines, trusting his memory to provide the missing text while he was preaching.) Nonetheless, he spent the lion's share of his time—every week—interpreting Scripture theologically, preaching it doctrinally (with trust in its transcendence and an unapologetically synthetic methodology) and applying it explicitly to the lives of those around him. He has often been depicted as a "spiritual" interpreter, a trait that may require explanation.[23]

Protestants typically pride themselves on literal exegesis, by which we usually mean discussion of the meaning of the Bible based on study in the grammar of and history behind its parts. Ever since the Reformation, we have distanced this method from the so-called allegorical, or spiritual, exegesis often used by Roman Catholics to authenticate teaching that is not clearly supported by a "plain" reading of Scripture. Our strategy has been to slice through the many centuries of exegetical excess—overwrought renderings and outright fabrication of symbolic biblical meanings—repristinating a simpler, apostolic reading of Scripture and the faith that it commends. This has involved a refutation of most traditional exegesis. But many other moderns, whether Protestant or not, have helped us cope with the destruction caused by such a critical method by affirming a dim view of the Catholic "dark ages" (i.e., the "Middle Ages," those between the more enlightened classical and modern periods of history) and their spiritual, and exegetical, barbarism.

Even early church fathers, though, advocated allegory. Origen, for example, spoke of three senses of Scripture—body, soul and spirit— suggesting that God had arranged for errors in the Bible's bodily sense (i.e., historical sense) in order to elevate our minds to its much "higher," spiritual sense.[24] Augustine proved more cautious, teaching

---

[23]See, for example, the highly regarded depiction of Stephen J. Stein, "The Quest for the Spiritual Sense: The Biblical Hermeneutics of Jonathan Edwards," *Harvard Theological Review* 70 (1977): 99-113.

[24]Origen, *On First Principles* (*De Principiis* in Latin; in Greek, *Periarchon*; c. 230), 4.2.4, 9. See the English translation of G. W. Butterworth (1936; Gloucester, Mass.: Peter Smith, 1973), pp.

that those interpreting Scripture must be sure to base their readings on the literal sense of the text, or "the intention of the writer through whom the Holy Spirit" spoke. Even he, though, thought that biblical texts could harbor multiple meanings and rejoiced that God revealed himself in multidimensional ways. "Could God have built into the divine eloquence a more generous or bountiful gift," he asked, "than the possibility of understanding the same words in several ways, all of them deriving confirmation from other no less divinely inspired passages [of Scripture]"?[25]

Through most of the Middle Ages, a moderated form of Origen's spiritual exegesis held sway within the world of serious Bible scholarship.[26] By the ninth century, in fact, most scholars had agreed that every passage in the Bible held *four* different senses: (1) a literal sense, conveyed by the "letter" of the text (from the Latin word *littera*); (2) an allegorical sense (from the Greek word ἀλληγορέω, "to speak figuratively"), also called the doctrinal, mystical or Christological sense,

---

275-87. Of course, more orthodox Fathers—Justin, Irenaeus, Clement of Alexandria, as well as a host of other worthies—also employed allegorical and typological methods of the interpreting the Bible.

[25]*De Doctrina Christiana* (*On Christian Doctrine*, completed in 426/27), 3.84-85. English translation from Augustine, *De Doctrina Christiana*, ed. and trans. R. P. H. Green, Oxford Early Christian Texts (Oxford: Clarendon, 1995), pp. 169-71.

[26]Academics often distinguish between Origen's "Alexandrian" school of biblical exegesis and the more temperate school of "Antioch," exemplified in textbooks by the likes of Lucian of Antioch, Diodorus of Tarsus, Theodore of Mopsuestia and John Chrysostom. It is said that Alexandrian exegesis was fanciful, full of allegorical excess, while the school of Antioch was much more careful and historical. The difference between these "schools" is often exaggerated, however. In point of fact, there never was a formal school of Antioch. Further, exegetes in both groups shared a great deal in common. Nevertheless, there were interpreters among the church fathers who opposed the lofty allegorizing found within the writings of a few of the Alexandrians. Diodorus of Tarsus (in *On the Difference between Theory and Allegory*, only fragments of which remain), Theodore of Mopsuestia (in *Concerning Allegory and History against Origen*, 5 vols., which is no longer extant) and John Chrysostom (in many sermons and commentaries which do survive), distanced their own exegesis from the methods of Origen. Their famous doctrine of "theoria" (θεωρία, a Greek word meaning "vision, insight or contemplation"), according to which the Hebrew prophets saw and recorded *both* the immediate (historical) and the future (Christological) significance of their prophecies, grounded the spiritual sense of Scripture squarely upon the literal sense. It also fixed the correlation between the biblical types and antitypes in the history of redemption. These "Antiochenes" contended that biblical meaning was clearly discernable, not hidden and mysterious, as in Alexandria.

---

symbolized by the objects of the Bible's literal sense; (3) a moral sense, referred to as the tropological sense (from the Greek word τροπολογέω, "to speak in tropes or figures of speech"), found when looking for the ethical or legal drift of the text; and (4) a heavenly sense, referred to as the anagogical sense (from ἀνάγω, "to lead up"), found when contemplating the eschatological import of the text.[27] This so-called four-horse chariot (*quadriga*) of medieval exegesis found its ultimate codification in the work of Thomas Aquinas.[28] It was memorized in schools with the help of a popular ditty:

> The letter shows us what God and our Fathers did;
> The allegory shows us where our faith is hid;
> The moral meaning gives us rules of daily life;
> The anagogy shows us where we end our strife.[29]

During the time of the Reformation, biblical learning was transformed. Great strides were made in the study of the ancient biblical languages, textual scholars emended scribal errors in the Bible (by making use of older, more reliable biblical manuscripts), and printing presses expedited the distribution of Bibles, biblical commentaries and other Christian treatises. Protestants, especially, touted improvements in the study of the Scriptures and their meaning. And

---

[27] Most of the early church fathers made only a broad, generic distinction between the literal and the spiritual sense of Scripture, though some did propose up to seven different senses. John Cassian was the first to promote the fourfold exegesis that became the standard during the Middle Ages. In his *Conferences* (*Collationes*, written during the 420s), 14.8-11, he wrote that on top of the literal sense "there are three kinds of spiritual lore, namely, tropology, allegory, and anagoge. . . . History embraces the knowledge of things which are past and which are perceptible. . . . What follows is allegorical, because the things which actually happened are said to have prefigured another mystery. . . . Anagoge climbs up from spiritual mysteries to the higher and more august secrets of heaven. . . . Tropology is moral teaching designed for the amendment of life and for instruction in asceticism." English translation from John Cassian, *Conferences*, trans. Colm Luibheid, The Classics of Western Spirituality (New York: Paulist Press, 1985), pp. 159-66.

[28] Thomas Aquinas *Summa Theologiae* Ia.1.10. Under Thomas's weighty influence, the three spiritual senses were often said to correspond to the three theological virtues: faith (allegorical), hope (anagogical) and love (tropological).

[29] *Littera gesta docet, quid credas allegoria,*
Moralis quid agas, quo tendas anagogia.

---

most Protestant Reformers followed Luther's lead in emphasizing literal exegesis.[30] In his well-known commentary on the epistle to the Galatians, when discussing chapter four, the *locus classicus* for those defending allegorical readings (Paul himself says there that his discussion of Hagar, Sarah, Ishmael and Isaac is "an allegory"),[31] Luther vouched for the usefulness of spiritual exegesis but insisted forcefully on the precedence of the literal.

> There are usually held to be four senses of Scripture. They are called the literal sense, the tropological, the allegorical, and the anagogical, so that Jerusalem, according to the literal sense, is the capital city of Judea; tropologically, a pure conscience or faith; allegorically, the church of Christ; and anagogically, the heavenly fatherland. Thus in this passage [Gal 4:24-31] Isaac and Ishmael are, in the literal sense, the two sons of Abraham; allegorically, the two covenants, or the synagog and the church, the Law and grace; tropologically, the flesh and the spirit, or virtue and vice, grace and sin; anagogically, glory and punishment, heaven and hell, yes, according to others, the angels and the demons, the blessed and the damned.
>
> This kind of game may, of course, be permitted to those who want it, provided they do not accustom themselves to the rashness of some, who tear the Scriptures to pieces as they please and make them uncertain. On the contrary, these interpretations add extra ornamentation, so to speak, to the main and legitimate sense, so that a topic may be more richly adorned by them, or—in keeping with Paul's example—so that those who are not well instructed may be nurtured in gentler fashion with milky teaching, as it were. But these interpretations should not be brought forward with a view to establishing a doctrine of faith. For that four-horse team (even though I do not disapprove of

---

[30]This emphasis, of course, had roots in ancient Christianity, as well as in the study of the literal meanings of Scripture initiated in twelfth-century France. See G. R. Evans, *The Language and Logic of the Bible: The Road to Reformation* (Cambridge: Cambridge University Press, 1985).

[31]Other Pauline statements cited traditionally as warrants for the spiritual exegesis of the Bible include the following: Rom 15:4; 1 Cor 2:6-7; 3:1-2; 9:9-12; 10:1-4; and 2 Cor 3:6. The book of Hebrews, for Edwards, was a Pauline text as well, one that was full of typological exegesis of the Old Testament.

it) is not sufficiently supported by the authority of Scripture, by the custom of the fathers, or by grammatical principles.[32]

By Edwards' day, the literal sense had come to prevail throughout the West, among both Protestants and others who now favored historical methods (and suspected the superfluity of Catholic exegesis). For the Puritans and their heirs, the reasons were largely pastoral. If the study of the Word was ever to captivate the laity, "learned and unlearned, young and old, men and women," then its meanings must be plain, in the main, to simple minds. As confessed by the divines who assembled at Westminster: "All things in Scripture are not alike plain in themselves, nor alike clear unto all; yet those things which are necessary to be known, believed, and observed, for salvation, are so clearly propounded and opened in some place of Scripture or other that not only the learned but the unlearned, in a due use of the ordinary means, may attain unto a sufficient understanding of them."[33] A "sufficient understanding" would require earnest effort. Some passages might not be understood by everyone. But the Bible's main storyline was given for all to read. Indeed, its message of redemption carried the power of God to save even the humblest of believers. Scholars should seek to clarify this message for the laity rather than dizzy them on learned flights of fancy.

Despite this stated Protestant preference for the literal sense of Scripture, spiritual exegesis did survive the Reformation. Luther himself often interpreted the Bible allegorically. Calvin came to master the art of biblical typology. The Puritans, as well, resorted to spiritual exegesis, particularly in places such as the Song of Solo-

---

[32]English translation from Martin Luther, *Lectures on Galatians, 1519*, trans. Richard Jungkuntz, in *Luther's Works*, vol. 27, ed. Jaroslav Pelikan and Walter A. Hansen (St. Louis: Concordia, 1964), p. 311. For the original Latin, see *D. Martin Luthers Werke: Kritische Gesamtausgabe* (Weimar: Hermann Böhlaus Nachfolger, 1883-), 2:550. N.B. Whereas for Origen the spiritual senses are given for the mature, for Luther they are mainly for the immature (though Luther himself made reference to them constantly, confirming his notion that all of us are beggars before the Word).

[33]The Westminster Confession of Faith (1647) 1.7.

---

mon.[34] Like many other early Protestants, then, Edwards practiced literal *and* spiritual exegesis. He majored in the literal sense. Scholars sometimes overwork his spiritualizing tendencies. He served as a parish pastor, though, a minister of the Word. He was called by God to preach the Bible whole, for the church. So he took advantage of *all* the tools that helped him make its contents come alive for those in his care. He sought to help them find their place in the grand story of redemption, which began in the Garden of Eden and is yet to be fulfilled.[35]

Edwards' best-known form of spiritual exegesis was typology. He trusted that God had filled the Bible with types, or vivid symbols, of the Messiah, human redemption and the coming kingdom of heaven—types that adumbrate and enrich our understanding of their antitypes, or things that God intended them to signify. As he penned in one of his notebooks during the mid-1740s, Scripture itself seemed to suggest "that it has ever been God's manner from the beginning of the world to exhibit and reveal future things by symbolical representations, which were no other than types of the future things revealed." He rarely publicized his theories about these images and shadows, but his notes effervesced with typological analysis. It helped him to discern the divine nature of reality, purposes in history and harmony of Scripture. According to Edwards, Adam,

---

[34]Significantly, in *The Faithfull Shepheard* Richard Bernard offered the Puritans several principles, or guidelines, for the control of allegory in their spiritual exegesis: "First, gather [allegories] after the true and naturall sense [i.e., the literal sense] be delivered, and not before. Secondly, let them not be too farre fetched, strained, obscure, or foolish: but agreeing with the Analogie of Faith, and other manifest Scriptures. . . . Thirdly, handle an allegorie briefly, and use them not too often. Fourthly, let the use and end be for instruction of life, but not for any proofe of doctrine. Fiftly [sic], let the ancient, grave, and wise collect them. It is not a safe way for young beginners not well exercised in the Scriptures, and grounded in the trueth. Allegories are delightfull, and therefore youth will (as I may say) *lascivire*, soone wax wanton immoderately herein, and so instead of using, abuse the Scripture." See Richard Bernard, *The Faithfull Shepheard: Or the Shepheards Faithfulnesse* (London: Printed by Arnold Hatfield for John Bill, 1607), pp. 53-54.

[35]For helpful advice on redemptive-historical biblical proclamation, see Daniel M. Doriani, *Getting the Message: A Plan for Interpreting and Applying the Bible* (Phillipsburg, N.J.: P & R, 1996); and Dennis E. Johnson, *Him We Proclaim: Preaching Christ from All the Scriptures* (Phillipsburg, N.J.: P & R, 2007).

Abraham and David were types of Christ, as each shadowed forth an aspect of his messianic role. The prophet Jonah was a type of Christ's death and resurrection, as he emerged from three days in the belly of a whale. The "future struggling of the two nations of the Israelites and Edomites was typified by Jacob's and Esau's struggling . . . in the womb." And in another, fairly representative typological comment, Edwards mused in one of his notebooks: "by Moses' being wonderfully preserved in the midst of . . . waters, though but a little helpless infant, . . . seems apparently to be typified the preservation and deliverance of his people."[36]

Edwards granted that "some types . . . are much more lively" than the others.[37] Compared to many medieval Christians, he discussed them with restraint. He warned that "persons ought to be exceeding careful in interpreting of types, that they don't give way to a wild fancy; not to fix an interpretation unless warranted by some hint in the New Testament of its being the true interpretation, or a lively figure and representation contained or warranted by an analogy to other types that we interpret on sure grounds."[38] He tried to show, in fact, that such restraint can yield a faithfully Protestant approach to biblical types. He sought a sound, golden mean "between those that cry down all types, and those that are for turning all into nothing but allegory and not having it to be true history; and also the way of the rabbis that find so many mysteries in letters."[39]

Still, Edwards had a fulsome, typological view of reality, one that gave his thought a unique and rather striking spiritual focus. Not

---

[36]Edwards, "Types of the Messiah" (Miscellanies No. 1069), in *Typological Writings*, pp. 192-95.

[37]Edwards, "Images of Divine Things," in *Typological Writings*, p. 114.

[38]Edwards, "Types," in *Typological Writings*, p. 148. As he suggests in this quotation, Edwards thought the surest types were those identified as such within the New Testament. The analogy of faith provided a strong, canonical warrant for his method of typology, and for some of his types as well. For according to this analogy, which dates from the church fathers, the clear and general teachings of Scripture were to be used to make sense of its more ambiguous texts and types, providing a theological framework for one's biblical exegesis that controlled and informed one's typological thinking.

[39]Ibid., p. 151.

content to restrict typology to the contents of the canon, he taught that *all the world* was laden with the emblems of the divine. To say that God created the universe *ex nihilo* (out of nothing), he thought, was to say that God created out of nothing but his own, internal, infinite resources. It was to say, then, that the universe reflected—by its design—the inner-trinitarian life of God. Human sin clouds our vision of the vestiges of God that remain outside the realm of supernatural revelation. The spectacles of Scripture and the Spirit are required to correct our view of the world's divine images and patterns. And yet for those with eyes to see, the world is full of signs, yea intentional reminders, of our origin and destiny in the providence of God. To those forgetful of their Maker, for example, there are signs given to warn them of the fearsome consequences of their sin. The "extreme fierceness and extraordinary power of the heat of lightning is an intimation of the exceeding power and terribleness of the wrath of God." For those who need a glimpse of the promise of the gospel, on the other hand, God provides a host of hopeful signs. "The silkworm is a remarkable type of Christ," Edwards wrote, "which, when it dies, yields us that of which we make such glorious clothing. Christ became a worm for our sakes," he continued, "and by his death finished that righteousness with which believers are clothed, and thereby procured that we should be clothed with robes of glory."[40]

Reality was grounded in the mighty acts of God. Salvation history gave the universe its purpose and coherence. And the gospel tied together all the contents of the Bible, transcending their diverse social contexts. Edwards knew that these convictions would not score him many points in the enlightened world of modern biblical scholarship. He expected, on the contrary, "by . . . ridicule and contempt to be called a man of a very fruitful brain and copious fancy." Nonetheless, he persisted on his typological path. As he once proclaimed defiantly, "I am not ashamed to own that I believe that the whole universe,

---

[40]Edwards, "Images of Divine Things," in *Typological Writings*, p. 59.

heaven and earth, air and seas, and the divine constitution and history of the holy Scriptures, be full of images of divine things, as full as a language is of words; and that the multitude of those things that I have mentioned are but a very small part of what is really intended to be signified and typified by these things."[41]

Edwards' God was real and powerful. His Word could not be relativized by modern unbelief, torn apart by biblical criticism or tamed by those too dull to see its spiritual signs and wonders. It was alive. It was active. And it testified to Christ—from the Pentateuch to the Apocalypse. "Had ye believed Moses," Jesus preached once in Jerusalem, "ye would have believed me: for he wrote of me" (Jn 5:46). Shortly after the resurrection, walking along the road to Emmaus, Jesus explained to two of his friends how the Scriptures spoke of him, making clear their gospel focus and thrilling the hearts of his companions: "beginning at Moses and all the prophets, he expounded unto them in all the Scriptures the things concerning himself. . . . And they said one to another, Did not our heart burn within us, while he talked with us by the way, and while he opened to us the Scriptures?" (Lk 24:27, 32).

In one of his early published sermons, titled "The Excellency of Christ," Edwards reinforced this notion of the Bible's Christocentrism, using all of Scripture to support his thesis statement: "There is an admirable conjunction of diverse excellencies in Jesus Christ." After a brief introduction to the context of his Scripture text, from Revelation 5, in which Jesus is depicted both as a mighty "Lion" of Judah and a lowly "Lamb" who was slain for the salvation of the world, Edwards devoted the rest of the sermon to a canonical orchestration of this Christological paradox. Using scores of Scripture references, from every part of the Bible, he showed his people that the Messiah had always been characterized this way. He was both a divine person, who is strong and mighty to save, as well as a humble Son

---

[41]Edwards, "Types," in *Typological Writings*, p. 152.

of Man, who condescended to befriend us. Edwards applied his doctrine boldly to the lives of those who listened, inviting all to "close" with a Savior who fulfills our every need:

> And thus is the affair of our redemption ordered, that thereby we are brought to an immensely more exalted kind of union with God, and enjoyment of him, both the Father and the Son, than otherwise could have been. For Christ being united to the human nature, we have advantage for a more free and full enjoyment of him, than we could have had if he had remained only in the divine nature. So again, we being united to a divine person, as his members, can have a more intimate union and intercourse with God the Father . . . than otherwise could be. Christ who is a divine person, by taking on him our nature, descends from the infinite distance and height above us, and is brought nigh to us; whereby we have advantage for the full enjoyment of him. And, on the other hand, we, by being in Christ a divine person, do as it were ascend up to God, through the infinite distance, and have hereby advantage for the full enjoyment of him also. . . . Christ has brought it to pass, that those that the Father had given him, should be brought into the household of God; that he, and his Father, and his people should be as it were one society, one family; that the church should be as it were admitted into the society of the blessed Trinity.[42]

By the mid-1730s, Edwards played a role in rocking the world by means of sermons like this, using the ministry of the Word to spread revival through the West.

---

[42]Jonathan Edwards, "The Excellency of Christ (1738)," in *The Sermons of Jonathan Edwards*, pp. 163, 195-96.

— Chapter 4 —

TRY THE SPIRITS

Beloved, believe not every spirit, but try the spirits whether they are of God: because many false prophets are gone out into the world. Hereby know ye the Spirit of God: Every spirit that confesseth that Jesus Christ is come in the flesh is of God: And every spirit that confesseth not that Jesus Christ is come in the flesh is not of God: and this is that spirit of antichrist, whereof ye have heard that it should come; and even now already is it in the world. . . . Beloved, let us love one another: for love is of God; and every one that loveth is born of God, and knoweth God. He that loveth not knoweth not God; for God is love.

I JOHN 4:1-3, 7-8

*T*he people of Northampton were no strangers to revival. Solomon Stoddard had overseen five "harvests" of their souls, as he called them, during his sixty years of ministry in their midst (in 1679, 1683, 1696, 1712 and 1718). But "just after" Stoddard died, the town had languished through "a time of extraordinary dullness in religion," Edwards wrote. "Licentiousness for some years greatly prevailed among the youth . . . ; they were many of them very much addicted to night-walking, and frequenting the tavern, and lewd practices, wherein some, by their example exceedingly corrupted others." Their pastor grew concerned, as he realized that his young people engaged in such practices "especially" on the evenings after corporate worship services. He addressed the problem publicly. Local circumstances aided his efforts at reform.[1]

REVIVAL STIRS THE REGION

Early in 1734, a revival had started to stir the nearby village of Pascommuck, roughly three miles from town. Then in April of that year, Northampton's youth were faced with the unexpected deaths of two of their friends—the first "a young man in the bloom of his youth," who was "violently seized with a pleurisy and . . . died in about two days"; the other

> a young married woman, who had been considerably exercised in mind about the salvation of her soul before she was ill, and was in great distress in the beginning of her illness; but seemed to have satisfying evidences of God's saving mercy to her before her death; so that she died very full of comfort, in a most earnest and moving manner warning and counseling others.

As Edwards noted of her passing, "this seemed much to contribute to the solemnizing of the spirits of many young persons: and there began evidently to appear more of a religious concern on people's minds."[2]

Taking advantage of this concern, Edwards spoke to the youth that fall, recommending that they turn their Thursday evening revelry into a time of "social religion," meeting in homes throughout the town for Christian fellowship and prayer. No sooner had they done so than the town was forced again to deal with a strange, surprising death—this time of a senior citizen. "Many were much moved and affected" by this tragedy.[3] Soon the adults in town followed the lead of their own children, meeting on Sunday nights for fellowship,

---

[1]Jonathan Edwards, *A Faithful Narrative*, in *The Great Awakening*, ed. C. C. Goen, *WJE*, vol. 4 (1972), pp. 146-47.
[2]Ibid., pp. 147-48.
[3]Ibid., p. 148.

prayer and hymn singing (the latter a controversial practice for de-scendants of the Puritans, but one that would soon characterize re-vivals everywhere).[4] Before long, these spiritual practices had yielded a transformation. Revival blazed through town, spreading up and down the Connecticut River valley.

Edwards, of course, was biased, but his testimony regarding this revival's holy fruit suggests a massive outpouring of the Spirit in Northampton.

> This work of God . . . soon made a glorious alteration in the town; so that in the spring and summer following [1735] . . . the town seemed to be full of the presence of God: it never was so full of love, nor so full of joy; and yet so full of distress, as it was then. There were remarkable tokens of God's presence in almost every house. It was a time of joy in families on the account of salvation's being brought unto them; parents rejoicing over their children as newborn, and hus-bands over their wives, and wives over their husbands.[5]

As usual, pious females offered the best examples to Edwards of regenerate spirituality. His statements on the revival pointed to two of them in particular whose conversions characterized the whole

---

[4]As noted above, the Puritans were a cappella psalm singers who ruled out hymnody from their corporate worship services. During the early eighteenth century, though, due in part to the awful sound of much of their psalmody (sung responsively and led by men with little or no training), but also to the knowledge that hymns were used in other circles to warm the hearts and ready the minds of earnest worshipers for the Word, some New Englanders began to favor the forming of "singing circles" (largely for educational purposes), the practice of "regular sing-ing" (singing by note, in harmony) and even the introduction of extrabiblical hymnody. Thomas Walter was the leader of the singing circle movement (in the early 1720s). The English dissenter Isaac Watts proved to be the most prolific composer of hymns and psalm paraphrases used in the region's churches. (His most famous publications included *Hymns and Spiritual Songs* [1707] and *The Psalms of David Imitated in the Language of the New Testament* [1719].) And Edwards was the most important pastor in New England to support the "New Way" of singing. For more information on these changes and their significance, see Laura L. Becker, "Ministers vs. Lay-men: The Singing Controversy in Puritan New England, 1720–1740," *New England Quarterly* 55 (March 1982): 79-96; and the first three chapters, by Mark A. Noll, Esther Rothenbusch Crookshank and Rochelle A. Stackhouse, in *Wonderful Words of Life: Hymns in American Protes-tant History and Theology*, ed. Richard J. Mouw and Mark A. Noll, Calvin Institute of Christian Worship Liturgical Studies Series (Grand Rapids: Eerdmans, 2004), pp. 3-66.
[5]Edwards, *A Faithful Narrative*, in *The Great Awakening*, p. 151.

work. The first was an ailing woman known as Abigail Hutchinson who died slowly from starvation after her throat had swollen shut "so that she could swallow nothing but what was perfectly liquid, and but very little of that, and with great and long strugglings and stranglings, that which she took in flying out at her nostrils till she at last could swallow nothing at all." Despite this miserable condition, Hutchinson's spiritual rebirth filled her soul with heavenly food and deep longing, not for healing, but "for persons in a natural state, that they might be converted, and for the godly that they might see and know more of God." She testified to the glory of God throughout her long ordeal, sharing the gospel with her friends while her body wasted away. She wanted nothing more than for everyone she knew to be with God. In fact, she pined for death herself so that "strong grace might have more liberty" with her beyond the grave, "without the clog of a weak body."[6]

Edwards' second main example of the power of this revival was a child, a four-year-old girl named Phebe Bartlet. She, too, was roundly converted as revival fires burned. Despite her age, she longed to be with God and point her friends to Jesus. She "often manifested a great concern for the good of others' souls: and has been wont many times affectionately to counsel the other children." Phebe also developed "an uncommon degree of a spirit of charity," as Edwards illustrated in this colorful anecdote:

A poor man that lives in the woods had lately lost a cow that the family much depended on, and being at the house, he was relating his misfortune, and telling of the straits and difficulties they were reduced to by it. [Phebe] took much notice of it, and it wrought exceedingly on her compassions; and after she had attentively heard him a while, she went away to her father, who was in the shop, and entreated him to give that man a cow: and told him that the poor man *had no cow!* That the hunters or something else *had killed his cow!* And

---

[6]Ibid., pp. 197, 199.

———

entreated him to give him one of theirs. Her father told her that they could not spare one. Then she entreated him to let him and his family come and live at his house: and had much more talk of the same nature.

Edwards ended this account by alluding to 1 John on the signs of true religion, suggesting that little Phebe, more than most adults in town, "manifested bowels of compassion to the poor" (1 Jn 3:17).[7]

In addition to the changes wrought in individual souls, this revival changed the nature of corporate worship in Northampton. "Our public assemblies were then beautiful," as Edwards later recalled:

> the congregation was alive in God's service, everyone earnestly intent on the public worship, every hearer eager to drink in the words of the minister as they came from his mouth; the assembly in general were, from time to time, in tears while the Word was preached; some weeping with sorrow and distress, others with joy and love, others with pity and concern for the souls of their neighbors.

He continued in a tone that indicates his early interest in the virtues of well-orchestrated congregational singing: "Our public praises were then greatly enlivened; God was then served in our psalmody, in some measure, in the beauty of holiness [Ps 96:9]":

> there has been scarce any part of divine worship, wherein good men amongst us have had grace so drawn forth and their hearts so lifted up in the ways of God, as in singing his praises. Our congregation excelled all that ever I knew in the external part of the duty before, generally carrying regularly and well three parts of music, and the women a part by themselves. But now they were evidently wont to sing with unusual elevation of heart and voice, which made the duty pleasant indeed.[8]

Edwards' experience as a leader of these musical performances eventuated in his use of hymns on Sunday afternoons in congrega-

---

[7]Ibid., pp. 204-5.
[8]Ibid., p. 151.

tional worship (which was far more controversial than the singing of hymns in homes or the singing of psalms in parts).[9]

It amazes one to consider that Edwards was barely thirty-one years old when he led this great revival. Sarah was twenty-four. Even contemporaries stood in awe of what was taking place. Edwards scribbled a breathless report to a senior colleague living in Boston,[10] who in turn spread the word along his own social network. Soon the news reverberated all the way to England. A detailed account was in demand across the sea, and Edwards stepped up to supply it in the form of his first book, *A Faithful Narrative of the Surprizing Work of God in the Conversion of Many Hundred Souls in Northampton, and the Neighbouring Towns and Villages of New-Hampshire in New-*

---

[9]Beginning in 1742, after Samuel Buell's stint as visiting preacher in Northampton, Edwards' congregation sang an occasional hymn in summertime during their Sunday services. As Edwards explained to a pastor-friend of his in Boston, Benjamin Colman, in the spring of 1744: "It has been our manner in this congregation, for more than two years past, in the summer time, when we sing three times upon the Sabbath, to sing an hymn, or part of a hymn of Dr. [Isaac] Watts' . . . at the conclusion of the afternoon exercise. I introduced it principally because I saw in the people a very general inclination to it. Indeed, I was not properly he that introduced it: they began it in my absence on a journey; and seemed to be greatly pleased with it; and sang nothing else, and neglected the Psalms wholly. When I came home I disliked not their making some use of the hymns, but did not like their setting aside the Psalms; and therefore used them principally, only in the manner that I have spoken of, and thus we continued to use them." In a treatise on the Awakening, Edwards defended this new practice in response to conservative critics: "what is . . . especially found fault with in the singing that is now practiced, is making use of hymns of human composure. And I am far from thinking that the Book of Psalms should be thrown by in our public worship, but that it should always be used in the Christian church, to the end of the world: but I know of no obligation we are under to confine ourselves to it. I can find no command or rule of God's Word, that does any more confine us to the words of the Scripture in our singing, than it does in our praying; we speak to God in both: and I can see no reason why we should limit ourselves to such particular forms of words that we find in the Bible, in speaking to him by way of praise, in meter, and with music, than when we speak to him in prose, by way of prayer and supplication. And 'tis really needful that we should have some other songs besides the Psalms of David: 'tis unreasonable to suppose that the Christian church should forever . . . be confined only to the words of the Old Testament, wherein all the greatest and most glorious things of the Gospel . . . are spoken of under a veil, and not so much as the name of our glorious Redeemer ever mentioned, but in some dark figure, or as hid under the name of some type." Jonathan Edwards to the Rev. Benjamin Colman, May 22, 1744, in *Letters and Personal Writings,* ed. George S. Claghorn, *WJE,* vol. 16 (1998), p. 144; and Jonathan Edwards, *Some Thoughts Concerning the Present Revival of Religion in New-England,* in *The Great Awakening,* pp. 406-7.

[10]See Edwards to the Rev. Benjamin Colman, May 30, 1735, in *Letters and Personal Writings,* pp. 48-58.

England (1737). Never mind that the London printers placed this work of God in New Hampshire (an understandable mistake, for Northampton lay in Massachusetts' rural Hampshire County). The book sold well. Within three years, it was reprinted both in Edinburgh and Boston, translated and republished in both German and Dutch editions (in Magdeburg and Amsterdam). It inspired other ministers to work toward revival. It compelled George Whitefield to resume his work in the colonies, encouraged John Wesley to practice outdoor preaching in England, and exerted a powerful force on the spread of the "Great Awakening," which would crest during the early 1740s (more on this below).[11]

Edwards gave the credit to the work of his sovereign God. But he knew that God is wont to work through prayer and gospel preaching. He prefers to work through circumstances, "secondary causes," to accomplish the work of redemption—so Christians ought to busy themselves in acts of spiritual service. In 1747, Edwards published a lengthy treatise on the need to pray for revival.[12] He preached for many years about the importance of praying persistently.[13] Late in

---

[11]For a brief, general history of the transatlantic Awakening, see Douglas A. Sweeney, *The American Evangelical Story: A History of the Movement* (Grand Rapids: Baker Academic, 2005), pp. 27-51. For longer accounts, see especially Mark A. Noll, *The Rise of Evangelicalism: The Age of Edwards, Whitefield, and the Wesleys*, A History of Evangelicalism: People, Movements and Ideas in the English-Speaking World (Downers Grove: InterVarsity Press, 2003); and Thomas S. Kidd, *The Great Awakening: The Roots of Evangelical Christianity in Colonial America* (New Haven: Yale University Press, 2007).

[12]Jonathan Edwards, *An Humble Attempt to Promote Explicit Agreement and Visible Union of God's People in Extraordinary Prayer for the Revival of Religion and the Advancement of Christ's Kingdom on Earth, Pursuant to Scripture-Promises and Prophecies concerning the Last Time*, in *Apocalyptic Writings*, ed. Stephen J. Stein, WJE, vol. 5 (1977), pp. 308-436. This treatise was based on a sermon Edwards preached in Northampton on a public day of fasting "for the coming of Christ's kingdom," February 3, 1747. His sermon text was Zechariah 8:20-22. For a transcription of the (incomplete) surviving manuscript, see "The Suitableness of Union in Extraordinary Prayer for the Advancement of God's Church," in *Sermons and Discourses, 1743–1758*, ed. Wilson H. Kimnach, WJE, vol. 25 (2006), pp. 197-206.

[13]Though Edwards defended a Calvinist doctrine of predestination, he also taught that prayer can change world history. In a sermon preached soon after this revival had subsided (January 8, 1736), he contended that "the Most High is a God that *hears prayer*." In fact, Edwards told his parishioners that "God is, speaking after the manner of men, overcome by humble and fervent prayer." No one changes God's mind, or even informs him, during prayer. God "is omniscient, and with respect to his knowledge unchangeable. . . . He knows what we want, a thousand

---

113

1734, he also began, prayerfully, to preach a gospel series on the sinner's justification and conversion by faith alone—a series used by God to effect the work of redemption in Northampton.

Justification and the New Birth

As seen in the chapters above, the doctrine of justification by faith had long been central to Edwards' ministry. He championed it at Yale by means of his master's *quaestio* (1723). He defended it in Boston during the week of Harvard's commencement (1731). By 1734, however, this doctrine had taken a beating amid what Edwards called "the great noise that was in this part of the country about Arminianism." Edwards probably never met an evangelical Arminian. He would later hear of the Wesley brothers' Methodist Arminianism. His own neck of the woods, though, was dominated by Calvinists. New Englanders associated Arminianism with liberalism—broad-minded, moralistic, rationalistic liberal-

---

times more perfectly than we do ourselves, before we ask him." Still, God commands us to pray to him for he wants us to depend on him. He wills from eternity, moreover, to answer prayer. See Jonathan Edwards, "The Most High a Prayer-Hearing God," in *The Works of Jonathan Edwards*, ed. Edward Hickman, 2 vols. (1834; Edinburgh: Banner of Truth Trust, 1974), 2:115 (this sermon did not make it into the Yale Edition of Edwards' works). Another helpful example of Edwards' Calvinist view of prayer may be found in "The Terms of Prayer," in *Sermons and Discourses, 1734–1738*, ed. M. X. Lesser, *WJE*, vol. 19 (2001), pp. 768-91. Surprisingly little has been written on Edwards' doctrine and practice of prayer, but see Glenn R. Kreider, "Jonathan Edwards's Theology of Prayer," *Bibliotheca Sacra* 160 (November–December 2003): 434-56; Glenn R. Kreider, "'God Never Begrutches His People Anything They Desire': Jonathan Edwards and the Generosity of God," *Reformation & Revival Journal* 12 (Summer 2003): 71-91; Donald S. Whitney, "Pursuing a Passion for God through Spiritual Disciplines: Learning from Jonathan Edwards," in *A God Entranced Vision of All Things: The Legacy of Jonathan Edwards*, ed. John Piper and Justin Taylor (Wheaton, Ill.: Crossway, 2004), pp. 109-28, which has a small section on prayer (pp. 114-15); W. Clark Gilpin, "'Inward, Sweet Delight in God': Solitude in the Career of Jonathan Edwards," *Journal of Religion* 82 (October 2002): 523-38; and especially Peter Beck, "The Voice of Faith: Jonathan Edwards's Theology of Prayer" (Ph.D. diss., The Southern Baptist Theological Seminary, 2007). On prayer among the Puritans and during the Great Awakening, see especially Charles Hambrick-Stowe, *The Practice of Piety: Puritan Devotional Disciplines in Seventeenth-Century New England* (Chapel Hill: University of North Carolina Press, 1982); Richard Lovelace, *Dynamics of Spiritual Life: An Evangelical Theology of Renewal* (Downers Grove, Ill.: InterVarsity Press, 1979); Iain H. Murray, *The Puritan Hope: A Study in Revival and the Interpretation of Prophecy* (London: Banner of Truth Trust, 1971), pp. 99-103; and Thomas S. Kidd, "'The Very Vital Breath of Christianity': Prayer and Revival in Provincial New England," *Fides et Historia* 36 (Summer/Fall 2004): 19-33.

---

ism. "Arminian," to Edwards, meant opposed to the Reformation and its glorious doctrines of grace, opposed to the biblical truth that sinners are saved supernaturally—and only supernaturally—by grace alone, through faith alone, in Christ alone. So in the fall of 1734, when Robert Breck, an "Arminian," was called to serve a nearby church in Springfield, Massachusetts (nineteen miles from Northampton), and William Rand of Sunderland (which was even closer to home) preached "new notions as to the doctrines of justification" to his flock, "the friends of vital piety trembled for fear" of the consequences, local clergy threw up their hands, and Edwards felt the need (again) to teach Reformed theology.[14]

He commenced his series of sermons in November of that year, leading off with a learned lecture, "Justification by Faith Alone." Four of these were published, along with a fifth preached long after the revival had receded, as *Discourses on Various Important Subjects, Nearly Concerning the Great Affair of the Soul's Eternal Salvation* (1738).[15] In Edwards' estimation, God had blessed the town with revival partly to honor his faithfulness in preaching Reformation doctrine. Some criticized him publicly for "meddling with the controversy." But "though it was ridiculed," his stress on justification by faith "proved a word spoken in season . . . and was most evidently attended with a very remarkable blessing of heaven to the souls of the people in this

---

[14]Edwards, *A Faithful Narrative*, in *The Great Awakening*, p. 148. We do not know for sure what William Rand actually preached, but that he preached "new notions" we read in the diary of another pastor, Stephen Williams of Longmeadow. See *The Great Awakening*, p. 17. Rand would later retract his errors under duress and keep his job, but he opposed the Great Awakening with the antirevival minority of the Hampshire County Association of Congregational ministers.

[15]The four revival sermons published were "Justification by Faith Alone," "Pressing into the Kingdom of God," "Ruth's Resolution" and "The Justice of God in the Damnation of Sinners." The fifth sermon included was "The Excellency of Jesus Christ" (quoted at length in chapter three). All of them are reprinted in *Sermons and Discourses, 1734–1738*, with Edwards' preface to the book, in which he explains why he included the final sermon: "What is published at the end, concerning the excellency of Christ, is added on my own motion; thinking that a discourse on such an evangelical subject, would properly follow others that were chiefly legal and awakening, and that something of the excellency of the Savior, was proper to succeed those things that were to show the necessity of salvation" (p. 797).

---

town."[16] Indeed, as Edwards construed the tumult in the "Preface" to his *Discourses:*

> The beginning of the late work of God in this place was so circum-stanced, that I could not but look upon it as a remarkable testimony of God's approbation of the doctrine of justification by faith alone, here asserted and vindicated:—By the noise that had a little before been raised in this county, concerning that doctrine, people here seemed to have their minds put into an unusual ruffle; some were brought to doubt of that way of acceptance with God, which from their infancy they had been taught to be the only way.

Edwards' homiletical efforts, though,

> seemed to be remarkably blessed, not only to establish the judgments of many in this truth, but to engage their hearts in a more earnest pursuit of justification, in that way that had been explained and de-fended; and at that time, while I was greatly reproached for defend-ing this doctrine in the pulpit, and just upon my suffering a very open abuse for it, God's work wonderfully brake forth amongst us, and souls began to flock to Christ, as the Savior in whose righteousness alone they hoped to be justified: So that this was the doctrine on which this work in its beginning was founded, as it evidently was in the whole progress of it.[17]

Edwards' lecture on justification started at Romans 4:5, "But to him that worketh not, but believeth on him that justifieth the un-godly, his faith is counted for righteousness." He took from the text this doctrine: "We are justified only by faith in Christ, and not by any manner of virtue or goodness of our own." And he expounded this doctrine with passion, making it clear that justification comes as a gift of God's free grace, not for anything we do, but because of what God effects when he unites us to his Son, by the power of the Spirit, making us part of his holy church, the mystical bride of Jesus Christ.

---

[16]Edwards, *A Faithful Narrative,* in *The Great Awakening,* pp. 148-49.

[17]"Appendix A: Preface to *Discourses on Various Important Subjects,*" in *Sermons and Discourses, 1734–1738,* p. 795.

Our faith is that by which we cling to Christ in spiritual union. God brings it to life in us; we merely exercise it "actively." And as we cling to Christ and trust in his merit for salvation, God sees that we are one with him and reckons his merit our own. "[W]hat is real in the union between Christ and his people, is the foundation of what is legal," Edwards postulated famously.

> That is, it is something really in them, and between them, uniting them, that is the ground of the suitableness of their being accounted as one by the Judge: and if there is any act, or qualification in believers, that is of that uniting nature, that it is meet on that account that the Judge should look upon 'em, and accept 'em as one [with Christ], no wonder that upon the account of the same act or qualification, he should accept the satisfaction and merits of the one, for the other, as if it were their satisfaction and merits.[18]

Like the Puritans before him, Edwards placed a high premium on the Christian's union with Christ as the basis of salvation. We are saved, he taught, not merely by assenting to the gospel. Even "the devils . . . believe, and tremble" (Jas 2:19). We are saved, as well, because the Holy Spirit inhabits our bodies, reorients our souls by uniting them with Christ, lets us share in the Lord's righteousness and bears fruit in our lives.

This teaching about the Holy Spirit's role in our salvation proved extremely important to Edwards. It might be said, in fact, to have been the defining feature of his ministry.[19] He lived in a time and place when everyone had to go to church and almost everyone affirmed the basic truths of the Christian faith. He worked as a tax-

---

[18]Jonathan Edwards, "Justification by Faith Alone," in *Sermons and Discourses, 1734–1738,* pp. 147, 149, 158.

[19]I will revisit this theme again in chapter five. For more on Edwards and the Spirit, see Robert W. Caldwell III, *Communion in the Spirit: The Holy Spirit as the Bond of Union in the Theology of Jonathan Edwards,* Studies in Evangelical History and Thought (Carlisle, U.K.: Paternoster, 2006). I have discussed the ecclesiological ramifications of Edwards' view of the Holy Spirit in Douglas A. Sweeney, "The Church," in *The Princeton Companion to Jonathan Edwards,* ed. Sang Hyun Lee (Princeton: Princeton University Press, 2005), pp. 167-89.

supported servant of his colony's state church, an institution that he knew was full of culture Protestantism. He loved his people dearly and believed that he would have to give an account someday for his ministry. So he labored tirelessly to help his hearers understand that there is a wide, eternal difference between authentic faith in Christ and perfunctory religion, or nominal Christianity. That difference, furthermore, has to do with the Holy Spirit and his work of regeneration, of quickening the soul, giving it spiritual life in Christ. "There is such a thing as conversion," Edwards pleaded earnestly: "'tis the most important thing in the world; and they are happy that have been the subjects of it and they most miserable that have not."[20] The subjects of conversion had the Spirit guiding their lives, rehabilitating their souls and giving them spiritual understanding. They had acquired a *taste* for God, a new and profound sense of joy and confidence in divine things. Or, as he put this point in his sermon "A Divine and Supernatural Light," they had "a true sense of the divine excellency of the things revealed in the Word of God, and a conviction of the truth and reality of them."[21]

In driving this point home, Edwards departed somewhat from an evangelistic practice of his Puritan forebears. The tendency of pastors in New England's early years was to comfort sinners anxious about the ultimate state of their souls by telling them God keeps his promises and works reliably through the usual means of grace (i.e., Scripture, sacraments, prayer and Christian fellowship). They may not be converted *yet*, but if they *prepare* themselves for conversion by

---

[20]Jonathan Edwards, "The Reality of Conversion," in *The Sermons of Jonathan Edwards: A Reader*, ed. Wilson H. Kimnach, Kenneth P. Minkema and Douglas A. Sweeney (New Haven: Yale University Press, 1999), pp. 83, 92. Cf. Jonathan Edwards, sermon on 2 Timothy 3:5 ("True grace in the heart is a powerful thing"), folder 805, box 11, Beinecke, another of his most compelling sermons on this theme.

[21]Jonathan Edwards, "A Divine and Supernatural Light, Immediately Imparted to the Soul By the Spirit of God, Shown to Be both a Scriptural, and Rational Doctrine (1734)," in *The Sermons of Jonathan Edwards*, p. 126. For a marvelous discourse on the Holy Spirit *as* the divine and supernatural light, the new, indwelling, vital principle in the souls of the converted, see Jonathan Edwards, "Treatise on Grace," in *Writings on the Trinity, Grace, and Faith*, ed. Sang Hyun Lee, *WJE*, vol. 21 (2003), pp. 149-97.

repenting of their sins, getting "in the way of grace," and making good on the grace received, they will be taking steps to salvation. Scholars refer to such counsel as the Puritans' "preparationism," dubbing its saving steps a standard "morphology of conversion."[22]

Edwards had qualms about it. He agreed that God is reliable. He trusted the means of grace and taught his people to do the same. But he feared that, all too often, preparationist advice coddled sinners in their sin, encouraged spiritual complacency and domesticated God. As we saw in chapter one, his own conversion failed to match the standard Puritan morphology. For a while, he wondered why it had not occurred "in those particular steps, wherein the people of New England . . . used to experience it."[23] Eventually, however, he came to see that God does not convert us all in the same way, that the substance of conversion matters much more than the form.[24] He also saw that *true* conversion was primarily supernatural. It is not something sinners effect by taking the right steps. They should certainly prepare for it, repenting and praying for mercy. But they could not make it happen by their practice of religion. God effects conversion. And the main thing he does when he converts a penitent sinner is give that person a new heart, reorient that person's "affections."[25] He fills her with his Spirit. He engenders in her soul a deep longing to walk with him, to know him better and to honor him in every-

---

[22]See especially Norman Pettit, *The Heart Prepared: Grace and Conversion in Puritan Spiritual Life* (New Haven: Yale University Press, 1966); and Edmund S. Morgan, *Visible Saints: The History of a Puritan Idea* (New York: New York University Press, 1963).

[23]Jonathan Edwards, "Diary," in *Letters and Personal Writings*, p. 779.

[24]For examples of this insight that deserve more careful scrutiny than they usually receive, see Edwards, *A Faithful Narrative*, in *The Great Awakening*, pp. 185-86; and Jonathan Edwards, "Charity Contrary to a Censorious Spirit," in *Ethical Writings*, pp. 283-92.

[25]"Affections" is a word that Edwards used frequently to refer to the matrix of desires, inclinations and aspirations that ground a person's moral life. In 1746, Edwards published a major treatise on what he called the religious affections, contending that "[t]rue religion, in great part, consists in holy affections," and defining affections (technically) as "the more vigorous and sensible exercises of the inclination and will of the soul." Jonathan Edwards, *Religious Affections*, ed. John E. Smith, *WJE*, vol. 2 (1959), pp. 95-96. There are two excellent paraphrases of this difficult spiritual classic: Gerald R. McDermott, *Seeing God: Jonathan Edwards and Spiritual Discernment* (Vancouver: Regent College Publishing, 2000); and Sam Storms, *Signs of the Spirit: An Interpretation of Jonathan Edwards' Religious Affections* (Wheaton, Ill.: Crossway, 2007).

---

thing she does. So when Edwards counseled sinners, he did not concern himself with where they stood along the morphology. He asked about their hearts. He wanted to find out what they loved, how they wished to spend their time, what they aspired to in life. Moreover, his burden during the rest of his revivalistic ministry was to help others discern the Spirit's presence in their lives—to "try the spirits," distinguishing God's Spirit from counterfeits.

He did so in a spate of publications on revival—*Distinguishing Marks of a Work of the Spirit of God* (1741), *Some Thoughts Concerning the Present Revival of Religion in New England* (1743), *Religious Affections* (1746) and *True Grace, Distinguished from the Experience of Devils* (1753)—which, taken together, represent the most important body of literature in all of Christian history on the challenge of discerning a genuine work of the Holy Spirit.[26] Here again, Edwards' strategy was to point people away from the externals of religion, red herrings of the faith, things he labeled "negative signs"—they neither confirm nor disprove the Spirit's presence and activity—and toward what he referred to as the "positive signs" of grace, things the Bible says result from true revival and conversion. The negative signs were things like strong emotions, loss of control (either physically or spiritually) and irregular worship practices. Such things had often attended God's regenerating work, but could also be the products of religious "hypocrites" (a term that Edwards used quite frequently) or even of the devil.

Edwards' positive signs, by contrast, included esteem for Jesus, opposition to the devil, "greater regard to the Holy Scriptures" and "a spirit of love to God and man," all things that guarantee that God is active in one's life. They cannot be fabricated. They are supernatural gifts. And the "chief" of all these gifts, the sign most clearly taught in Scripture as an indicator of grace, was the sign of "Christian prac-

---

[26]The first two of these works are available in *The Great Awakening*, pp. 213-530. *Religious Affections* constitutes volume two of the Yale Edition. *True Grace, Distinguished from the Experience of Devils* may be found in *Sermons and Discourses, 1743–1758*, pp. 605-40.

tice," or biblical "holiness."[27] This was no red herring. It was the sum of true religion and, in Edwards' estimation, it had characterized Northampton for a period of several months—like never before in local history—from December of 1734 through summer of 1735.

DECLINE, DESPAIR AND DIVISION

Unfortunately, however, this revival of the Spirit and its signs of grace would fade—nearly as fast as they had appeared—during the dog days of summer. For despite, or rather because of these positive signs of saving grace, the devil was haunting the town by spring, trying to thwart the work of God by spreading melancholy, doubt and even suicidal urges.

On March 25, "a poor weak man" named Thomas Stebbins slit his own throat in a fit of despair. (He is reputed to have suffered from a mental handicap.) "[B]eing in great spiritual trouble" at the height of the revival, he was "hurried" by the devil "with violent temptations" to hurt himself. He failed to end his own life. However, after he had recovered, he "continued . . . exceeding[ly] overwhelmed with melancholy."[28] On June 1, a different townsman did succeed in killing himself. Unlike Stebbins, furthermore, Joseph Hawley was a prominent civic leader in Northampton. He was Solomon Stoddard's son-in-law, Jonathan Edwards' uncle. (He had married Rebekah Stoddard, a sister of Edwards' mother, Esther.) Hawley had served for many years as Northampton's town clerk. He was also a leading businessman, the first one in town to sell forks and knives for eating. Edwards described him as "a gentleman, . . . religious in his behavior, and an useful honorable person in the town." Like Steb-

---

[27]Edwards delineates his negative signs and positive signs in two major works: *Distinguishing Marks of a Work of the Spirit of God* (1741), in which he lists nine negative signs and five positive signs; and *Religious Affections* (1746), in which he lists twelve of each. The quotations from this paragraph are taken from Jonathan Edwards, *The Distinguishing Marks of a Work of the Spirit of God*, in *The Great Awakening*, pp. 253, 255; and *Religious Affections*, pp. 383, 406.

[28]Edwards, *A Faithful Narrative*, in *The Great Awakening*, pp. 205-6. Stebbins would finally succeed at suicide in 1752, when he threw himself down a well.

bins, however, Hawley also suffered from depression, which intensified his turmoil in the throes of the revival.

> He had, from the beginning of this extraordinary time, been exceedingly concerned about the state of his soul. . . . Towards the latter part of his time, he grew much discouraged, and melancholy grew amain upon him, till he was wholly overpowered by it, and was in great measure past a capacity of receiving advice, or being reasoned with to any purpose. The Devil took the advantage, and drove him into despairing thoughts. He was kept awake anights, meditating terror; so that he had scarce any sleep at all. . . . And it was observed at last, that he was scarcely well capable of managing his ordinary business, and was judged delirious by the coroner's inquest.[29]

The revival did him in. It overwhelmed his constitution. Hawley despaired of his salvation. Spiritual pressure drove him mad.

Things grew worse from that point forward. "[I]t began to be very sensible," both to Edwards and his people, "that the Spirit of God was gradually withdrawing from us, and after this time Satan seemed to be more let loose, and raged in a dreadful manner." Many other local citizens entertained despairing thoughts. In fact, as Edwards admitted shamefully,

> multitudes in this and other towns seemed to have it strongly suggested to 'em, and pressed upon 'em, to do as this person [Hawley] had done. And many that seemed to be under no melancholy, some pious persons that had no special darkness, or doubts about the goodness of their state, nor were under any special trouble or concern of mind about anything spiritual or temporal, yet had it urged upon 'em, as if somebody had spoke to 'em, "Cut your own throat, now is good opportunity: *now*, NOW!" So that they were obliged to fight with all their might to resist it.[30]

By summer's end the revival had stalled in a slough of spiritual cra-

---

[29]Ibid., p. 206.
[30]Ibid., pp. 206-7.

ziness. Many reverted to sinful patterns of strife and partisan bickering. Edwards was embarrassed, but submitted to God's providence. He resolved to guard against religious confusion in the future.[31]

Making matters worse, by the end of 1735 Northampton's people were embroiled in what became a lengthy dispute about their meeting house. The current building was dilapidated. The town approved construction of a new one in November. Not surprisingly, however, at least to other active church folk, they disagreed—at length—about expenses and location. Ten months later a frame was raised (September 16–27, 1736), but the building was not completed. To Edwards' chagrin, in fact, it would not be finished for several more months.[32]

Then on March 13, 1737, disaster struck. During Sunday morning worship, "soon after the beginning of [the] sermon, the whole gallery—full of people, with all the seats and timbers, suddenly and without any warning—sunk and fell down, with the most amazing noise, upon the heads of those that sat under, to the astonishment of the congregation." As one would anticipate, "[t]he house was filled with dolorous shrieking and crying; and nothing else was expected than to find many people dead, or dashed to pieces." After the dust had cleared, however, the church's leaders moved in quickly and discovered that, surprisingly, "every life was preserved; and though

---

[31]As Edwards recounted some of this humbly in a letter to a friend: "Contention and a party spirit has been the old iniquity of this town; and as God's Spirit has been more and more withdrawn, so this spirit has of late manifestly revived. . . . I am ashamed, and ready to blush, to speak or think of such an appearance of strife, and division of the people into parties as there has been, after such great and wonderful things as God has wrought for us, which others afar off are rejoicing in, and praising God for. . . . God is pleased to let us see how entirely and immediately the great work lately wrought was his, by withdrawing, and letting us see how little we can do, and how little effect great things have without him." Edwards to the Rev. Benjamin Colman, May 19, 1737, in *Letters and Personal Writings*, pp. 67-68.

[32]Local historian James Trumbull reported that 76 men, 49 gallons of rum, and 36 pounds of sugar were required to raise the frame, "and twenty gallons seem to have been consumed while the framing was in progress, making in all sixty-nine gallons of liquor that were required for this part of the work, besides a number of barrels of 'cyder,' as well as several barrels of beer. . . . Notwithstanding the amount of intoxicants consumed," Trumbull assures us, "the laborious task of raising the huge frame was accomplished without accident." James Russell Trumbull, *History of Northampton, Massachusetts, from Its Settlement in 1654* (Northampton: Press of Gazette Printing Co., 1902), 2:70-71.

---

many were greatly bruised, and their flesh torn, yet there [was] not . . . one bone broken, or so much as put out of joint." The people praised God for this miraculous deliverance. And as Edwards testified in a well-known letter to Benjamin Colman, they found it "unreasonable" to interpret this prodigious episode in any other terms than those of divine "providence, in disposing the motions of every piece of timber, and the precise place of safety where every one should sit and fall, when none were in any capacity to care for their own preservation."[33]

They also viewed this episode as a sign from God to hurry up and finish their new building. They did so during the summer, raising its spire in July. (The old facility had no spire.)[34] They "seated" the church in autumn, assigning pews to local residents. They dedicated the building on none other than Christmas day (though they still did not celebrate Christmas). Early in 1738, they started to use the new facility. And on May 5, the men convened "to pull down the old meeting-house" and reallocate its remnants.[35]

Adding to Edwards' discouragement over the waning of the revival were the criteria employed in seating the meeting house. In the old church facility, all the men sat on one side, women and children on the other. Adolescents were allowed to sit together in the gallery. Seats were allotted by age, by men's "usefulness" in town and then by family estate or wealth, the most important people sitting front and center on the sabbath. In the new house, however, seats were assigned differently. For the most part, the sexes sat separately as before, although couples could opt to sit together in one of the thirty-five family boxes skirting the ground

---

[33]Edwards to the Rev. Benjamin Colman, March 19, 1737, in *Letters and Personal Writings*, pp. 65-66.

[34]Boston's class-conscious Brattle Street Church was the first Congregational church in the region to boast a spire, raised in 1699. See Joseph A. Conforti, *Imagining New England: Explorations of Regional Identity from the Pilgrims to the Mid-Twentieth Century* (Chapel Hill: University of North Carolina Press, 2001), p. 70.

[35]Trumbull, *History of Northampton*, 2:77.

floor. With permission from their parents, adolescents sat in the balcony (again, like before). However, seats on the main floor were now allotted first by wealth, only secondly by age and last by civic usefulness. Without the blessing of the pastor, wealth had jumped from third to first among the criteria now employed to determine people's social rank. Edwards was incensed. He did not mind the hierarchy, but he did oppose the materialism tainting the proceedings. He preached from John 14 at the dedication ceremony ("In my Father's house are many mansions"), calling his people to greater concern about the place they had in heaven—if indeed they had a place—than about their seats on Sunday. "'Tis very little worth the while . . . to pursue after honor in this world," he suggested, "when the greatest honor is but a bubble, and will soon vanish away. And death will level all."

> Some have more stately houses than others; some are in higher offices than others; and some are richer than others, and have higher seats in the meetinghouse than others. But all graves are upon a level. One rotting, putrefying corpse is as ignoble as another. The worms are as bold with one carcass as another. . . . if it be worth the while much to prize one seat before another in the house of worship, only because it is the pew or seat that is reckoned first in number, and to be seen here for a few days; how well it is worth the while to seek an high mansion in God's temple above, and in that glorious palace that is the everlasting habitation of God and all his children. You that are pleased with your seats in this house, because you are seated high; or in a place that is looked upon honorable by those that sit round about, and because many sit behind you; consider how short a time you will enjoy this pleasure.[36]

Unfortunately, we do not know how the congregation responded.

---

[36]Jonathan Edwards, "The Many Mansions," in *Sermons and Discourses, 1734–1738,* pp. 745-46. The committee responsible for submitting the plan of seating to the town was comprised of five prominent Christian laymen: John Stoddard, Esq. (Edwards' uncle); Ebenezer Pomeroy, Esq.; Timothy Dwight, Esq. (whose son would marry Edwards' daughter Mary); Samuel Mather; and Deacon Samuel Allyn. See Trumbull, *History of Northampton,* 2:74.

THE GREAT AWAKENING

Despite this letdown in the wake of his first revivalistic boon, Edwards continued to grow spiritually during the later 1730s. As he told Aaron Burr, in fact, at the end of his "Personal Narrative" (1740), this time was one of steady and even expansive Christian growth. "Though it seems to me," he wrote, "that in some respects I was a far better Christian, for two or three years after my first conversion, than I am now, yet of late years, I have had a more full and constant sense of the absolute sovereignty of God, and a delight in that sovereignty; and have had more of a sense of the glory of Christ."[37] This was also a season peppered with powerful spiritual epiphanies. For example, on several occasions Edwards enjoyed quasi-mystical encounters with the Lord, such as this one, which occurred sometime in 1737:

> having lit from my horse in a retired place, as my manner commonly has been, to walk for divine contemplation and prayer; I had a view, that for me was extraordinary, of the glory of the Son of God; as mediator between God and man; and his wonderful, great, full, pure and sweet grace and love, and meek and gentle condescension. This grace, that appeared to me so calm and sweet, appeared great above the heavens. The person of Christ appeared ineffably excellent, with an excellency great enough to swallow up all thought and conception. Which continued, as near as I can judge, about an hour; which kept me, the bigger part of the time, in a flood of tears, and weeping aloud. I felt withal, an ardency of soul to be . . . emptied and annihilated; to lie in the dust, and to be full of Christ alone; to love him with a holy and pure love; to trust in him; to live upon him; to serve and follow him, and to be totally wrapt up in the fullness of Christ; and to be perfectly sanctified . . . with a divine and heavenly purity.[38]

Edwards' "Narrative" concludes with the report of a similar incident, which occurred on a Saturday night, shortly before his Sunday services, in January of 1739:

---

[37]Edwards, "Personal Narrative," in *Letters and Personal Writings*, p. 803.
[38]Ibid., p. 801.

[I] had such a sense, how sweet and blessed a thing it was, to walk in the way of duty, to do that which was right and meet to be done, and agreeable to the holy mind of God; that it caused me to break forth into a kind of a loud weeping, which held me some time; so that I was forced to shut myself up, and fasten the doors. I could not but as it were cry out, "How happy are they which do that which is right in the sight of God! They are blessed indeed, they are the happy ones!" I had at the same time, a very affecting sense, how meet and suitable it was that God should govern the world, and order all things according to his own pleasure; and I rejoiced in it, that God reigned, and that his will was done.[39]

Edwards' piety was not as tame as many people think.

This spiritual growth prepared Edwards for his region's Great Awakening, an extension of the revival that had rocked the river valley during the mid-1730s, but which also sank deep roots in spiritual soil overseas, where revival had been sprouting since at least the 1720s. The story of this Awakening has been told many times.[40] It began in the middle of Europe, quickly spread to the British Isles and Britain's North American colonies, and impressed the entire West with the power of regeneration. It launched the modern, interdenominational, evangelical cause. It connected conservative Protestants all over the Western world with cords of common religious experience, international concerts of prayer, a flurry of pious letter writing, Christian periodicals, itinerant gospel preaching and a host of new institutions. It also played a formative role in American social history, granting colonists a common sense of spiritual identity that paved a way for the rise of American nationalism.

The most important individual to the transatlantic Awakening was George Whitefield, thought by some to be the greatest preacher

---

[39]Ibid., pp. 803-4.

[40]The most accessible accounts of this Awakening include Sweeney, *The American Evangelical Story*, pp. 27-51; Noll, *The Rise of Evangelicalism*; and Frank Lambert, *Inventing the "Great Awakening"* (Princeton: Princeton University Press, 1999). The most important account is W. R. Ward, *The Protestant Evangelical Awakening* (Cambridge: Cambridge University Press, 1992).

in history. Only twenty-six years old at the height of this work of God, Whitefield spoke to larger crowds than anyone else in colonial history—at times to tens of thousands—long before the invention of microphones and amplifiers. A poor man from England with distinctly crossed eyes, he was blessed by God with a booming voice, a flair for the dramatic and a remarkable gift of extemporaneous speech. (It was said that he could make a person swoon simply by saying "Mesopotamia.") He preached a basic gospel message from all over the biblical canon. He told stories with élan. The most compelling stories he told as he progressed from place to place had to do with the spread of revival through the Anglo-American world. He personified the Awakening and its international scope. He made seven trips to the colonies, preaching all the time and telling the hordes who flocked to hear him of the work of God in places they had only heard about, but which he knew firsthand. He was the era's greatest celebrity. God used his fame to extend the work of redemption.

During his second trip to the colonies, soon after his arrival, Whitefield sent a letter to Edwards asking permission to visit his church. "I rejoice for the great things God has done for many souls in Northampton," Whitefield wrote his senior colleague (based on Edwards' *Faithful Narrative*). "I hope, God willing, to come and see them in a few months."[41] Edwards replied warmly. He knew of Whitefield's record as a winsome gospel preacher and he longed for help renewing the work of revival in Northampton. "I apprehend, from what I have heard," he said, "that you are one that has the blessing of heaven attending you wherever you go; and I have a great desire . . . that such a blessing . . . may descend on this town, and may enter mine own house."[42] By the spring of 1740, Edwards' parish started to show the signs of another work of God, especially among the youth.

---

[41] This letter is dated November 16, 1739, and is most readily available in Iain H. Murray, *Jonathan Edwards: A New Biography* (Edinburgh: Banner of Truth Trust, 1987), p. 156.

[42] Jonathan Edwards to the Rev. George Whitefield, February 12, 1740, in *Letters and Personal Writings*, p. 80.

Then when Whitefield finally arrived—on Friday, October 17, eleven months after he had written to ask for Edwards' hospitality—these sparks were fanned into flame, and Northampton joined the ranks of the Great Awakening.[43]

Whitefield stayed for three days. He spoke twice on the day he arrived, once in church and once at the manse; once the following afternoon (after another sermon in Hadley, nearly five miles away); and twice more "upon the sabbath." Edwards reported to a friend that his "congregation was extraordinarily melted by every sermon; almost the whole assembly being in tears for a great part of sermon time." Edwards "wept" as well, "during the whole time" of the Sunday morning service, according to Whitefield. God's Spirit was at work, as nearly everyone could tell. Sarah described Whitefield's ministry in a letter to her brother:

> It is wonderful to see what a spell he casts over an audience by pro-
> claiming the simplest truths of the Bible. I have seen upwards of a
> thousand people hang on his words with breathless silence, broken
> only by an occasional half-suppressed sob. He impresses the ignorant,
> and not less the educated and refined. . . . our mechanics shut up
> their shops, and the day-labourers throw down their tools, to go and
> hear him preach, and few return unaffected. . . . He speaks from a
> heart all aglow with love, and pours out a torrent of eloquence which
> is almost irresistible.[44]

While in town for only three days, Whitefield played a crucial role in drawing Edwards' flock back into the Great Awakening.

---

[43]Edwards' most detailed account of this second major revival during his ministry in Northampton lies in a letter to the Rev. Thomas Prince (of Boston), December 12, 1743, in *Letters and Personal Writings*, pp. 115-27.

[44]Jonathan Edwards to the Rev. Thomas Prince, December 12, 1743, in *Letters and Personal Writings*, p. 116; *George Whitefield's Journals*, ed. Iain Murray (Edinburgh: Banner of Truth Trust, 1960), pp. 476-77; and Sarah Edwards to the Rev. James Pierpont, October 24, 1740, in Luke Tyerman, *The Life of the Rev. George Whitefield*, vol. 1 (New York: Anson D. F. Randolph & Co., 1877), p. 428. Sarah's letter does not survive in its original manuscript. This, combined with the fact that our earliest "copy" of it comes from a man known for fabricating similar documents for the sake of promoting Christian piety, has led some specialists to doubt its authenticity.

Whitefield was also rather impetuous, though, at times spiritually arrogant. He had earned a reputation for judging other pastors rashly, claiming that many—maybe most—were unconverted. So as Edwards traveled with him to his next few preaching stations (mainly in Suffield and East Windsor, near the river in northern Connecticut,[45] where the two of them would spend some quality time with Edwards' parents), he advised the young star that it could be dangerous to rely too much on spiritual "impulses" without help from the Word of God. He also said that, while he affirmed Whitefield's emphasis on the need for clergy themselves to be converted, he believed it inappropriate to judge precipitately which of their colleagues were regenerate—and which of them were not.[46] He listened to Whitefield preach to several thousand in the fields, thanked him

---

[45]Technically speaking, Suffield (and nearby Enfield, mentioned later in this chapter) were part of Massachusetts until 1749, when boundaries were redrawn and they were transferred to Connecticut.

[46]Edwards' advice was timely. Whitefield had started to side publicly with the testy Gilbert Tennent, a Presbyterian revivalist admired by Edwards himself (Edwards knew his father William), who had recently published a sermon against "Pharisee-Teachers" (i.e., unregenerate pastors) titled *The Danger of an Unconverted Ministry* (Philadelphia: Benjamin Franklin, 1740). A few years later, Edwards would have to hurry to Whitefield's defense—and his own—as a result of Whitefield's spotted reputation. In 1744, Yale's President Thomas Clap—who had shut the college down when the students grew unruly at the height of the revival, later expelling a couple students for attending a "New Light" (i.e., pro-revival) service in defiance of his rules—said publicly at Harvard that, as Edwards told him recently, Whitefield hoped to replace most of the ministers in New England with more suitable evangelicals from England, Scotland and Ireland. Edwards was mortified. He claimed he had never said any such thing. Still, the rumor was out, Whitefield's reputation made it credible, and Edwards had to refute it in a turgid paper war. See Thomas Clap, *A Letter from the Rev. Mr. Thomas Clap . . . to a Friend in Boston* (Boston: T. Fleet, 1745); Jonathan Edwards, *Copies of the Two Letters Cited by the Rev. Mr. Clap* (Boston: S. Kneeland and T. Green, 1745); Thomas Clap, *A Letter from the Rev. Mr. Thomas Clap . . . to the Rev. Mr. Edwards* (Boston: T. Fleet, 1745); Jonathan Edwards, *An Expostulatory Letter from the Reverend Mr. Edwards . . . to the Rev. Mr. Clap . . . concerning the Rev. Mr. Whitefield* (Boston: S. Kneeland and T. Green, 1745); and Edwards, *Letters and Personal Writings*, pp. 153-72. Cf. Kidd, *The Great Awakening*, pp. 169-73. Edwards also defended Whitefield in a letter to Scottish friends, responding to widespread allegations regarding his difficult personality. See *Letters and Personal Writings*, pp. 174-79, where Edwards also includes a report on Whitefield's second (and last) visit to Northampton (July 1745): "He with his lady [i.e., his new wife, a former widow named Elizabeth James Whitefield] was here at Northampton . . . and behaved himself so, that he endeared himself much to me; he appeared in a more desirable temper of mind and more solid and judicious in his thoughts, and prudence in his conduct, than when he was here before" (p. 178).

heartily for his labors, and returned home, hopeful for the future. Right away, he preached a series on the parable of the sower (Mt 13), exhorting his people not to be star-struck by Whitefield's obvious "eloquence," but to live as the kind of soil in which the Word can bear fruit.[47]

Within the next couple of months, Northampton bore abundant fruit. "[T]here was a great alteration in the town," Edwards testified, particularly among the local children. "By the middle of December a very considerable work of God appeared among those that were very young, and the revival of religion continued to increase; so that in the spring, an engagedness of spirit about things of religion was become very general amongst young people and children, and religious subjects almost wholly took up their conversation." Edwards' thank you note to Whitefield reinforces this account. "I have joyful tidings to send you concerning the state of religion in this place," he exclaimed:

> It has been gradually reviving and prevailing more and more, ever since you was here. Religion is become abundantly more the subject of conversation; other things that seemed to impede it, are for the present laid aside. I have reason to think that a considerable number of our young people, some of them children, have already been savingly brought home to Christ. I hope salvation has come to this house since you was in it, with respect to one, if not more, of my children. The Spirit of God seems to be at work with others of the family. That blessed work seems now to be going on in this place, especially amongst those that are young.[48]

Edwards' girls had now come under the saving work of the Holy Spirit. Many other children, as well, had been affected by the gos-

---

[47]This series was six sermons long. The original manuscripts are located in folders 462-63, 465-467, and 469, box 6, Jonathan Edwards Collection, Beinecke. Cf. Ava Chamberlain, "The Grand Sower of the Seed: Jonathan Edwards's Critique of George Whitefield," *New England Quarterly* 70 (September 1997): 368-85.

[48]Edwards to the Rev. Thomas Prince, December 12, 1743, and Edwards to the Rev. George Whitefield, December 14, 1740, in *Letters and Personal Writings*, pp. 116-17, 87.

pel. Edwards later described this time as "the most wonderful work among children that ever was in Northampton."[49] It rekindled his flame for revival and conversion in New England.

HELLFIRE AND BRIMSTONE

During the following spring and summer, Edwards himself was called upon to serve as a traveling gospel preacher. Inspired by Whitefield's example, he did more of this than ever during 1741, preaching with few and sketchy notes in places like Hadley, Suffield, Hartford and New Haven (among others). He is best known, of course, for the sermon he preached in Enfield, a satellite of Suffield, on a sultry day in July. He had preached this sermon before to his own congregation (from a complete manuscript, and to little recorded effect). As he preached it on the road, however, amazing things happened. Edwards' text was very brief, "Their foot shall slide in due time" (Deut 32:35); his doctrine somewhat longer and more memorable today, "There is nothing that keeps wicked men, at any one moment, out of hell, but the mere pleasure of God." He applied this doctrine at length, however, in words that went down in history, scaring the hell—quite literally—out of his hearers:

> The wrath of God is like great waters that are dammed for the present; they increase more and more, and rise higher and higher, till an outlet is given, and the longer the stream is stopped, the more rapid and mighty is its course, when once it is let loose. 'Tis true, that judgment against your evil works has not been executed hitherto; the floods of God's vengeance have been withheld; but your guilt in the meantime is constantly increasing, and you are every day treasuring up more wrath; the waters are continually rising and waxing more and more mighty; and there is nothing but the mere pleasure of God that holds the waters back that are unwilling to be stopped, and press

---

[49]Edwards to the Rev. Thomas Prince, December 12, 1743, in *Letters and Personal Writings*, p. 119. We do not have details about what happened to Edwards' girls, but at the time of Whitefield's visit, Edwards' daughter Sarah was 12, Jerusha 10, Esther 8, and Mary 6.

hard to go forward; if God should only withdraw his hand from the floodgate, it would immediately fly open, and the fiery floods of the fierceness and wrath of God would rush forth with inconceivable fury, and would come upon you with omnipotent power; and if your strength were ten thousand times greater than it is, yea ten thousand times greater than the strength of the stoutest, sturdiest devil in hell, it would be nothing to withstand or endure it.

The bow of God's wrath is bent, and the arrow made ready on the string, and justice bends the arrow at your heart, and strains the bow, and it is nothing but the mere pleasure of God, and that of an angry God, without any promise or obligation at all, that keeps the arrow one moment from being made drunk with your blood.

Thus are all you that never passed under a great change of heart, by the mighty power of the Spirit of God upon your souls; all that were never born again, and made new creatures, . . . (however you may have reformed your life in many things . . . and may keep up a form of religion in your families and closets, and in the house of God, and may be strict in it), you are thus in the hands of an angry God; 'tis nothing but his mere pleasure that keeps you from being this moment swallowed up in everlasting destruction.[50]

So goes the famous sermon "Sinners in the Hands of an Angry God," a truly frightening piece of work, but one that is also full of love and passionate literary artistry. The Rev. Stephen Williams, Edwards' cousin, heard him preach it to the people of Enfield (as was mentioned in chapter two). He kept a diary, which contains a vivid account of the response:

---

[50]Jonathan Edwards, "Sinners in the Hands of an Angry God," in *The Sermons of Jonathan Edwards*, pp. 49-50, 56-57. Edwards preached this sermon in Enfield on July 8, 1741. Though his text was from Deuteronomy, the sermon resonated just as clearly with Psalm 7, from which he re-preached "Sinners" on at least one other occasion: "God is angry with the wicked every day. If he turn not, he will whet his sword; he hath bent his bow, and made it ready. He hath also prepared for him the instruments of death; he ordaineth his arrows against the persecutors. Behold, he travaileth with iniquity, and hath conceived mischief, and brought forth falsehood. He made a pit, and digged it, and is fallen into the ditch which he made. His mischief shall return upon his own head, and his violent dealing shall come down upon his own pate" (Ps 7:11-16).

We went over to Enf[ield]—where we met dear Mr E[dwards] of N[orth]H[ampton]—who preached a most awakening sermon from these words—Deut. 32-35 and before sermon was done—there was a great moaning and crying out through [the] whole House—What Shall I do to be saved—oh I am going to Hell—Oh what shall I do for Christ [etc.] So [that the] minister was obliged to desist—[the] shrieks & cries were piercing & Amazing—after Some time of waiting the Congregation were Still so [that] a prayer was made . . . & after that we descended from the pulpit and discoursed with the people . . . and Amazing and Astonishing [the] power [of] God was seen—& Several Souls were hopefully wrought upon [that] night, & oh [the] cheerfulness and pleasantness of their countenances [that] received comfort—oh [that] God would strengthen and confirm—we sung an hymn & prayed & dismissed [the] Assembly.[51]

One of the first times I read this sermon to evangelical students, a young man in the back of the room called its rhetoric "barbaric." This sentiment is shared by many other students as well, many of whom have read "Sinners" in their high school English classes. What teachers of those classes almost always fail to mention, though, is that Edwards stood in a long line of Puritan hellfire preachers, few of whom liked to preach such messages, none of whom preached them frequently, but all of whom felt a compelling sense of moral obligation to warn their people of the dangers faced by unconverted sinners.

Edwards preached dozens of hellfire sermons during his thirty-five years of ministry, many of which survive. Like the Puritans before him, he did so in the manner of the "watchman" of Ezekiel, whom God held responsible to sound a trumpet clearly when his people were threatened with danger. For as God told Ezekiel:

Son of man, I have made thee a watchman unto the house of Israel: therefore hear the word at my mouth, and give them warning from

---

[51]A typescript of Stephen Williams' diary is housed at the Storrs Memorial Library, Long-meadow, Massachusetts. The snippet quoted above can also be found in Murray, *Jonathan Edwards*, p. 169.

me. When I say unto the wicked, Thou shalt surely die; and thou givest him not warning, nor speakest to warn the wicked from his wicked way, to save his life; the same wicked man shall die in his iniquity; but his blood will I require at thine hand. Yet if thou warn the wicked, and he turn not from his wickedness, . . . he shall die in his iniquity; but thou hast delivered thy soul. Again, When a righteous man doth turn from his righteousness, and commit iniquity, and I lay a stumblingblock before him, he shall die: because thou hast not given him warning, he shall die in his sin, and his righteousness which he hath done shall not be remembered; but his blood will I require at thine hand. Nevertheless if thou warn the righteous man, that the righteous sin not, and he doth not sin, he shall surely live, because he is warned; also thou hast delivered thy soul. (Ezek 3:17-21)[52]

This was serious business. Edwards believed that he was a watchman for the people in his care. He believed, as he proclaimed at one of his colleagues' ordinations, that "ministers of the gospel have the precious and immortal souls of men committed to their care and trust by the Lord Jesus Christ." He believed that he would give an account on Judgment Day for his ministry. He believed in the words of Hebrews, as he said once in Northampton, that his "God is a Consuming fire that will burn up all that resist him." So he preached from time to time on the dangers of damnation. "If there be really a hell," he wrote in 1741,

of such dreadful, and never-ending torments, . . . that multitudes are in great danger of, and that the bigger part of men in Christian countries do actually from generation to generation fall into, for want of a sense of the terribleness of it, and their danger of it, and so for want of taking due care to avoid it; then why is it not proper for those that have the care of souls, to take great pains to make men sensible of it? Why should not they be told as much of the truth as can be? If I am in danger of going to hell, I should be glad to know as much as possibly I can of the dreadfulness of it: if I am very prone to neglect due care

---

[52]Cf. Ezekiel 33, which extends this very theme.

to avoid it, he does me the best kindness, that does most to represent to me the truth of the case, that sets forth my misery and danger in the liveliest manner.[53]

Such preaching saw success at the apex of the Awakening.[54] Thousands were converted—in America alone—during 1741. Edwards was summoned to give a speech at Yale's commencement that September, helping the college boys sort through the spiritual wonders all around.[55] Recent Yale College graduates resorted to him for help, living in Edwards' parsonage to prepare for ministry.[56] Edwards gained a reputation for adept spiritual counsel, both to children and adults, a reputation that survived him for a century after his death. In fact, *Advice to Young Converts*, which began as a letter of counsel Edwards wrote for a teenage girl converted in 1741, became a steady bestseller read by hundreds of thousands of people over the course of the nineteenth century.[57]

---

[53]See Jonathan Edwards, "The Great Concern of a Watchman for Souls," in *Sermons and Discourses, 1743–1758*, p. 63 (preached at the ordination of Jonathan Judd, June 8, 1743); Edwards' ms. sermon on Hebrews 12:29, L. 3, r., folder 839, box 11, Jonathan Edwards Collection, Beinecke; and *The Distinguishing Marks of a Work of the Spirit of God*, in *The Great Awakening*, pp. 246-47. Edwards went on to clarify for Judd the eternal importance of his watch: "suffer me, dear brother, to tell you, that you must another day meet these souls that you are now going to take the charge of, before the judgment seat of Christ; and if by means of your faithfulness towards them, in your work, you shall meet them at the right hand of Christ in glory, how joyful a meeting will it be to you! They will be indeed your crown of rejoicing in that day. But if you behold 'em with devils at the left hand, in horror and despair, your conscience accusing you of unfaithfulness towards them, and it appears that they are lost through your neglect, how amazing will the sight of 'em be to you!" (p. 74).

[54]As I try to make clear in the rest of this book, Edwards preached on many other topics as well, including heaven (on this, see chapter seven). In fact, he tried to preach what used to be called "the whole counsel of God," treating all the important doctrines of the Bible in their turn. On Edwards' understanding of heaven and its importance for our lives, see also Stephen J. Nichols, *Heaven on Earth: Capturing Jonathan Edwards's Vision of Living in Between* (Wheaton, Ill.: Crossway, 2006).

[55]This speech was later published as *Distinguishing Marks of a Work of the Spirit of God* (Boston: S. Kneeland and T. Green, 1741).

[56]Several students did this over the course of his career. The first were the Rev. Joseph Bellamy (1736–1737) and the Rev. Samuel Hopkins (1741–1742).

[57]See Edwards to Deborah Hatheway, June 3, 1741, in *Letters and Personal Writings*, pp. 90-95. Hatheway was 18 years old and a resident of Suffield at the time of her conversion. First published in 1807, *Advice to Young Converts* had circulated in 328,000 copies by 1875.

HOPES DASHED, HEARTS HARDENED

Edwards hoped that this Awakening would hasten the millennium, a golden age of heightened spirituality.[58] Late in 1741, however, the work began to recede. It continued intermittently till 1743. But by that time, it had been overwhelmed by a host of holy rollers, Christian hypocrisy and contentiousness—a wash of "enthusiasm" that gave opponents of the revival an excuse to throw the baby out with the bath water. Poorly educated preachers started to upstage the work, substituting their personalities and spiritual one-upmanship for careful biblical ministry. They called upon the laity to leave their dry churches, burn the books of wiser pastors (for their cold, dead pretentiousness) and join their own services, where trances and visions abounded and where extrabiblical claims to immediate revelation carried more weight than Scripture itself.[59] They split well over a hundred congregations in New England. The Connecticut General Assembly passed a law against their itinerancy. Edwards labored diligently to distinguish their extremes from the work of the Holy Spirit. But by 1743, many agreed with Charles Chauncy (a respected pastor in Boston who opposed the Great Awakening) that the revival must be stopped.[60]

---

[58]He was a postmillennialist, who believed that Christ would not return to earth until after an age of intense, sustained revival (i.e., the great millennial age). He thought this age would start sometime around the year 2000, probably in the Holy Land, and hoped that the Awakening was its harbinger. As he said in *Some Thoughts Concerning the Present Revival of Religion in New England*, "'Tis not unlikely that this work of God's Spirit, that is so extraordinary and wonderful, is the dawning, or at least a prelude, of that glorious work of God, so often foretold in Scripture, which in the progress and issue of it, shall renew the world of mankind" (*The Great Awakening*, p. 353). For more on Edwards and the end times, see Brandon G. Withrow, "A Future of Hope: Jonathan Edwards and Millennial Expectations," *Trinity Journal* 22 (Spring 2001): 75-98.

[59]The most notorious of these extremists were James Davenport (who was eventually deemed insane), Andrew Croswell (a Harvard man who shared his pulpit with children and slaves, but whose congregation dwindled to seven members before he died) and Daniel Rogers (who left a large and fascinating diary, housed today at the New York Historical Society). In March of 1743, Edwards would chair a council of clergymen who met in New London, Connecticut, trying to "reclaim" the laity led astray by Davenport. My thanks to Tommy Kidd for teaching me most of what I know about Daniel Rogers.

[60]Chauncy toured New England, New York and New Jersey before he published a 400-page exposé of these excesses, *Seasonable Thoughts on the State of Religion in New-England* (Boston: Printed by Rogers and Fowle, for Samuel Eliot, 1743).

Even in Edwards' own church, things began to go downhill. The pastor pleaded, pushed and prodded his congregation to cooperate with God in spreading revival. He reminded them that the eyes of all the world were now upon them. But despite his best efforts, things continued to devolve. He thought that perhaps a public renewal of Northampton's church covenant would fire up his parish, but it landed with a thud and failed to generate much heat.[61] He commenced a weekly offering for the needs of the local poor, but this too was received grudgingly and yielded sour fruit.[62] He said that many in his care exhibited spiritual "stupidity." He feared they were "sermon proof." His frustration grew palpable. He needled his people incessantly, aggravating his flock.[63]

Then in the mid-1740s he traversed a series of landmines, which injured his relationships with hundreds in his care. In 1744, he mishandled an affair known as the "Bad Book Controversy." Several young men in town had viewed an illustrated manual for early modern midwives—the closest thing to pornography that most of them

---

[61]The new church covenant, which was affirmed at a public worship service held on March 16, 1742, "a Day of Fasting and Prayer for the Continuance and Increase of the Gracious Presence of God," is available in Edwards to the Rev. Thomas Prince, December 12, 1743, in *Letters and Personal Writings*, pp. 121-25.

[62]As Edwards had preached to his congregation early in 1741, God discloses himself to those who care for others. "It would be the way to have much of the Holy Spirit poured out upon a people, for them to be much in deeds of charity. Remarkable outpourings of the Spirit of God and an abounding in the practice of the duty [of charity] have been wont to accompany one another." See "Much in Deeds of Charity," in *The Sermons of Jonathan Edwards*, p. 210. Though Edwards had pushed it for several years, the church did not begin this offering until 1743.

[63]Evidence of frustration riddles his sermons from this period. To take just one example, Edwards preached one of the hottest hellfire sermons ever written to the people of Northampton in July of 1747, "Yield to God's Word, or Be Broken by His Hand." Addressing those in the congregation unawakened by the gospel, he moaned: "How dark does your case appear! And, indeed, when I went about preparing this discourse it was with considerable discouragement: I thought it was now some time since I had offered any discourse of this nature, but so many had been offered with so little apparent effect that I thought with myself, I know not what to say further. But, however, because I must warn you from God—whether you will hear or whether you will forbear—I have warned you again." He hoped aloud, further, that his people would not "continue in your stupidity to the last." *Sermons and Discourses, 1743–1758*, p. 220. Edwards' concern about the potential of his people to grow "sermon proof" dates back to the death of Stoddard early in 1729. See "Living Unconverted under an Eminent Means of Grace," in *Sermons and Discourses, 1723–1729*, ed. Kenneth P. Minkema, *WJE*, vol. 14 (1997), pp. 365, 367.

---

would see—and had used it to harass several adolescent girls. Edwards cracked down hard on the boys, attacking the problem publicly (even from the pulpit), embarrassing the relatives of everyone involved, inciting the young culprits to rebel against his leadership and failing to facilitate a reconciliation.[64] Later that year, he initiated a lengthy conversation with the town about his salary. He asked for a permanent contract to avoid the annual scrutiny his family had endured regarding their high standard of living (high, that is, by local standards—even poorly paid pastors in America today live much better than Edwards did). Negotiations took three years. In the end he got his way, but had to promise not to ask for another raise ever again.[65] Then from 1747 till the summer of 1749, he stumbled through two nasty fornication cases in town, trying (but failing) to force two men, Elisha Hawley and Thomas Wait, to marry the girls who carried their babies, Martha Root and Jemima Miller.[66] All in all, these events took a heavy toll on Edwards. When considered in conjunction with the epidemic illnesses of the later 1740s, which eventually killed well over a tenth of the people in Northampton,[67] the threat of Indian raids feared in 1746, which led to the "fort[ing] in" and quartering of the parsonage with soldiers,[68] the death of his

---

[64]For more on this affair, see the documentary evidence in *A Jonathan Edwards Reader*, ed. John E. Smith, Harry S. Stout and Kenneth P. Minkema (New Haven: Yale University Press, 1995), pp. 172-78; and the historical analysis of Ava Chamberlain, "Bad Books and Bad Boys: The Transformation of Gender in Eighteenth-Century Northampton, Massachusetts," in *Jonathan Edwards at Home and Abroad: Historical Memories, Cultural Movements, Global Horizons*, ed. David W. Kling and Douglas A. Sweeney (Columbia: University of South Carolina Press, 2003), pp. 61-81.

[65]Despite this promise, the town gave Edwards another raise shortly thereafter, increasing his pay by £170 in 1749. By the end of the 1740s, Edwards enjoyed a higher salary than any other pastor in western New England. On the dispute about his salary, see Jonathan Edwards to the First Precinct, Northampton, November 8, 1744, and March 4, 1745, in *Letters and Personal Writings*, pp. 149-51, 162-63; and Trumbull, *History of Northampton*, 2:195-97.

[66]Hawley was Edwards' cousin and a son of the Joseph Hawley who had earlier killed himself. For more on these and other disciplinary cases in Northampton, consult Sweeney, "The Church," pp. 183-84, 188 n. 23; and "Timetable: Landmarks in the History of Edwards' Development as a Minister," in the front matter.

[67]Trumbull, *History of Northampton*, 2:101.

[68]On Edwards' military context, see especially "Colonial Wars," in George M. Marsden, *Jonathan Edwards: A Life* (New Haven: Yale University Press, 2003), pp. 306-19.

daughter Jerusha early in 1748, whom Edwards once referred to as "the flower of the family,"[69] not to mention the usual blows sustained by busy parish pastors, they can be understood to have weakened his effectiveness in ministry.

EDWARDS IS EJECTED

Early in 1749, the camel's back began to break. For many years, Edwards had harbored reservations about his church's sacramental policy. Pioneered by Solomon Stoddard, it allowed the unconverted to present themselves for communion (and present their children for baptism). In 1672, Stoddard had undergone a powerful experience of the assurance of God's saving love for him while presiding at communion. Ever since, he had called communion a "converting ordinance" (an act that aids in one's conversion), permitting all within the parish who professed belief in Christ and lived a decent moral life to participate.[70] By the late 1720s, Edwards disagreed with this, but kept his scruples to himself. As he explained his inconsistency in 1749:

> I have formerly been of [Stoddard's] opinion, which I imbibed from
> his books, even from my childhood, and have in my proceedings con-
> formed to his practice; though never without some difficulties in my
> view, which I could not solve: yet, however, a distrust of my own un-
> derstanding, and deference to the authority of so venerable a man,
> the seeming strength of some of his arguments, together with the

---

[69]As Edwards wrote to a friend in Scotland, "It has pleased God . . . sorely to afflict this family by taking away by death . . . my second daughter [Jerusha] in the eighteenth year of her age, a very pleasant and useful member of this family, and that was generally esteemed the flower of the family. Herein we have a great loss; but the remembrance of the remarkable appearances of piety in her, from her childhood, in life, and also at her death, are very comfortable to us, and give us great reason to mingle thanksgiving with our mourning. I desire your prayers, dear Sir, that God would make up our great loss to us in himself." Edwards to the Rev. John Erskine, August 31, 1748, in *Letters and Personal Writings*, pp. 249-50.

[70]Stoddard laid out his position in a series of publications, including *The Doctrine of Instituted Churches Explained and Proved from the Word of God* (London: Ralph Smith, 1700); *The Inexcusableness of Neglecting the Worship of God, under a Pretence of Being in an Unconverted Condition . . .* (Boston: B. Green, 1708); and *An Appeal to the Learned: Being a Vindication of the Right of Visible Saints to the Lords Supper, Though They Be Destitute of a Saving Work of God's Spirit on Their Hearts . . .* (Boston: B. Green, 1709).

---

success he had in his ministry, and his great reputation and influence, prevailed for a long time to bear down my scruples.[71]

By the late 1740s, though, his scruples overcame his great esteem for Stoddard's legacy. Sacraments, he thought, were signs and seals of saving grace. They functioned as false, confusing signs when shared by those who stood outside God's saving covenant of grace— even those who lived good lives and practiced nominal Christianity.[72] There is such a thing as conversion and it makes a world of difference. Christians ought to give an account of the Spirit's work in their souls before presenting themselves for communion (or presenting their children for baptism). No one needed to specify her place along the morphology, or fit within a procrustean bed of uniform conversion. But as Edwards summarized his view to the people in his parish: "'Tis the mind and will of God that none should be admitted to full communion in the church of Christ but such as in profession, and in the eye of a reasonable judgment, are truly saints or godly persons."[73]

---

[71]Jonathan Edwards, *An Humble Inquiry into the Rules of the Word of God, Concerning the Qualifications Requisite to a Compleat Standing and Full Communion in the Visible Christian Church* (1749), in *Ecclesiastical Writings*, ed. David D. Hall, *WJE*, vol. 12 (1994), p. 169. For background on the history of the sacraments in New England, start with E. Brooks Holifield, *The Covenant Sealed: The Development of Puritan Sacramental Theology in Old and New England, 1570-1720* (New Haven: Yale University Press, 1974).

[72]According to the *Westminster Confession of Faith* (1647), which Edwards did affirm: "Sacraments are holy signs and seals of the covenant of grace, immediately instituted by God, to represent Christ and His benefits; and to confirm our interest in Him; as also, to put a visible difference between those that belong unto the Church and the rest of the world; and solemnly to engage them to the service of God in Christ, according to His Word" (Article 27). Edwards once said to a Scottish friend who wanted to make him a Presbyterian: "As to my subscribing to the substance of the Westminster Confession, there would be no difficulty." See Edwards to the Rev. John Erskine, July 5, 1750, in *Letters and Personal Writings*, p. 355.

[73]Jonathan Edwards, "Lectures on the Qualifications for Full Communion in the Church of Christ," in *Sermons and Discourses, 1743-1758*, p. 354. Technically speaking, while this controversy had mainly to do with communion, it also pertained to church membership and baptism. Edwards sought to reserve church membership to those who could testify (even with help) to regeneration. In his view, moreover, only regenerate church members—only those who had real membership in the covenant of grace—had a biblical right to present their children for baptism. For more on Edwards' view of the sacraments and the doctrine of the church, see Sweeney, "The Church" (on the communion controversy, see esp. pp. 180-85).

Late in 1748, a young man about to be married sought admission to the church and, by implication, to the sacraments. Edwards told him he would have to give an account of his conversion. After some deliberation, the man claimed to be converted but declined to apply for membership in Edwards' new way. Word spread quickly through the grapevine of the pastor's change of mind. Then in February, Edwards informed "the committee of the church" (i.e., the leading board of laymen) of his plan to change their policy on membership and sacraments. He offered to explain himself in public from the pulpit. "This was strenuously opposed," however, "by several" in the group. The committee recommended that he print his views instead. Edwards did so right away, releasing a book on his views in August and agreeing that if and when the congregation read the book and still opposed his change of mind, he would offer to resign. In the meantime, Mary Hulbert, a parishioner who was willing to give an account of her conversion, sought admission to the church—but the committee refused to proceed with her for fear of a general fracas. The pastor and his people found themselves in a deadly stalemate.[74]

These events must have gone by very slowly for Edwards himself, though they seem centuries later to have raced by all too quickly. By the winter of 1750, Edwards faced stiff resistance from his local power brokers, some of whom were working behind the scenes to have him fired. He retained the allegiance of many women and young people, those with whom he had long enjoyed the greatest success. But the "leading men" in town, many of whom had come of age under his grandfather's tutelage, prevented him from purifying the

---

[74]Most accounts of the details of this lengthy controversy are based in one way or another on Edwards' "Narrative of Communion Controversy," in *Ecclesiastical Writings*, pp. 507-619 (quotations from p. 508). Edwards' first book on the matter was *An Humble Inquiry into the Rules of the Word of God, Concerning the Qualifications Requisite to a Compleat Standing and Full Communion in the Visible Christian Church* (1749), in *Ecclesiastical Writings*, pp. 166-348. He would later publish another book, defending himself from criticism, *Misrepresentations Corrected, and Truth Vindicated, in a Reply to the Rev. Mr. Solomon Williams's Book, intitled, The True State of the Question concerning the Qualifications Necessary to Lawful Communion in the Christian Sacraments* (1752), in *Ecclesiastical Writings*, pp. 350-503.

church.[75] Both Edwards and his opponents made appeals to other pastors. Edwards' change of heart became a cause célèbre throughout New England. In the end, however, he fell short of mustering a majority of the parish to his side.[76] Few of them ever read his book. He was prohibited from leading a conversation on the subject.[77] And on June 22, he was fired.

He played the part of the watchman even after his ejection. In his "Farewell Sermon," which he gave just nine days later (July 1, 1750), Edwards repeated that he would meet his flock again on Judgment Day. He said that the Lord would "judge between them, as to any controversies," and he pondered aloud the account he would give of his ministry:

> Faithful ministers will then give an account with joy, concerning those who have received them well, and made a good improvement of their ministry; and these will be given 'em, at that day, as their crown of rejoicing. And at the same time they will give an account of the ill-treatment, of such as have not well received them and their messages from Christ: they will meet these, not as they used to do in this world, to counsel and warn them, but to bear witness against them, and as their judges, and assessors with Christ, to condemn them. And on the other hand, the people will at that day rise up in judgment against wicked and unfaithful ministers, who have sought their own temporal interest, more than the good of the souls of their flock.

[75]Kenneth P. Minkema, "Old Age and Religion in the Writings and Life of Jonathan Edwards," *Church History* 70 (December 2001): 674-704. One might argue that Edwards has always appealed to young people most, as evidenced today in a recent piece by Collin Hansen, "Young, Restless, and Reformed: Calvinism Is Making a Comeback—and Shaking Up the Church," *Christianity Today*, September 2006, pp. 32-38.

[76]It should be noted here that many of Edwards' pro-revival colleagues took his side in this dispute, including Anglicans like Whitefield. What is more, by century's end a large preponderance of the region's Congregationalists would side with him, reserving church membership and access to the sacraments for those who were converted.

[77]After several more denials of his request to preach on the subject, Edwards delivered a series of optional weekday "Lectures on the Qualifications for Full Communion in the Church of Christ" (February and March 1750), strongly opposed by the leading men, which were "thinly attended," writes Kimnach, "outsiders sometimes far outnumbering members of the congregation." *Sermons and Discourses, 1743-1758*, pp. 349-440.

Then he directed his attention to his unconverted listeners:

My parting with you is in some respects in a peculiar manner a melancholy parting; inasmuch as I leave you in most melancholy circumstances; because I leave you in the gall of bitterness and bond of iniquity, having the wrath of God abiding on you. . . . Your consciences bear me witness, that while I had opportunity, I have not ceased to warn you and set before you your danger. . . . I have diligently endeavored to find out and use the most powerful motives to persuade you to take care for your own welfare and salvation. . . . You and I are now parting one from another as to this world; let us labor that we may not be parted, after our meeting at the last day. If I have been your faithful pastor (which will that day appear, whether I have or no), then I shall be acquitted, and shall ascend with Christ. O do your part, that in such a case, it may not be so, that you should be forced eternally to part from me, and all that have been faithful in Christ Jesus. This is a sorrowful parting that now is between you and me; but that would be a more sorrowful parting to you than this. This you may perhaps bear without being much affected with it, if you are not glad of it; but such a parting in that day will most deeply, sensibly and dreadfully affect you.[78]

The Great Awakening proved divisive. But it also crystallized the crucial importance of conversion and of living life with eschatological urgency. Whatever one thinks of his personality or his ministerial methods, Edwards' genius for conveying these priorities was great. As we will see further below, moreover, his courage in living them out was even greater.

---

[78]Jonathan Edwards, "A Farewell Sermon Preached at the First Precinct in Northampton, After the People's Public Rejection of Their Minister . . . on June 22, 1750," in *The Sermons of Jonathan Edwards*, pp. 221, 231-33.

— *Chapter 5* —

WITH ALL THY MIND

*Then one of them, which was a lawyer, asked him a question, tempt-
ing him, and saying, Master, which is the great commandment in the
law? Jesus said unto him, Thou shalt love the Lord thy God with all
thy heart, and with all thy soul, and with all thy mind. This is the first
and great commandment. And the second is like unto it, Thou shalt
love thy neighbor as thyself. On these two commandments hang all the
law and the prophets.*

MATTHEW 22:35-40

Edwards' ejection from Northampton proved a blessing in dis-
guise—at least to the rest of the Christian church—for it freed him
up to focus on some major writing projects. None of them took precedence over the work of pastoral ministry. He remained from first to
last a faithful minister of the Word. But unlike many parish pastors,
Edwards realized that his usefulness depended on careful study. He
also knew that God had gifted him for intellectual service and had
called him to defend the faith in light of recent challenges. So he paid
close attention to the literary world—not only to orthodox material,
but to anything that could help him understand its recent trends and
articulate the goodness, truth and beauty of the divine in terms his
peers would find persuasive. He loved the Lord with his mind. He

also burned with holy passion for the welfare of his neighbors, which he knew could be advanced only insofar as they grew in the knowledge, joy and love of God. In the words of Henry Scougal, a Scottish divine whose popular book, *The Life of God in the Soul of Man* (1677), would resonate through Edwards' life:

> The soul of man is of a vigorous and active nature, and hath in it a raging and unextinguishable thirst, an immaterial kind of fire, always catching at some object or other, in conjunction where with it thinks to be happy; and were it once rent from the world, and all the bewitching enjoyments under the sun, it would quickly search after some higher and more excellent object, to satisfy its ardent and importunate cravings; and being no longer dazzled with glittering vanities, would fix on that supreme and all-sufficient Good, where it would discover such beauty and sweetness as would charm and overpower all its affections. . . . Amidst all our pursuits and designs, let us stop and ask ourselves, For what end is all this? At what do I aim? Can the gross and muddy pleasures of sense, or a heap of white and yellow earth, or the esteem and affection of silly creatures, like myself, satisfy a rational and immortal soul? . . . Oh! What a poor thing would the life of man be, if it were capable of no higher enjoyment.[1]

Edwards lived the life of the mind in order to satisfy such "cravings" and to help his many readers come to know this "higher enjoyment."

In the near term, despair over the people of Northampton sucked

---

[1] *The Life of God in the Soul of Man,* by Henry Scougal, to Which Is Added, *Rules and Instructions for a Holy Life,* by Robert Leighton (Fearn, Ross-shire, Scotland: Christian Focus Publications, 1996), pp. 109-11. Scougal was ordained in the Church of Scotland and served as professor of divinity at the University of Aberdeen. He died tragically of consumption (tuberculosis) at the age of 27. *The Life of God in the Soul of Man* is listed in Edwards' "Catalogue" (a lengthy manuscript in which he listed the books he sought to acquire), where Edwards notes that it was "the Book that first Enlightned mr Whitefield." Indeed, the edition of Scougal's work released amidst the Great Awakening had an endorsement on its title page from Whitefield: "Altho' I had fasted, watched and prayed, and received the sacrament so long, yet I never knew what true religion was, 'till God sent me that excellent treatise." See Henry Scougal, *The Life of God in the Soul of Man: or The Nature and Excellency of the Christian Religion* . . . (Boston: G. Rogers and D. Fowle, for H. Foster in Cornhill, 1741). The quotation from Edwards' "Catalogue" may be found in *Catalogues of Books,* ed. Peter J. Thuesen, *WJE,* vol. 26 (2008), p. 219.

the wind out of his sails. It depleted his mental reserves, drained his intellectual energy. He managed to publish another treatise in 1752. But when compared to the 1740s, the first few years of the 1750s yielded little scholarly fruit. It was as if the psychological strain of the turmoil in Northampton overtook him after his firing, slowing his pen and casting a pall over his study.[2]

However, by 1753, Edwards was writing in earnest again. And after the spring of 1755, he scribbled more than ever. His suffering made him stronger and his separation from those he had been serving for so long intensified his sense of calling to the larger kingdom of God. He finished four lengthy treatises in the last five years of his life (1753–1758), as well as hundreds of pages of notes toward the works he left undone (which are discussed in chapter three). In 1754, he published *Freedom of the Will*, a tour de force that he had toyed with since the mid-1740s. In 1757, he ended a book on *Original Sin*, which would be published shortly after his death in 1758. He also completed *Two Dissertations* that would be published posthumously (1765): a brilliant *Dissertation Concerning the End for Which God Created the World*; and its oft-reprinted companion, a less dogmatic *Dissertation Concerning the Nature of True Virtue*.[3]

The purpose of this chapter is to pause from telling the story of Edwards' life and pastoral labors and to summarize the achievements of these final published works, which secured his reputation in the academic world. I warn my readers to prepare themselves for

---

[2]*Misrepresentations Corrected* (1752), which was mentioned in chapter four, proved to be little more than a variation on themes already sounded in the more famous *Humble Inquiry* (1749). See *Ecclesiastical Writings*, ed. David D. Hall, WJE, vol. 12 (1994), pp. 350-503. As will be seen in chapter six, Edwards' move in 1751 to the frontier Stockbridge mission also took time away from his writing. For more on the pace of Edwards' literary output during these years, see my "Editor's Introduction" to The *"Miscellanies," 1153-1360*, WJE, vol. 23 (2003), pp. 4-9.

[3]Though often published separately, Edwards' *Two Dissertations* were originally bound together (when released by Edwards' student and executor, Samuel Hopkins [1721–1803]). Many argue that they can only be interpreted well together. See especially Paul Ramsey, "Editor's Introduction" to Jonathan Edwards, *Ethical Writings*, WJE, vol. 8 (1989), pp. 5-6. Their full, original title was *Two Dissertations, I. Concerning the End for which God created the World. II. The Nature of True Virtue* (Boston: S. Kneeland, 1765).

strenuous mental exertion. Oliver Wendell Holmes compared the work discussed below to "the unleavened bread of the Israelite: holy it may be," he said, "but heavy it certainly is."[4] Heavy indeed, and hard to chew. However, these books are worth the effort. They offer compelling presentations of traditional Protestant doctrines aimed at thinkers who are enamored with the spirit of the Enlightenment. They involved Edwards deeply in the leading thought of his day. And they demonstrate his genius for repackaging the faith so as to meet the existential needs of keen but troubled minds. Readers tempted to skip this chapter are the ones who need it most. As we will see in the conclusion, it is difficult to apply Edwardsian insights to our lives if we neglect the mental labor that was central to his life.[5]

THE FREEDOM OF THE WILL

Among the books discussed below, Edwards' *Freedom of the Will* has garnered the most sustained attention from the widest array of readers—parish pastors, missionaries, academic theologians, even a host of non-Christians.[6] Published in multiple editions, read all over the Western world (the East as well in recent years), it fueled the rise of modern missions (discussed at length in chapter six), shaped the growth of America's first indigenous school of Christian thought ("the New England Theology," mentioned again briefly in chapter seven),[7] and supported the spread of revival by Reformed evangelicals. Pitched as a critique of Arminian views of moral agency (or of "the

---

[4]Oliver Wendell Holmes, "Jonathan Edwards," *The International Review* 9 (July 1880): 3.

[5]At this point in the story it should go without saying, but Edwards' work was always full of exegesis. Even the heavy-duty books discussed below (in this chapter) offer hundreds of Scripture references, allusions and quotations. Edwards wrote them in defense of Calvinistic Bible doctrine. I have resisted the temptation to discuss these many references in detail for the sake of economical expression.

[6]On its reception in America to the time of the Civil War, see especially Allen C. Guelzo, *Edwards on the Will: A Century of American Theological Debate* (Middletown, Conn.: Wesleyan University Press, 1989).

[7]On the New England Theology, see Douglas A. Sweeney and Allen C. Guelzo, eds., *The New England Theology: From Jonathan Edwards to Edwards Amasa Park* (Grand Rapids: Baker Academic, 2006).

---

modern prevailing notions of that freedom of will, which is *supposed* to be essential to moral agency, vertue and vice, reward and punishment, praise and blame"),[8] it also fleshed out Edwards' doctrine of the sovereignty of God and its relationship to human responsibility.

Edwards' foils in this treatise were all departed English "Arminians": Thomas Chubb, Daniel Whitby and Isaac Watts.[9] Each in his own way had undermined traditional Calvinist conceptions of the will in favor of less deterministic views of human moral potential, thus contributing to what Edwards called an Arminian notion of liberty (or freedom of the will). According to Edwards' summary, this Arminian notion of liberty stipulated three conditions of actual freedom and personal moral culpability: A person is truly free, it said, and liable for her actions *if and only if* her behavior is altogether self-determined; performed from a state of perfect moral equilibrium (a state in which there is "no prevailing motive" in her mind); and genuinely contingent (in no way necessary, which can only be true if she could have acted otherwise).[10]

Edwards thought that this was nonsense. Only God is self-determined, he said. The rest of us behave in ways that are shaped by outside forces. There is no such thing, he claimed, as moral equilibrium, for all of us have preferences and act with motivation. Contingence, furthermore, does not comport with Christian faith. Even Arminians grant that God predestines all that comes to be. They disagree

---

[8]These words are found in the long, original title of the work: *A Careful and Strict Enquiry into The modern prevailing Notions of That Freedom of Will, Which is supposed to be essential to Moral Agency, Vertue and Vice, Reward and Punishment, Praise and Blame* (Boston: S. Kneeland, 1754).

[9]None of these men was an Arminian in the most technical sense of the term (though Daniel Whitby was close). Rather, Chubb (1679–1747) began as an Arian and died a well-known Deist. Whitby (1638–1726) was an Anglican with Unitarian tendencies. Watts (1674–1748) was a hesitant Calvinist and evangelical hymn writer (as noted in chapter four), though he was claimed (controversially) by Arians after his death. The works of these three writers addressed in *Freedom of the Will* were Thomas Chubb, *A Collection of Tracts on Various Subjects* (London: T. Cox, 1730); Daniel Whitby, *Discourse on the Five Points*, 2nd ed. (London: Aaron Ward and Richard Hett, 1735); and Isaac Watts, *An Essay on the Freedom of Will in God and in Creatures* (London: n.p., 1732).

[10]Edwards lists these three features of an Arminian notion of liberty in *Freedom of the Will*, pp. 164-65. He discusses them at length throughout the treatise.

with Calvinists over the manner, not the fact, of God's predestinating will.[11] And if God predestines a moral act, it cannot be contingent (at least not in the moment).

The key to Edwards' doctrine of the freedom of the will lies in his definition of terms, especially "will" and moral "freedom." The will, he said, is "that by which the mind chooses anything." And "freedom" of the will is but the "power, opportunity, or advantage, that anyone has, to do as he pleases."[12] In Edwards' view, the will is not an independent faculty, a loose moral cannon, but an integral part of the soul, related closely to the mind, heart, emotions and affections. The choices of the will take their rise from the affections. They follow upon what Edwards called the dictates of the mind. Further, as finite moral agents, all of us find ourselves with a limited range of moral possibilities, with thoughts and inclinations shaped in part by social context. Unconverted people find themselves with sin-sick minds, indeed with fallen inclinations and desires that lead to vice. They do not *want* to do God's will. They still behave with genuine freedom, with power to do what they please. No one forces them to sin. Yet despite the "natural" freedom they enjoy to do as they wish, they sin by "moral" necessity—for "the will always is as the greatest

---

[11]Arminians taught that God predestines the lives of moral agents based on his "foreknowledge" of their free decisions. With regard to salvation, this means that God predestines some to glory (and passes over others) based on his knowledge of their responses to the gospel in time and space. He does this eternally, or in a way that is logically prior to their historical decisions. (For Arminians, God predestines all that comes to be "before" it happens in our world.) Still, he elects the saints because he knows they will follow him. This is known as the doctrine of "conditional election." It was defined in opposition to Calvin's teaching that God elects "unconditionally," in a manner *not* based on (conditioned by) the deeds that people do. Edwards discusses these concerns at length in *Freedom of the Will* (pp. 257-69), but exhibits little patience for Arminian views of foreknowledge. An expert treatment of conditional election is available in Richard A. Muller, *God, Creation, and Providence in the Thought of Jacob Arminius: Sources and Directions of Scholastic Protestantism in the Era of Early Orthodoxy* (Grand Rapids: Baker, 1991). For an Arminian perspective, see F. Stuart Clarke, *The Ground of Election: Jacobus Arminius' Doctrine of the Work and Person of Christ*, Studies in Christian History and Thought (Milton Keynes, U.K.: Paternoster, 2006). See also Roger E. Olson, *Arminian Theology: Myths and Realities* (Downers Grove: InterVarsity Press, 2006), esp. pp. 179-99, who offers a softer, more paradoxical, insider's view of Arminian predestination.

[12]Edwards, *Freedom of the Will*, pp. 137, 163.

apparent good is."[13] The will always chooses what the moral agent prefers. People act according to their strongest inclinations—and do so necessarily, whenever they make a choice.

Attentive readers will have seen by now that Edwards' doctrine hinges on a distinction he maintained between a fallen sinner's "natural ability" (constitutional capacity) to repent and live a life that honors God and her "moral inability" (ineradicable unwillingness) to do the very same (without the help of saving grace). Edwards insisted that all people have a natural capacity to do what God requires, even though everyone also acts by moral necessity. (Even Christians doing good deeds *always* do what they desire.) Moral necessity and freedom of will, for him, were fully compatible. Scholars refer to this teaching as "compatibilism."[14]

Edwards explained this crucial distinction with an analogy. He told of two fictional prisoners, the first

> a man who has offended his prince, and is cast into prison; and after he has lain there a while, the king comes to him, calls him to come forth to him; and tells him that if he will do so, and will fall down before him, and humbly beg his pardon, he shall be forgiven, and set at liberty, and also be greatly enriched, and advanced to honor: the prisoner heartily repents of the folly and wickedness of his offense against his prince, is thoroughly disposed to abase himself, and accept of the king's offer; but is confined by strong walls, with gates of brass, and bars of iron.[15]

---

[13]Ibid., p. 142.

[14]Many of Edwards' Calvinistic forebears also favored compatibilism. Few of them, however, affirmed the doctrine of natural ability. In fact, Francis Turretin (1623–1687), one of Edwards' favorite thinkers, fought fiercely against this doctrine as articulated at the French Reformed Academy of Saumur, even going so far as to make sure the doctrine was condemned in Canons 21 and 22 of the Swiss Reformed confession published in 1675, *Helvetic Formula Consensus*. For more on this doctrinal history, see Douglas A. Sweeney, *Nathaniel Taylor, New Haven Theology, and the Legacy of Jonathan Edwards*, Religion in America Series (New York: Oxford University Press, 2003), pp. 73-74, 201-3. For Edwards' admiration of Turretin, see Jonathan Edwards to the Rev. Joseph Bellamy, January 15, 1747, in *Letters and Personal Writings*, ed. George S. Claghorn, WJE, vol. 16 (1998), p. 217; and Jonathan Edwards, *Religious Affections*, ed. John E. Smith, WJE, vol. 2 (1959), p. 289 n. 4. For the condemnation itself, see the English translation of the *Helvetic Formula Consensus* in Martin I. Klauber, "The Helvetic Formula Consensus (1675): An Introduction and Translation," *Trinity Journal* 11 (Spring 1990): 103-23.

[15]Edwards, *Freedom of the Will*, p. 362.

He is *teased,* that is, with pardon. While physically constrained, he is naturally unable to meet the terms of his release and so should not be blamed for failing. The second prisoner, though, proves to be a different man,

> of a very unreasonable spirit, of a haughty, ungrateful, willful disposition; and moreover, [he] has been brought up in traitorous principles; and has his heart possessed with an extreme and inveterate enmity to his lawful sovereign; and for his rebellion is cast into prison, and lies long there, loaden with heavy chains, and in miserable circumstances. At length the compassionate prince comes to the prison, orders his chains to be knocked off, and his prison doors to be set wide open; calls to him, and tells him, if he will come forth to him, and fall down before him, acknowledge that he has treated him unworthily, and ask his forgiveness; he shall be forgiven, set at liberty, and set in a place of great dignity and profit in his court. But he is so stout and stomachful, and full of haughty malignity, that he can't be willing to accept the offer: his rooted strong pride and malice have perfect power over him, and as it were bind him, by binding his heart: the opposition of his heart has the mastery over him, having an influence on his mind far superior to the king's grace and condescension, and to all his kind offers and promises.

Edwards concluded this analogy by stressing the practical import of the distinction he was making:

> Now, is it agreeable to common sense, to assert and stand to it, that there is no difference between these two cases, as to any worthiness of blame in the prisoners; because, forsooth, there is a necessity in both, and the required act in each case is impossible? 'Tis true, a man's evil dispositions may be as strong and immovable as the bars of a castle. But who can't see, that when a man, in the latter case, is said to be "unable" to obey the command, the expression is used improperly, and not in the sense it has originally and in common speech? And that it may properly be said to

be in the rebel's power to come out of prison, seeing he can easily do it if he pleases?[16]

The moral of the story was that unconverted sinners had only themselves to blame for their sin—even though they sinned by necessity. Listeners who resisted when the gospel was proclaimed were like the second, not the first, of Edwards' prisoners. (The first prisoner was only a foil, for no one is ever *teased* with pardon, according to Edwards.)[17] They had a capacity to convert and find release from the bonds of sin. Nothing material stood in their way. However, their hearts were hard, recalcitrant, too proud to submit to God. Nothing hindered their repentance but their own free wills.[18]

As one can imagine, this contention not only rattled the Arminians but revised the approach of many other Calvinists to evangelism. For much of the eighteenth century, English Calvinists, in particular, had struggled to reconcile their biblical trust in predestination with the Scripture texts suggesting God wants good news preached to all (Jn 3:16-17; 1 Tim 2:3-4; 2 Pet 3:3-4, 8-9). Some worried about the revival and what they called its doubtful method of "indiscriminate evangelism," questioning the truthfulness of calling perfect strangers—who may not be predestined for the blessings of salvation—to repent and be reborn. Edwards helped such doubters see that whether or not all those who heard them stood among the Lord's elect, all possessed a natural ability to do what God requires. Reformed revivalists and missionaries could preach the gospel freely, then, to those they had

---

[16]Ibid., pp. 362-63.

[17]Arminians and others have often objected at this point (and at many other points!), noting that Edwards had a Calvinistic view of predestination in which God elects some and not others for salvation unconditionally. As Edwards granted elsewhere, only those predestined to glory will ever be given a new heart, or given the *will* to turn to God. No matter what Edwards claimed about the sinner's natural ability, then, his doctrine of salvation seemed to tease the non-elect. They may well sin voluntarily but they also lack the power, in Edwards' view, to renovate their own affections (or to engender moral ability in themselves).

[18]Edwards developed this theme further in two other well-known places: Jonathan Edwards, "The Justice of God in the Damnation of Sinners," in *Sermons and Discourses, 1734–1738*, ed. M. X. Lesser, *WJE*, vol. 19 (2001), pp. 336-76; and Jonathan Edwards to the Rev. John Erskine, August 3, 1757, in *Letters and Personal Writings*, pp. 718-24.

not met, believing that God was working through them to redeem his chosen people while the reprobate rejected him voluntarily.[19]

ORIGINAL SIN

Edwards' work on *Original Sin* reinforced this way of interpreting the sinner's culpability for flouting the will of God, for it probed the massive scope and murky depths of human depravity, absolving God from blame regarding the origin of evil—in both Eden and our hearts. Most of the contents of this treatise seem predictable today to those well-versed in Calvinist doctrine (or even that of Augustine). In Edwards' age of "enlightenment," though, they bore emphatic, winsome and well-pointed repetition. As he parleyed with his rivals over the field of human iniquity, moreover, part of his argument involved some rare maneuvers.

"The following discourse," he began, "is intended not merely as an answer to any particular book" against original sin, "but as a *general defense* of that great important doctrine. Nevertheless," he continued, "I have in this defense taken notice of the main things said against this doctrine" by "the more noted opposers of it." The most notable opposers, Edwards thought, were John Taylor and George Turnbull, highly regarded British liberal theologians. Throughout the 1740s, they had published major books against the Calvinist view of sin.

---

[19]"Indiscriminate evangelism" was the practice of extending gospel promises to all, without emphasizing that God redeems only the elect. Those opposed to this practice have been labeled "hyper-Calvinists." They argued that one should preach the gospel freely, indiscriminately, only in a rightly ordered, covenant community (whose members had the advantage of the signs and seals of grace, tokens of God's covenant promises regarding their salvation). In early modern England, they included Tobias Crisp (1600–1643), Richard Davis (1658–1714), Joseph Hussey (1660–1726), and especially John Gill (1697–1771) and John Brine (1703–1765). Those who affirmed a freer evangelism, appealing to Edwards for help, included many of the founders of the English missions movement, such as the well-known Baptist leaders Andrew Fuller (1754–1815) and William Carey (1761–1834), whose best-known books were based in part on Edwards' argument: Andrew Fuller, *The Gospel of Christ Worthy of All Acceptation: or the Obligations of Men Fully to Credit, and Cordially to Approve, Whatever God Makes Known* (Northampton, U.K.: T. Dicey & Co., [1785]); and William Carey, *Enquiry into the Obligations of Christians to Use Means for the Conversion of the Heathens* (Leicester, England: Ann Ireland, 1792). For more on the history of this issue, see Sweeney, *Nathaniel Taylor, New Haven Theology*, pp. 124-25, 230-31.

Moreover, in Edwards' estimation, "no one book has done so much towards rooting out of [western] New England" the views of "our pious . . . forefathers," and "alienating . . . many from . . . [the] doctrines of the gospel, as that which Dr. Taylor has published against . . . original sin."[20]

Taylor's *Scripture-Doctrine of Original Sin Proposed to Free and Candid Examination* (1740) rocked New England, knocking Calvinists back on their heels.[21] It accused traditional Protestants of hindering moral progress by promoting gloomy views of human nature and potential. We are not as bad as you think, it said, and God does not resemble Calvin's arbitrary tyrant, damning creatures for behavior over which they lack control. Taylor granted that sin was rampant, that it captivated some, but eschewed several other, related Calvinistic doctrines: total depravity, Adam's tragic fall from original righteousness and God's imputation of Adam's guilt to the human race. He said that children sin primarily by parroting poor examples, attributing moral failure more to nurture than to nature. He taught that we have stumbled by misusing our freedom and reason, not collapsed by expressing our native depravity. He agreed that death is a consequence of Adam's first sin, but denied that it is punitive; God sent it, rather, to wean us from the world and foster virtue, which all of us can cultivate with practice.[22]

---

[20]Jonathan Edwards, *Original Sin*, ed. Clyde A. Holbrook, *WJE*, vol. 3 (1970), p. 102. John Taylor (1694–1761) was a Hebrew scholar and Presbyterian minister best known as a tutor at the Warrington Academy (Cheshire, England). George Turnbull (1698–1748) was a liberal moral philosopher from Scotland who wound up in the Church of England, serving as Rector of Drumachose. Both epitomized the sunny approach to human moral potential characteristic of the so-called British Enlightenment.

[21]For more on this controversy, see H. Shelton Smith, *Changing Conceptions of Original Sin: A Study in American Theology Since 1750* (New York: Charles Scribner's Sons, 1955). For more on Edwards' doctrine of sin, see C. Samuel Storms, *Tragedy in Eden: Original Sin in the Theology of Jonathan Edwards* (Lanham, Md.: University Press of America, 1985); and Oliver D. Crisp, *Jonathan Edwards and the Metaphysics of Sin* (Aldershot, England: Ashgate, 2005).

[22]Edwards owned the third edition of Taylor's *Scripture-Doctrine . . .* (Belfast: J. Magee, for John Hay Bookseller at the Two Bibles in Bridge Street, 1746). The other works by Taylor and Turnbull to which Edwards paid attention were John Taylor, *A Paraphrase with Notes on the Epistle to the Romans: To Which Is Prefix'd, a Key to the Apostolic Writings . . .* (Dublin: A. Reilly, for John Smith at the Philosophers Heads on the Blind-quay, 1746); and George Turnbull, *The Principles*

Edwards knew that the best defense is often a comprehensive offense. Thus he mounted an aggressive, systematic plan of attack, taking shots at Taylor and others along the way. He spent the bulk of his time demonstrating that "all mankind do constantly in all ages" sin,[23] and that Scripture says we do so as a result of Adam's fall. Nearly half of Edwards' treatise is devoted to examining the "evidence" from Scripture "proving" Adam fell from grace and took the human race down with him. The remainder is devoted to an empirical study of deviance and "answers to objections" from his liberal "adversaries."

"[W]hen God made man at first," Edwards explained, "he implanted in him two kinds of principles."

> There was an *inferior* kind, which may be called *natural*, being the principles of mere human nature; such as self-love, with those natural appetites and passions, which belong to the nature of man, in which his love to his own liberty, honor and pleasure, were exercised: these when alone, and left to themselves, are what the Scriptures sometimes call *flesh*. Besides these, there were *superior* principles, that were spiritual, holy and divine, summarily comprehended in divine love; wherein consisted the spiritual image of God, and man's righteousness and true holiness; which are called in Scripture the *divine nature*.

The superior principles, actuated by the Holy Spirit, were given to govern the lower principles, "to possess the throne" and exercise "dominion in the heart." As long as they did so, Adam's passions would be oriented properly, in "peace and beautiful harmony." Our first parents' affections would be fittingly attuned. As soon as Adam sinned, however,

> and broke God's Covenant, and fell under his curse, these superior principles left his heart: for indeed God then left him; that communion with God, on which these principles depended, entirely ceased;

---

of *Moral Philosophy* . . . , 2 vols. (London: John Noon, 1740).
[23]Edwards, *Original Sin*, p. 107.

the Holy Spirit, that divine inhabitant, forsook the house. Because it would have been utterly improper . . . and inconsistent with the covenant and constitution God had established, that God should still maintain communion with man, and continue . . . to dwell . . . in him, after he was become a rebel. . . . and thus man was left in a state of darkness, woeful corruption and ruin; nothing but flesh, without spirit. The inferior principles of self-love and natural appetite, which were given only to serve, being alone, and left to themselves, of course became . . . absolute masters of the heart. The immediate consequence of which was a *fatal catastrophe.*

Deprived of God's Spirit, Adam's passions ran amuck. His natural appetites consumed him. And the race became *depraved.* Adam's children entered the world in the same confused moral condition. They were *born* bereft of the supernatural aid that he enjoyed. Unless and until they are born again, they live their lives without the Spirit, choosing to fill the God-shaped vacuum they feel aching in their hearts with lesser things, created good but used corruptly sincethe Fall by those with misdirected affections.[24]

---

[24]Ibid., pp. 381-83. The God-shaped vacuum metaphor is quite common to Augustinians, most famously Blaise Pascal (1623–1662). The sentiment behind it derives ultimately from Augustine (354-430) *Confessions* 1.1. Edwards has often been criticized for failing to answer the question: Why did Adam sin in the first place if he had the Holy Spirit? It is true that Edwards did not provide an exhaustive answer to this. (How could anyone respond well to such a conjectural query, one that Scripture does not address with specificity?) But his tendency was to say that while Adam had power not to sin (in the language of the scholastics he was *posse non peccare*), he would not become impeccable (*non posse peccare*) till his time of trial had ended (when either he proved himself righteous by resisting the devil's inducements or God glorified his fallen soul in heaven). While Adam and Eve were on probation, they were given genuine freedom to obey the Lord or not, blessed with the aid of the Holy Spirit, but remained susceptible to affectional change in response to Satan's counterfeit delights. In a sermon preached in Northampton on their tragic fall from grace (one that is always overlooked by those who blame him of neglect), Edwards addressed this issue squarely: Before he fell, Adam "had the Sp[irit] of G[od] dwelling in him," but "he had not so much assistance given him as to make him impeccable—to Render it Impossible for him to sin[—]yet he had so much as was sufficient with proper care [and] watchfulness and a due improvem[en]t forever to prevent his sinning." Further: "If any enq[uire] how our first P[arents] could exercise such lusts when they had none[,] I answ[er]: Lust begins in the soul at the first conception of this sin in the Heart. [T]his sin was there before [it] was conc[ei]ved in the H[eart,] before it was perpetuated in outw[ard] act. There was first an hankering Inclination and then a deliberation [and] so the progress was from one step to another till all was finished in outw[ard] act—so that tho[ugh] no lust could be exercised

Like many early Calvinists, Edwards was a federalist. He taught that God had ordained that Adam should serve as our federal head (much as Christ would be the head of the church, united to him by faith). If Adam stood, the world would stand; if Adam fell, the world would fall. As most believe, moreover, he fell. And as St. Paul informed the church in Rome: "by one man's offence death reigned. . . . by the offence of one judgment came upon all men to condemnation. . . . by one man's disobedience many were made sinners" (Rom 5:12-21 [quote vv. 17-19]; cf. 1 Cor 15:22). Edwards delineated original sin accordingly:

> as Adam's nature became corrupt, without God's implanting or infusing any evil thing into his nature; so does the nature of his *posterity*. God dealing with Adam as the head of his posterity . . . and treating them as one, he deals with his posterity as having *all sinned in him*. And therefore, as God withdrew spiritual communion and his vital gracious influence from the common head, so he withholds the same from all the members, as they come into existence; whereby they come into the world . . . entirely under the government of natural and inferior principles; and so become wholly corrupt, as Adam did.[25]

Edwards was also what the philosophers call an ontological realist. He believed that human nature really exists, objectively, uniting human beings universally (across time, space and cultural difference). In his work on original sin, this meant that Edwards thought that Adam was a *real* federal head, the father of the race in whom all people are united, not a distant representative like federal politi-

---

before the first Conscious act of the H[eart,] yet it began with the Heart's first inward act and so was [exercised] thenceforwards in all the progress of the conc[ei]ved sin till it [was] brought forth and Perfected in that external deed." The first sin emerged, that is, by the incremental formation of a disposition to sin, not a settled disposition like that which led to sin thereafter. See Jonathan Edwards, sermon on Genesis 3:11 (February 1739), L. 20r., L. 24r-v., folder 2, box 1, Jonathan Edwards Collection, Beinecke.

[25]Edwards, *Original Sin*, p. 383. For more on the federal theology, pioneered in Heidelberg during the early 1560s at the hands of Zacharias Ursinus (1534–1583) and Caspar Olevianus (1536–1587), see David A. Weir, *The Origins of Federal Theology in Sixteenth-Century Reformation Thought* (New York: Oxford University Press, 1990).

cians.[26] We were there with him in Eden—not bodily, of course, but ontologically, seminally, like an oak tree is present in an acorn. We were joined in Adam's fall and so are implicated in it.[27] God does not consider us guilty for our sin capriciously. We are culpable *in Adam.* Human nature is corrupt and we are all our brothers' keepers. Edwards' summary of this point, though rather difficult to read, confirms the justice of God in counting humans guilty for depravity:

> the derivation of the evil disposition to the hearts of Adam's posterity, or rather the *coexistence* of the evil disposition, implied in Adam's first rebellion, in the root and branches, is a consequence of the union, that the wise Author of the world has established between Adam and his posterity: but not properly a consequence of the imputation of his sin; nay, rather *antecedent* to it, as it was in Adam himself. The first depravity of heart, and the imputation of that sin, are both the consequences of that established union: but yet in such order, that the evil disposition is *first,* and the charge of guilt *consequent;* as it was in the case of Adam himself.[28]

As in *Freedom of the Will,* here again in *Original Sin* Edwards leaves the hard of heart without excuse. He finds them guilty—as charged—*even for their inclinations.* Their guilt did not precede and cause their evil disposition; rather, their disposition led to their in-

---

[26]Most later Reformed thinkers would maintain Edwards' federalism without his realism, reducing Adam to a modern-style federal representative (like senators and congressmen) and holding the race responsible for a fall to which it has no ontological connection. The trouble this caused for those attempting to make the imputation of Adam's guilt to all humanity sound reasonable led many to drop the doctrine of imputation. See George Park Fisher, "The Augustinian and the Federal Theologies of Original Sin Compared," *New Englander* 27 (June 1868): 468-516.

[27]In Edwards' view, God does not hold the race responsible for *everything* involved in Adam's sin. Rather, some of it was unique to him as father of mankind. "G[od] don't Impute that to us and Require us to Lament that and be humbled for that as what we are Guilty of that we don't and can't Know any thing of. . . . Hence it follows that there were some aggravations of that sin that Concerned Adam personally that ben't Imputed to us." Edwards, sermon on Genesis 3:11, L. 6r.

[28]Edwards, *Original Sin,* p. 391. In arguing this way, Edwards employed "Stapfer's scheme" for the defense of imputation, named for Johann Friedrich Stapfer (1708–1775), one of his favorite theologians. See Stapfer, *Institutiones Theologiae Polemicae Universae* (Tiguri: Heideggerum and Socios, 1743–1747), 1.3.856-57, 4.16.60, 61, and 4.17.78 (Edwards himself provided some English translation of this in *Original Sin,* pp. 392-93 n.).

---

dictment. So they should quit blaming God and feeling sorry for themselves, leaving excuses for their decadence behind.

THE TWO DISSERTATIONS: GOD'S DESIGN AND TRUE VIRTUE

Edwards' *Two Dissertations* builds upon *Original Sin* to argue that no one is born with "principles" sufficient for true virtue.[29] All are born with natural ability to live a righteous life. All retain the natural principles of conscience, self-love, human sympathy and longing for the welfare of their loved ones. But no one enters the world equipped with the higher moral principles of genuine benevolence—the godliness, holiness and all-around good will that pleases God and guarantees a just and wholesome civic life. Conversion is required. All of us need the Holy Spirit to guide our natural inclinations if we ever hope to exercise *true* virtue.[30]

---

[29]Edwards said as much at the end of *Original Sin*: "As to the arguments made use of by many late writers . . . to shew that we are born into the world with principles of virtue; with a natural prevailing relish, approbation, and love of righteousness, truth, and goodness, and of whatever tends to the public welfare; with a prevailing natural disposition to dislike, to resent and condemn what is selfish, unjust, and immoral; a native bent in mankind to mutual benevolence, tender compassion, etc. those who have had such objections against the doctrine of original sin, thrown in their way, and desire to see them particularly considered, I ask leave to refer them to a *Treatise on the Nature of True Virtue*, lying by me prepared for the press, which may ere long be exhibited to public view" (p. 433). The "objections" Edwards had in mind were made not only by Taylor and Turnbull, but also by the thinkers known as the British moralists, especially Anthony Ashley Cooper (1671–1713), the Third Earl of Shaftesbury; Francis Hutcheson (1694–1746), his foremost Scottish disciple; and David Hume (1711–1776), the most famous of them all. For a smattering of their work, see D. D. Raphael, ed., *British Moralists, 1650–1800*, 2 vols. (Oxford: Clarendon, 1969).

[30]The *Two Dissertations* also rested on a 15-sermon series Edwards preached on 1 Corinthians 13 (in mid-1738). Published in 1852, *Charity and Its Fruits* dealt at length with the nature of genuine virtue. See *Charity and Its Fruits*, in *Ethical Writings*, pp. 123-397. There is a great deal of scholarship on Edwards' ethical writings, but the best works are those by Paul Ramsey, "Editor's Introduction," in *Ethical Writings*, pp. 1-121; Roland Delattre, *Beauty and Sensibility in the Thought of Jonathan Edwards: An Essay in Aesthetics and Theological Ethics* (New Haven: Yale University Press, 1968); William J. Danaher, *The Trinitarian Ethics of Jonathan Edwards* (Louisville: Westminster John Knox, 2004); Norman Fiering, *Jonathan Edwards's Moral Thought and Its British Context* (Chapel Hill: University of North Carolina Press, 1981); Gerald R. McDermott, *One Holy and Happy Society: The Public Theology of Jonathan Edwards* (University Park: Pennsylvania State University Press, 1992); and John E. Smith, "Christian Virtue and Common Morality," in *The Princeton Companion to Jonathan Edwards*, ed. Sang Hyun Lee (Princeton: Princeton University Press, 2005), pp. 147-66.

Edwards erected the general framework of this argument in the *Dissertation Concerning the End for Which God Created the World*. Addressing the question of God's "original ultimate end" in the creation, he claimed that God created in order to glorify himself—or, more technically, to do so by repeating, or communicating, the glory of his inner-trinitarian life in the world. In Edwards' own words, "a disposition in God, as an original property of his nature, to an emanation of his own infinite fullness, was what excited him to create the world; and . . . the emanation itself was" God's "last end of . . . creation."[31] God's purposes do not depend on humans for success. "God's joy" as the Creator "is dependent on nothing besides his own act, which he exerts with . . . absolute . . . power." Yet God's creatures do participate in magnifying his glory as they shine it back to him in lives of virtue.[32]

Edwards illustrated the creature's role in glorifying God in one of the most beloved sections of his writings. It sounds unduly abstract to many pious Christian readers, but Edwards thought it epitomized the meaning of our lives.

> The emanation or communication of the divine fullness, consisting in the knowledge of God, love to God, and joy in God, has relation indeed both to God and the creature: but it has relation to God as its fountain, as it is an emanation from God; and as the communication itself, or thing communicated, is something divine, something of God, something of his internal fullness; as the water in the stream is something of the fountain; and as the beams are of the sun. And again, they have relation to God as they have respect to him as their object: for the knowledge communicated is the knowledge of God; and so God is the object of the knowledge: and the love communicated, is the love of God; so God is the object of that love: and the happiness communicated, is joy in God; and so he is the object of

---

[31]Jonathan Edwards, *Dissertation Concerning the End for Which God Created the World*, in *Ethical Writings*, p. 435.
[32]Ibid., p. 447.

the joy communicated. In the creature's knowing, esteeming, loving, rejoicing in, and praising God, the glory of God is both exhibited and acknowledged; his fullness is received and returned. Here is both an *emanation* and *remanation*. The refulgence shines upon and into the creature, and is reflected back to the luminary. The beams of glory come from God, and are something of God, and are refunded back again to their original. So that the whole is *of* God, and *in* God, and *to* God; and God is the beginning, middle and end in this affair.[33]

We cannot increase God's fullness—add water to his fountain, multiply the rays of the sun—or effect his end in creation. God will glorify himself whether or not we honor him. But as we praise him with our lives, we participate in the end for which he made the universe—by acknowledging, returning, remanating and reflecting glory back to its original, magnifying his fullness through the cosmos.[34]

This is impossible for us to do, however, without his grace. We are morally unable to live according to God's design; we resist the highest forms of human virtue in our lives unless the Holy Spirit redirects our natural appetites, helping us fill the God-shaped vacuum in our hearts with God himself. Natural principles can generate a lesser kind of virtue. They can lead to good deeds that look at first like true virtue. But ultimately, the moral fruit of unconverted people proves rotten at the core. Their works are not performed in keeping with God's blessed purposes in creation.[35]

Edwards specified the differences between true virtue and its taw-

---

[33]Ibid., p. 531.

[34]That Christians magnify but do not increase God's fullness is only the most poignant of Edwards' several paradoxes. (Others: the notion that our actions are both free and morally necessary; the notion that sinners are able and unable to convert.) He was a both/and thinker, who tried to speak persuasively to the many paradoxes of life.

[35]George Turnbull taught the use of natural reason in morality. The British moralists founded their approach to virtuous living on the steady cultivation of our common moral sentiments. Edwards dealt directly with these naturalistic teachings, appreciating what he labeled secondary virtue, but showing how it languished when compared to the genuine article, the fruit of the Holy Spirit. For an upbeat assessment of Edwards' take on "the splendor of common morality," see Paul Ramsey, "Editor's Introduction," in *Ethical Writings*, pp. 33-53.

dry imitations in his well-known *Dissertation Concerning the Nature of True Virtue*. "[T]here is a distinction to be made," he contended famously, "between some things which are truly virtuous, and others which only seem to be virtuous, through a partial and imperfect view of things." True virtue, he suggested, "most essentially consists in benevolence to Being in general. Or perhaps to speak more accurately, it is that consent, propensity and union of heart to Being in general, that is immediately exercised in a general good will." Being in general, he explained, is both God (the highest Being) as well as the whole system of being God created for his glory. A truly virtuous man is one who lives for that glory. Most others exhibit benevolence to members of their family, to those they find attractive and to those with something to give them. But the truly virtuous person exhibits good will categorically. He loves other people in the service of God and the world. His "disinterested benevolence," in fact, finds expression even in self-defeating ways (or ways that *appear* to be self-defeating). Let me be clear: Edwards did not teach that self-love and passion have no place in the moral life. Quite to the contrary, he taught that virtuous people are *most* passionate and joyful in well doing. Their self-love finds *fulfillment* in the service of Being in general. They are happiest, in fact, when sharing the love of God promiscuously. In Edwards' summary, then, "it appears that a truly virtuous mind, being as it were under the sovereign dominion of *love to God*, does above all things seek the *glory of God*, and makes *this* his supreme, governing, and ultimate end." He strives with heart, soul and mind to manifest the love and glory of God in the world.[36]

---

[36] Edwards, *Dissertation Concerning the Nature of True Virtue*, in *Ethical Writings*, pp. 539-40, 559. The notion that a truly virtuous man takes delight in serving God, that his self-love finds fulfillment in the greater love of God, and that God wants him to be happy are part Edwards' Christian eudaemonism, or Christian "hedonism" (a much less accurate term), promoted recently by John Piper. See Piper, *Desiring God: Meditations of a Christian Hedonist* (Sisters, Ore.: Multnomah, 1986); *The Pleasures of God* (Sisters, Ore.: Multnomah, 1991); and *God's Passion for His Glory: Living the Vision of Jonathan Edwards* (Wheaton, Ill.: Crossway, 1998). Cf. Douglas A. Sweeney, "Expect Joy," *Christian History* 22, no. 1 (2003): 42-43, reprinted in John Piper, ed., *1703–2003: Reflections on Jonathan Edwards 300 Years Later* (Minneapolis: Desiring God Min-

◇   ◇   ◇

In all of Edwards' major works, the Holy Spirit is seen to play a leading role within the lives of people flourishing in the world. As mentioned in chapter four, in fact, this pneumatological[37] theme might well be called the defining feature of his ministry. He was an evangelical leader called to serve a state church amidst the age of the Enlightenment. He felt a responsibility, then, to help complacent Christians and free-thinking intellectuals understand that God is real and vitally active in our world, that he designed us to cooperate in his kingdom purposes, and that we need his Spirit to do so. There is such a thing as conversion, Edwards recited ceaselessly, a divine and supernatural light available to us even now. It can show you divine truth. It can liberate your will from self-destructive inclinations. It can help you find fulfillment in the things that truly satisfy. It can put you in touch with God, save your soul and make your daily life exciting and important.

What could be more useful than to present this urgent message in a clear and compelling manner? Yet Edwards did this only insofar as he carved out time for study. He loved the Lord with his *mind*—more than most of us do today. He really *believed* that God can use the greater ministry of the Word to change the world and bring it in line with its "original ultimate end." This faith made Edwards great. People do not regard him today as the most important Protestant clergyman in all of American history because he was well-liked or entertaining. He remains influential, rather, because he invested prayer, sweat and tears in the life of the mind. Such commitment requires trust that God will use the Word as he says. We ought to ask ourselves today whether we have that kind of trust.

---

istries, 2003). Edwards summarized this teaching in many Sunday sermons as well. See especially Jonathan Edwards, "The Pleasantness of Religion," in *The Sermons of Jonathan Edwards: A Reader*, ed. Wilson H. Kimnach, Kenneth P. Minkema and Douglas A. Sweeney (New Haven: Yale University Press, 1999), pp. 13-25; and Edwards, "Charity Contrary to a Selfish Spirit," in *Ethical Writings*, pp. 252-71. I have addressed this teaching at greater length in Sweeney, *Nathaniel Taylor, New Haven Theology*, pp. 115-123.

[37]Pneumatology is a theological term that refers to the study of and doctrine of the Spirit.

— *Chapter 6* —

AS THE WATERS
COVER THE SEA

*And there shall come forth a rod out of the stem of Jesse, and a Branch
shall grow out of his roots: And the spirit of the LORD shall rest upon
him, the spirit of wisdom and understanding, the spirit of counsel and
might, the spirit of knowledge and of the fear of the LORD; And shall
make him of quick understanding in the fear of the LORD: and he shall
not judge after the sight of his eyes, neither reprove after the hearing
of his ears: But with righteousness shall he judge the poor, and reprove
with equity for the meek of the earth: and he shall smite the earth with
the rod of his mouth, and with the breath of his lips shall he slay the
wicked. And righteousness shall be the girdle of his loins, and faithfulness the girdle of his reins. The wolf also shall dwell with the lamb,
and the leopard shall lie down with the kid; and the calf and the young
lion and the fatling together; and a little child shall lead them. And the
cow and the bear shall feed; their young ones shall lie down together:
and the lion shall eat straw like the ox. And the sucking child shall
play on the hole of the asp, and the weaned child shall put his hand
on the cockatrice' den. They shall not hurt nor destroy in all my holy
mountain: for the earth shall be full of the knowledge of the LORD, as
the waters cover the sea.*

ISAIAH 11:1-9

$\mathcal{I}$magine what it was like, before paved roads, telephones, electric telegraphs or even a steady system of mail delivery, to be fired from a church that you had served for twenty-four years. In colonial New England, pastors served their churches for life. They did not expect to move as often as pastors do today. They prized stability and commitment. Leaving a congregation was onerous, finding a new assignment difficult. Not only were the vacant pulpits few and far between, but moving furniture and family members across the region's wilderness was physically forbidding and emotionally exhausting.

Edwards was forty-six when ejected from his church, somewhat older than the average age at death for men in his world.[1] He had a very large family (nine children living at home),[2] an unusually large salary and little hope of landing a church as large as the one he was leaving. As he wrote to a friend in Boston on the eve of his ejection:

> If I should be wholly cast out of the ministry, I should be in many respects in a poor case. I shall not be likely to be serviceable to my generation, or get a subsistence in a business of a different nature. I am by nature very unfit for secular business; and especially am now unfit, after I have been so long in the work of the ministry. I am now comfortably settled, have as large a salary settled upon me as most have out of Boston, and have the largest and most chargeable family of any minister, perhaps within an hundred miles of me. . . . I need the prayers of my fathers and brethren who are friendly to me, that I may have wisdom given me by my great master, and that I may be

---

[1] Scholars continue to debate mortality rates in colonial New England. There were numerous variables. A male surviving to adulthood had much better chances of living to become a senior citizen. But most agree that the *average* life expectancy in Edwards' world was in the mid-30s (women living slightly longer than men). See David J. Hacker, "Trends and Determinants of Adult Mortality in Early New England: Reconciling Old and New Evidence from the Long Eighteenth Century," *Social Science History* 21 (Winter 1997): 481-519. Cf. John Demos, *Past, Present, and Personal: The Family and the Life Course in American History* (New York: Oxford University Press, 1986); and David Hackett Fischer, *Growing Old in America* (New York: Oxford University Press, 1977).

[2] Baby Pierrepont was two months old in June of 1750. Jonathan and Sarah had 11 children in all, but daughter Jerusha had died in February of 1748 and daughter Sarah was married on June 11, 1750, only 11 days before her father's firing.

enabled to conduct with a steady faithfulness to him, under all trials and whatever may be the issue of this affair. I seem . . . to be casting myself off from a precipice; and have no other way, but to go on, . . . blindfold, i.e. shutting my eyes to everything else but the evidences of the mind and will of God, and the path of duty; which I would observe with the utmost care.[3]

Despite his trust in God's providence, Edwards clearly feared for his pecuniary prospects.

THE DUST SETTLES SLOWLY

Ironically, Northampton's First Church was frightened too. They had a terrible time finding someone to stand in Edwards' shoes. Several people preached supply, most with rather poor results. Two young men were called to serve the church, but neither agreed to settle there. Lightning struck the meeting house in 1751. In short, it took three years of want and work to find a willing replacement. At last, on September 17, 1753, Northampton voted unanimously to extend a call to a young alumnus of Yale, John Hooker, who accepted and agreed to settle permanently. Although basically a Calvinist, Hooker received the right hand of fellowship during his ordination and installation service from Robert Breck, one of Edwards' Arminian foes (see chapter four). According to evangelical lore, the church was never the same again.[4]

Edwards himself preached supply on several occasions in Northampton, buying time to find a new pulpit while exemplifying

---

[3]Jonathan Edwards to the Rev. Thomas Foxcroft, May 24, 1749, in *Letters and Personal Writings*, ed. George S. Claghorn, *WJE*, vol. 16 (1998), p. 284. Foxcroft (1697–1769) was the pastor at the First Church in Boston who facilitated the printing of Edwards' writings (functioning as his literary agent).

[4]Hooker was ordained on December 5, 1753. For more on these events, see James Russell Trumbull, *History of Northampton, Massachusetts, from Its Settlement in 1654*, vol. 2 (Northampton: Press of Gazette Printing Co., 1902), pp. 235-42, who reports that the meeting house "was considerably damaged" by the bolt of lightning. "The lightning struck the weathercock, and ran down the spire to the ground. Whether it was considered a direct visitation of the Providence of God frowning upon the people for dismissing their pastor, is not recorded" (p. 236).

---

humility and mercy to his opponents. As he wrote to Thomas Foxcroft just six weeks after his firing,

> The committee for supplying the pulpit have got me to preach three Sabbaths since I preached my farewell sermon; but it is with great reluctance. They from week to week do their utmost to get the pulpit otherwise supplied. They have taken much pains to get the neighboring ministers to take their turns to preach here, but meet with difficulty. They have talked of hiring somebody for the present, that they have no thoughts of settling, till they can hear of some likely candidate to hire on probation; but they don't know who to get.[5]

By late November, the town could not endure the embarrassment that Edwards' pulpit presence caused its leaders. In the words of Samuel Hopkins, "a great uneasiness was manifested by many . . . at his preaching there." The local group in charge of filling the pulpit called a meeting and the town decided not to hear from Edwards ever again. Consequently, Hopkins explained, even when "Edwards was in town, and they had no other minister to preach to them, they carried on publick worship among themselves, and without any preaching, rather than to invite Mr. Edwards!" Their former shepherd led them "twelve Sabbaths in all" after his firing. By the end of 1750, though, his thoughts were focused elsewhere.[6]

He had preached beginning in August at a church in Canaan, Connecticut, whose people wanted to call him as their pastor. He also preached from time to time in several other congregations, stretching from Boston south to Middletown (Connecticut) and west to Long-

---

[5]Jonathan Edwards to the Rev. Thomas Foxcroft, July 31, 1750, in *Letters and Personal Writings*, p. 359.

[6]Samuel Hopkins, *The Life and Character of the Late Reverend Mr. Jonathan Edwards* (Boston: S. Kneeland, 1765), p. 62; and Trumbull, *History of Northampton*, 2:227, 236. Interestingly, Trumbull expressed minor doubts as to whether the meeting described by Hopkins in late November ever transpired, as he could find no mention of it in the records of Northampton. Manuscript evidence suggests that Edwards continued to preach occasionally in the homes of former parishioners through October of 1751. See "Appendix: Dated Sermons, January 1743–February 1758, Undated Sermons, and Sermon Fragments," in *Sermons and Discourses, 1743–1758*, ed. Wilson H. Kimnach, *WJE*, vol. 25 (2006), pp. 738-42.

meadow (Massachusetts). Friends in Virginia worked quietly to find him a church there.[7] Friends in Scotland wrote to ask whether Edwards would cross the sea and join the Presbyterian Kirk. Edwards' answer, although negative, has long thrilled the souls of Presbyterians everywhere. As he wrote to John Erskine two weeks after his ejection:

> You are pleased, dear Sir, very kindly to ask me whether I could sign the Westminster Confession of Faith, and submit to the Presbyterian form of church government; and to offer to use your influence to procure a call for me to some congregation in Scotland. I should be very ungrateful if I were not thankful for such kindness and friendship.
>
> As to my subscribing to the substance of the Westminster Confession, there would be no difficulty: and as to the Presbyterian government, I have long been perfectly out of conceit with our unsettled, independent, confused way of church government in this land. And the Presbyterian way has ever appeared to me most agreeable to the Word of God, and the reason and nature of things, though I cannot say that I think that the Presbyterian government of the Church of Scotland is so perfect that it can't in some respects be mended.[8]

Friends in New York continued to think of Edwards as their pulpits emptied.[9] Friends in Northampton even sought to form a splinter

---

[7]As Edwards reported to Erskine, "I was, in the latter part of the last summer [1751], applied to with much earnestness and importunity, by some of the people of Virginia, to come and settle among them in the work of the ministry; who subscribed very handsomely for my encouragement and support, and sent a messenger to me with their request and subscriptions. But I was installed at Stockbridge, before the messenger came." See Jonathan Edwards to the Rev. John Erskine, July 7, 1752, in *Letters and Personal Writings*, p. 492. For more on the work of friends in Virginia to secure a church for Edwards—chief among them Samuel Davies (1723–1761), the region's leading evangelical Presbyterian minister—see Iain H. Murray, *Jonathan Edwards: A New Biography* (Edinburgh: Banner of Truth Trust, 1987), pp. 364-65.

[8]Jonathan Edwards to the Rev. John Erskine, July 5, 1750, in *Letters and Personal Writings*, p. 355. For more on Edwards' relationship to Scottish Presbyterianism, see Christopher W. Mitchell, "Jonathan Edwards's Scottish Connection," in *Jonathan Edwards at Home and Abroad: Historical Memories, Cultural Movements, Global Horizons*, ed. David W. Kling and Douglas A. Sweeney (Columbia: University of South Carolina Press, 2003), pp. 222-47.

[9]Most significantly, Edwards' former church in New York City sought a pastor in 1754. The congregation first called Edwards' student Joseph Bellamy and later considered Edwards. However, everyone seemed to sense that Edwards' (and Bellamy's) pure church principles would prove to be divisive in New York. Neither Bellamy nor Edwards took the assignment.

congregation, filled with Edwards' loyal followers, to rival the First Church. But rather than take a common, tall-steeple British congregation, Edwards chose to move to the sticks of frontier Stockbridge, Massachusetts, and assume the life of a crosscultural missionary.

EDWARDS AND MODERN MISSIONS

As the Australian church historian Stuart Piggin has declared, "Jonathan Edwards was massively constitutive of modern Protestant missions."[10] Not only did his *Freedom of the Will* inspire Calvinists to practice "indiscriminate," intercultural evangelism (discussed in chapter five), but his role as a promoter of the cause of world missions, his *Life of David Brainerd* and his work with Native Americans inspired a surge of institutional, crosscultural ministries.[11]

In 1747, Edwards wrote a minor treatise, missiological in nature, which is often overlooked by Edwards scholars. Based on Zechariah 8, it was published in support of a transatlantic concert of prayer (proposed by Scottish evangelicals) and spelled out Edwards' hope for world missions. Its lengthy title said it all: *An Humble Attempt to Promote Explicit Agreement and Visible Union of God's People in Extraordinary Prayer for the Revival of Religion and the Advancement of Christ's Kingdom on Earth, Pursuant to Scripture-Promises and Prophecies Con-*

---

[10]Stuart Piggin, "The Expanding Knowledge of God: Jonathan Edwards's Influence on Missionary Thinking and Promotion," in *Jonathan Edwards at Home and Abroad: Historical Memories, Cultural Movements, Global Horizons*, ed. David W. Kling and Douglas A. Sweeney (Columbia: University of South Carolina Press, 2003), p. 266. For more on modern Protestant missions, see Douglas A. Sweeney, *The American Evangelical Story: A History of the Movement* (Grand Rapids: Baker Academic, 2005), pp. 79-106; and Martin Klauber and Scott M. Manetsch, eds., *The Great Commission: Evangelicals and the History of World Missions* (Nashville: Broadman & Holman, 2008).

[11]For more on Edwards' legacy in international missions, see Ronald E. Davies, *Jonathan Edwards and His Influence on the Development of the Missionary Movement from Britain* (Cambridge, U.K.: Currents in World Christianity Project, 1996); Andrew F. Walls, "Missions and Historical Memory: Jonathan Edwards and David Brainerd," in *Jonathan Edwards at Home and Abroad: Historical Memories, Cultural Movements, Global Horizons*, ed. David W. Kling and Douglas A. Sweeney (Columbia: University of South Carolina Press, 2003), pp. 248-65; and Douglas A. Sweeney, "Evangelical Tradition in America," in *The Cambridge Companion to Jonathan Edwards*, ed. Stephen J. Stein (New York: Cambridge University Press, 2007), pp. 222-25.

cerning the Last Time.[12] Like many in the heyday of the transatlantic Awakening, Edwards was an ardent postmillennialist.[13] He thought revival would continue to spread throughout the known world, leading eventually to the great millennial age—an extended time of heightened spirituality—when the earth would be full of the knowledge of God "as the waters cover the sea" (Is 11:9),[14] most of the globe would turn to Christ, and he would come again in glory. "If the Spirit . . . should be . . . poured out," Edwards speculated anxiously,

> and that great work of God's power and grace should now begin, which in its progress and issue should complete this glorious effect [i.e., bring on the millennial age]; there must be an amazing and unparalleled progress of the work and manifestation of divine power to bring so much to pass, by the year 2000. Would it not be a great thing, to be accomplished in one half century, that religion, in the power and purity of it, should so prevail, as to gain the conquest over all those many things that stand in opposition to it among Protestants, and gain the upper hand through the Protestant world? And if in another [half century], it should go on so to prevail, as to get the victory

---

[12]The first edition was printed in Boston: D. Henchman, 1747. The definitive edition is found in *Apocalyptic Writings*, ed. Stephen J. Stein, *WJE*, vol. 5 (1977), pp. 308-436. Edwards' text was Zechariah 8:20-22, "Thus saith the LORD of Hosts; It shall yet come to pass, that there shall come people, and the inhabitants of many cities: and the inhabitants of one city shall go to another, saying, Let us go speedily to pray before the LORD, and to seek the LORD of Hosts: I will go also. Yea, many people and strong nations shall come to seek the LORD of Hosts in Jerusalem, and to pray before the LORD."

[13]The boundaries between "postmillennialism," "premillennialism" and "amillennialism" would be drawn more clearly in the nineteenth century than they were in Edwards' day. Edwards did not refer to the terms. Still, for the sake of comprehension it should be noted that postmillennialists believe that Christ will return to earth *after* the golden millennial age (see Rev 20), which will be ushered in with unprecedented revival and social improvement. Premillennialists, by contrast, teach that Christ will return to earth *before* the millennial age, inaugurating it personally and reigning on earth for a thousand years before the final judgment (many have viewed the thousand years symbolically, or approximately). Amillennialists, for their part, teach a spiritual millennium, one in which Christ is said to be reigning now with the saints who are in heaven. (Amillennialists deny a literal, thousand-year interlude between the present history and judgment day.) For more on Edwards' eschatology and its practical significance, see Brandon Withrow, "Jonathan Edwards: Revival, Millennial Expectations, and the Vials of Revelation," *Trinity Journal* 22 (Spring 2001): 75-98.

[14]This biblical prophecy occurs in five places (in somewhat different versions): Num 14:21; Ps 72:19; Is 6:3; 11:9; Hab 2:14.

over all the opposition and strength of the kingdom of Antichrist, so as to gain the ascendant in that which is now the popish world? And if in a third half century, it should prevail and subdue the greater part of the Mahometan world, and bring in the Jewish nation, in all their dispersions? And then in the next whole century, the whole heathen world should be enlightened and converted to the Christian faith, throughout all parts of Africa, Asia, America and Terra Australis, . . . and this attended with an utter extirpation of the remnant of the Church of Rome, and all the relics of Mahometanism, heresy, schism and enthusiasm, and a suppression of all remains of open vice and immorality, and every sort of visible enemy to true religion, through the whole earth, and bring to an end all the unhappy commotions, tumults, and calamities occasioned by such great changes, and all things so adjusted and settled through the world, that the world thenceforward should enjoy an holy rest or sabbatism?[15]

Edwards was not a gentle ecumenist. He believed the Roman Catholic Church was evil—it was "Antichrist"—and strove for a day when evangelical faith would rule the world. His biases are striking in our own, more liberal age.[16] However, he knew that his millennium would never come to pass, not even by Y2K,[17] without coop-

---

[15]Edwards, *An Humble Attempt*, in *Apocalyptic Writings*, p. 411. Terra Australis ("southern land") was an imaginary continent in the southern hemisphere, which appeared on many early modern European maps (until the early nineteenth century). The etymological root of the name of modern-day Australia, it was thought to be much larger than the land "down under" is. Before the age of exploration, many thought that it extended across much of the space above the South Pole.

[16]In early Protestant history, many pastors and theologians—Martin Luther, John Calvin and a host of lesser worthies—said the Roman Church, or the papacy, was antichrist. In fact, the best-known history of world missions in Edwards' day advocated Protestant missions largely for anti-Catholic reasons. Robert Millar (1672–1752), a Presbyterian, feared that Catholics could win the world by means of their "unwearied Diligence." He goaded fellow Protestants with questions such as this: "Shall the Popish Missionaries compass Sea and Land to make Proselytes, and we Protestants loiter, sit still, and do nothing?" Edwards owned a copy of Millar, *The History of the Propagation of Christianity and Overthrow of Paganism*, 2 vols., 2nd ed. (London: G. Strahan, 1726). Quotations from 1:xii and 2:592.

[17]Edwards was long said to have taught, in the words of Yale's editor of *Some Thoughts Concerning the Present Revival of Religion in New England*, that "the millennium [would] probably . . . dawn in America." That this is not quite true never occurred to most scholars, who ignored the bulk of his writings on the subject (all of which are heavily exegetical). He did say the following: "'Tis not unlikely that this work of God's Spirit [the Great Awakening], that is so extraordinary and

erative evangelism. He did whatever he could to inculcate a global consciousness among his Protestant readers, to support the cause of revival and evangelism abroad, and to lead by bold example in the mission field. By the early nineteenth century, many leaders of the Anglo-American Protestant missions movement hearkened to Edwards as a herald of their cause.

THE LIFE OF DAVID BRAINERD

He was best known among them as the author of the blockbuster *Life of David Brainerd,* published in 1749, which told the story of a martyr in the work of Indian missions.[18] Born in woodsy Haddam, Connecticut, in 1718, Brainerd lost his father and mother by the age of fourteen. He made it to Yale but was expelled during the fervor

---

wonderful, is the dawning, or at least a prelude, of that glorious work of God, so often foretold in Scripture, which in the progress and issue of it, shall renew the world of mankind [the great millennial age]. . . . And if we may suppose that this glorious work of God shall begin in any part of America, I think, if we consider the circumstances of the settlement of New England, it must needs appear the most likely of all American colonies, to be the place whence this work shall principally take its rise. And if these things are so, it gives us more abundant reasons to hope that what is now seen in America, and especially in New England, may prove the dawn of that glorious day . . . the beginning or forerunner of something vastly great." However, in several other writings treating eschatological themes, Edwards also specified that, in the best case scenario, the millennial age would finally dawn about the year 2000, probably in the Holy Land. He only hoped that God would use New England's Great Awakening to pave a way for it. As Edwards wrote to a Scottish friend, William McCulloch, in 1744: "It has been slanderously reported and printed concerning me, that I have often said that the millennium was already begun, and that it began at Northampton. . . . but the report is very diverse from what I have ever said. Indeed, I have often said, as I say now, that I looked upon the late wonderful revivals of religion as forerunners of those glorious times so often prophesied of in the Scripture, and that this was the first dawning of that light, and beginning of that work which in the progress and issue of it would at last bring on the church's latter-day glory. But there are many that know that I have from time to time added, that there would probably be many sore conflicts and terrible convulsions, and many changes, revivings and intermissions, and returns of dark clouds, and threatening appearances, before this work shall have subdued the world, and Christ's kingdom shall be everywhere established and settled in peace, which will be the beginning of the millennium." Jonathan Edwards, *Some Thoughts Concerning the Present Revival of Religion in New England,* in *The Great Awakening,* ed. C. C. Goen, *WJE,* vol. 4 (1972), pp. 353, 358; and Jonathan Edwards to the Rev. William McCulloch, March 5, 1744, in *Letters and Personal Writings,* pp. 135-36. Cf. Gerald R. McDermott, *One Holy and Happy Society: The Public Theology of Jonathan Edwards* (University Park: Pennsylvania State University Press, 1992), pp. 37-92.

[18]For more on the role of this book in the rise of modern Protestant missions, see especially Joseph Conforti, "David Brainerd and the Nineteenth-Century Missionary Movement," *Journal of the Early Republic* 5 (Fall 1985): 309-29.

---

of the Awakening. (He was overheard complaining about the tepid spirituality of Tutor Chauncey Whittelsey—"He has no more grace than this chair," Brainerd told a group of students—and refused to repent of this in public.)[19] He burned his candle at both ends and died young, at twenty-nine. But during his final years of life, he exhibited the sort of truly gracious Christian piety that Edwards had been championing for years.

In November of 1742, Brainerd won a commission from the Society in Scotland for Propagating Christian Knowledge to work as a missionary to Indians. He prepared for this with the Rev. John Sergeant, a student of Edwards and a former Yale tutor, at the Stockbridge Indian mission. Crossing the Hudson soon thereafter, he commenced his work in Kaunaumeek (New York) and then moved south to work with the Delawares of Pennsylvania. Ordained a Presbyterian in 1744 (by the "New Side," or pro-revival, New York Presbytery), he spent the final years of his ministry in New Jersey. He founded an Indian congregation in the village of Crossweeksung, moved this church to nearby Cranbury in 1746 and, by the time he had to leave this group in 1747, the congregation boasted 85 communicants (43 adults and 42 children).

Never a very healthy man, Brainerd contracted tuberculosis, lived for a while with Jonathan Dickinson in Elizabethtown, New Jersey (from November of 1746 to March of 1747), and thus is sometimes called the first student at Princeton College. (The College of New Jersey, later Princeton University, began in the Dickinson parson-

---

[19]See Jonathan Edwards, *The Life of David Brainerd*, ed. Norman Pettit, *WJE*, vol. 7 (1985), p. 155. In September 1740, at the height of the Great Awakening, Yale's trustees had passed a rule requiring that if "any Student of this College shall directly or indirectly say, that the Rector, either of the Trustees or Tutors are Hypocrites, carnall or unconverted Men, he shall for the first offence make a publick confession in the Hall, and for the Second Offence be expelled." See the *Minutes of the Yale University Corporation and the Prudential Committee* (RU 307), 1716–1760, Manuscripts and Archives, Yale University Library, as quoted and explained by John Grigg, "'A Principle of Spiritual Life': David Brainerd's Surviving Sermon," *New England Quarterly* 77 (June 2004): 274-75. I have adapted the following four paragraphs from Douglas A. Sweeney and Allen C. Guelzo, eds., *The New England Theology: From Jonathan Edwards to Edwards Amasa Park* (Grand Rapids: Baker Academic, 2006), pp. 47-48.

age in 1746.) In the spring of 1747, Brainerd moved to New England where he convalesced with the Edwardses. He formed an intimate friendship with their teenage daughter, Jerusha, before dying of consumption in a bedroom at the parsonage, on October 9, 1747. (Jerusha died at age eighteen just four months later. She is buried next to Brainerd in Northampton's cemetery.)[20]

From a worldly point of view, Brainerd did not know much success. He lived a short, grueling life without renown or temporal gain. As Edwards himself pointed out, he also wrestled with personal demons. He was "prone to melancholy" and "excessive in his labors." He neglected to take "due care to proportion his fatigues to his strength."[21] But through the leaves of Edwards' *Life*, Brainerd quickly became a hero to the evangelical world. Thousands traveled in spiritual pilgrimage to Brainerd's humble grave. Many more determined to follow him into the mission field.[22]

Edwards implied that Brainerd ranked among "the best saints in this world."[23] And in the midst of the spiritual turmoil of the era's Great Awakening, he could think of no one better to frame as a picture of Protestant piety. Brainerd had a knack for limning the differences between authentic faith and rank hypocrisy, true virtue and its counterfeits. He demonstrated a longing to mature in sanctification, refusing to rest secure on his spiritual laurels. In a eulogy delivered at Brainerd's funeral in Northampton, Edwards emphasized that Brainerd "abhorred the way of such, as live on their first work [of grace], as though they had now got through their work, and are thencefor-

---

[20]Contrary to rumors that have persisted over the years since Brainerd's death, he and Jerusha were never engaged to be married.

[21]Edwards, *Life of David Brainerd*, pp. 91, 95.

[22]These claims are well documented. See Norman Pettit's "Editor's Introduction" to Edwards, *Life of David Brainerd*, pp. 3-4, 55-56; and Conforti, "David Brainerd and the Nineteenth-Century Missionary Movement," pp. 309-29. Less appreciated is Brainerd's vast influence on the everyday spiritual lives of long-forgotten lay Christians. For just one of many examples, see the recently published diary of an eighteenth-century housewife, *The World of Hannah Heaton: The Diary of an Eighteenth-Century New England Farm Woman*, ed. Barbara E. Lacey (Dekalb: Northern Illinois University Press, 2003), pp. 84-85.

[23]Edwards, *Life of Brainerd*, p. 95.

ward, by degrees, settled in a cold, lifeless, negligent, worldly frame." He exalted Brainerd's life as an example to his people of regenerate spirituality unfettered by the kind of self-absorption and religious ostentation that had plagued the region's churches since the revivals. "He greatly nauseated a disposition in persons to much noise and show in religion," Edwards noted,

> and affecting to be abundant in publishing and proclaiming their own experiences; though he did not condemn, but approved of Christians' speaking of their experiences, on some occasions, and to some persons, with modesty, discretion and reserve. He abominated the spirit and practice of the generality of the separatists in this land. I heard him say, once and again, that he had been much with this kind of people, and was acquainted with many of them, in various parts; and that by this acquaintance, he knew that what was chiefly and most generally in repute amongst them, as the power of godliness, was entirely a different thing from that vital piety recommended in the Scripture and had nothing in it of that nature.[24]

Though still an opinionated man, Brainerd had clearly come a long way since leaving New Haven. No longer holier-than-thou, he seems

---

[24]See Jonathan Edwards, "True Saints, When Absent from the Body, Are Present with the Lord," in *Sermons and Discourses, 1743–1758*, pp. 222-56 (quotations from pp. 247-48). Based on 2 Cor 5:8, this sermon was preached on October 12, 1747, and published first by D. Henchman of Boston, 1747. Yet another salient feature of Edwards' view of Brainerd's life is the perspective he offers on Brainerd's manner of prayer: "His manner of praying was very agreeable; most becoming a worm of the dust, and a disciple of Christ, addressing to an infinitely great and holy God, and Father of mercies; not with florid expressions, or a studied eloquence; not with any intemperate vehemence, or indecent boldness; at the greatest distance from any appearance of ostentation, and from everything that might look as though he meant to recommend himself to those that were about him, or set himself off to their acceptance; free too from vain repetitions, without impertinent excursions, or needless multiplying of words. He expressed himself with the strictest propriety, with weight, and pungency; and yet what his lips uttered seemed to flow from the fullness of his heart, as deeply impressed with a great and solemn sense of our necessities, unworthiness, and dependence, and of God's infinite greatness, excellency, and sufficiency, rather than merely from a warm and fruitful brain. . . . In his prayers, he insisted much on the prosperity of Zion, the advancement of Christ's kingdom in the world, and the flourishing and propagation of religion among the Indians. And he generally made it one petition in his prayer, that we might not outlive our usefulness." Edwards, *Life of David Brainerd*, p. 446. Cf. Edwards, "True Saints, When Absent from the Body, Are Present with the Lord," in *Sermons and Discourses, 1743–1758*, p. 245.

to have grown the most critical of the very sins that characterized his youth.

Edwards' great esteem for Brainerd also shaped his own decision to be a missionary. Less than two years after Brainerd died, Sergeant died too (in July of 1749), depriving Stockbridge of the ministry of the Word. Edwards himself had helped to found the fledgling Indian mission there, so as he looked for a new assignment after June of 1750, Stockbridge occupied his thoughts.

THE STOCKBRIDGE INDIAN MISSION

In 1734, Edwards' brother-in-law, the Rev. Samuel Hopkins of West Springfield,[25] had led a conversation about the need for an Indian mission. In March of that year, Edwards orchestrated a meeting of Northampton's leading citizens to generate support.[26] By 1736, the commissioners of the Society for Propagating the Gospel among the Indians of North America—also called the New England Company—opened the Stockbridge mission for business.[27] After consulting with a group of regional Housatonic Indians, they hired Sergeant to serve as founding minister at the mission and appointed Timothy Woodbridge (yet another friend of Edwards) to run its school. Edwards continued to raise funds for this throughout the 1740s. His relatives, the Williams clan (comprised of a motley crew of Edwards' uncles, aunts and cousins), moved to Stockbridge and engaged in trade and speculation in land. By the time that Sergeant died, the village boasted an English church,[28] a larger Indian congregation, an

---

[25]N.B. This is a different Samuel Hopkins from the one who studied with Edwards and published his earliest biography. Samuel Hopkins of West Springfield (1693–1755) was married to Edwards' sister Esther.

[26]This meeting was held in the home of Edwards' uncle, John Stoddard (1682–1748), a wealthy merchant, politician and local power broker.

[27]On the history of this society, see William Kellaway, *The New England Company, 1649–1776: Missionary Society to the American Indians* (London: Longmans, 1961).

[28]Technically, the Williamses were Welsh. There were approximately twelve English/Welsh families living near the mission. See Kevin Michael Sweeney, "River Gods and Related Minor Deities: The Williams Family and the Connecticut River Valley, 1637–1790" (Ph.D. diss., Yale University, 1986).

Indian school, as well as a boarding school for gifted Indian boys (hoping to work some day with the English). The mission became a meeting place for Indians and English at a time when their relations proved tenuous at best. By 1749, there were 218 Native American residents in Stockbridge, primarily Mahicans with a smaller and less constant group of Mohawks from New York (who were attracted by the school).[29] Sergeant himself had baptized 129 of these inhabitants. (He baptized 182 at the mission altogether.) The Native American church included 42 full members (who received the Lord's Supper). The school served 55, and the boarding program 12.

Edwards preached in Stockbridge in October of 1750. Then from January to March he served as a regular pastor there. Its people called him to settle permanently on the 22nd of February. In keeping with the custom of New England's Congregationalists, however, Edwards sought the counsel of others before responding. Pastors in New England typically called together a regional council of sympathetic clergymen for prayerful conversation before deciding to make a move. Edwards' council finally congregated on May 16. They had to discuss not only the offer on the table from the mission, but the hope of some in Northampton that he would start a new church there. In the end, they concluded that Edwards should settle at the mission. So he moved there right away and was installed on August 8. On

---

[29]The Mohawks were part of the famous Iroquois federation centered in (eastern) upstate New York. They had to travel quite a distance to participate in Stockbridge. On the history of these tribes (often called the "Stockbridge Indians") and their experience at the mission, see Frederick E. Hoxie, ed., *Encyclopedia of North American Indians* (Boston: Houghton Mifflin, 1996), pp. 390-91, 611; Samuel Hopkins, *Historical Memoirs, Relating to the Housatunnuk Indians: or, An account of the methods used, and pains taken, for the propagation of the Gospel among that heathenish-tribe, and the success thereof, under the ministry of the late Reverend Mr. John Sergeant* (Boston: S. Kneeland, 1753); Rachel Wheeler, *To Live Upon Hope: Mohicans and Missionaries in the Eighteenth-Century Northeast* (Ithaca, N.Y.: Cornell University Press, 2008); Daniel Richard Mandell, "Behind the Frontier: Indian Communities in Eighteenth-Century Massachusetts" (Ph.D. diss., University of Virginia, 1993); Patrick Frazier, *The Mohicans of Stockbridge* (Lincoln: University of Nebraska Press, 1992); Philip S. Colee, "The Housatonic-Stockbridge Indians: 1734–1749" (Ph.D. diss., SUNY at Albany, 1977); Sarah Cabot Sedgwick and Christina Sedgwick Marquand, *Stockbridge: 1739–1974* (Stockbridge: Berkshire Traveler Press, 1974); and Lion G. Miles, "The Red Man Dispossessed: The Williams Family and the Alienation of Indian Land in Stockbridge, Massachusetts, 1736–1818," *New England Quarterly* 67 (March 1994): 45-76.

October 18, the rest of his family members arrived.[30]

The Edwardses decided to make their home among the Indians. When Sergeant had moved to Stockbridge back in 1736, he had determined to do the same, building a humble house by the mission in the valley running through town. But after he married in 1739, his wife, Abigail Williams,[31] asked for a finer, English home upon the bluff above the mission. The newlyweds ascended to the English part of town, near the rest of the Williams family, never to move back down again. This did not seem right to Edwards, whose relationship with the Williamses was never warm and cozy. So he renovated Sergeant's first house and settled there.[32]

As he took the mission's reins, its congregations carried on much like they had in Sergeant's day. However, its schools quickly became a bone of contention. Edwards emerged as a defender of the Indians and their needs over against the frequent encroachments of the Williamses. Most of the Williams clan supported the Great Awakening and its fruit, including the cause of Native American education. But they also swindled Indian land and used the mission for gain. Well before Edwards moved to town, they had assumed control of its schools and did not appear to care much for its students. In 1748, they had appointed one of their lackeys, Martin Kellogg—an elderly man with little experience teaching—to run the boarding school for boys. Then in 1752, they tried to foist their daughter Abigail, now recently remarried, on a similar school for girls. Edwards grew in-

---

[30]As usual, Sarah bore the brunt of the logistical details. The Edwards' property in Northampton would not sell until February of 1752.

[31]Abigail Williams (1721–1791) was the daughter of the mission's leading citizen, Colonel Ephraim Williams Sr. (1691–1754), an opponent of Edwards' ministry. She married John Sergeant (1710–1749) at the age of 17. Some people think she turned him against the Great Awakening. Shortly after Edwards' arrival, she would marry Colonel Joseph Dwight (1703–1765) and turn him against Edwards (he had once been Edwards' friend). In evangelical accounts of Edwards' work at the Stockbridge mission, Abigail Williams Sergeant Dwight is often depicted as a Jezebel.

[32]Though Edwards' house no longer survives, Sergeant's second house has since been moved back down to the Stockbridge plain, where it functions as a museum (called the Mission House) on the corner of Main Street and Sergeant Street.

---

censed. He knew that neither of these locals served the interests of the students. And he worried about the effect of Abigail upon the Indians. Not only had she pulled her first husband from the mission. She also seems to have pulled him away from evangelical Calvinism. Sergeant was a follower of Edwards in his youth. He had studied at the parsonage in Northampton. But after tying the knot with Abigail, he joined the "Old Light" critics of the region's Great Awakening and sponsored Chauncy's book against revival (chapter four).[33]

Edwards labored tirelessly to win control of the schools, appealing constantly to the powers that be in Massachusetts government and the mission's ruling bodies.[34] He was not an ideal missionary. He preached and taught in English (always speaking through a translator). Even at the mission he was something of a racist. He thought its schools should play a role in "civilizing" the Indians (i.e., making them more English). But he also thought the Indians were *spiritually* his *equals* and he argued more than once that they could teach their English neighbors a lesson or two about religion. Most importantly, perhaps, he demonstrated solidarity with the Indians and their cause. Rather than use his time in Stockbridge as a retreat from worldly affairs, he poured his life into Native American ministry.[35]

By February of 1754, he proved victorious. The mission's leading patron sided publicly with Edwards.[36] The New England Company

---

[33]Charles Chauncy, *Seasonable Thoughts on the State of Religion in New-England* (Boston: Printed by Rogers and Fowle, for Samuel Eliot, 1743).

[34]The New England Company was governed from London but managed by commissioners whose work was centered in Boston. Edwards wrote numerous letters to leaders in both places asking for help with the mission's schools.

[35]For more on Edwards' struggles as a defender of the Indians, consult the many letters he wrote on his work at the Stockbridge mission (both to power brokers and friends), in *Letters and Personal Writings*, pp. 374-738. See also Rachel M. Wheeler, "Edwards as Missionary," in *The Cambridge Companion to Jonathan Edwards*, ed. Stephen J. Stein (New York: Cambridge University Press, 2007), pp. 196-214; and Rachel Wheeler, "Lessons from Stockbridge: Jonathan Edwards and the Stockbridge Indians," in *Jonathan Edwards at 300: Essays on the Tercentenary of His Birth*, ed. Harry S. Stout, Kenneth P. Minkema and Caleb J. D. Maskell (Lanham, Md.: University Press of America, 2005), pp. 131-40. Though full of historical inaccuracies, Elizabeth George Speare's historical novel, *The Prospering* (Boston: Houghton Mifflin, 1967), offers a vivid account of everyday life at the mission.

[36]This was Isaac Hollis (1699–1774), a Baptist preacher and philanthropist in High-Wycombe,

gave him full control of the Stockbridge schools. The Williamses' attempts to box him out had come to an end.[37] Edwards could finally drop his guard and fix his mind on spiritual things. Tragically, however, terrible damage had been done. A year before, the schoolhouse used by Indian boys had been destroyed (in a mysterious case of arson). Scores of students left in disappointment at their treatment. Edwards stood alone atop a shambles. He spent the next few years rebuilding. Nearly everyone knew that his victory had been Pyrrhic.

As if this were not enough, the so-called French and Indian War (or better, the Seven Years' War) began as soon as Edwards' battle for the mission came to an end. A frontier outpost, Stockbridge stood in constant danger of attack. And in the spring of 1754, its threat level was raised. Two English horse thieves murdered a Native American bystander during a local crime spree. Stockbridge feared retaliation. Edwards' house was quartered with soldiers in the summer of that year. Nevertheless, a raid occurred. On September 1, 1754, the town was stormed. Four inhabitants were slain at the hands of a band of "Canada Indians; which occasioned a great alarm to us and great part of New England." Stockbridge went unscathed throughout the rest of this bloody war. But Edwards and others lived in fear. "What will become of us, God only knows," he wrote his colleague Gideon Hawley.[38]

Making matters worse, Edwards succumbed to a serious illness as hostilities began—no coincidence for one whose body had always buckled in seasons of emotional distress. In July of 1754, he was hit with what he depicted as "the longest and most tedious sickness that

---

England, whose unusual (and rather enthusiastic) evangelicalism was largely unknown to Edwards. See R. E. Davies, "Missionary Benefactor and Strange Bedfellow: Isaac Hollis, Jonathan Edwards' English Correspondent," *Baptist Quarterly* 41 (January 2006): 263-80.

[37] The Williams family had been struggling to rid themselves of Edwards since November of 1752, when Colonel Joseph Dwight (Abigail Williams' second husband) wrote to the Massachusetts General Assembly asking for his ouster.

[38] See Jonathan Edwards to the Rev. William McCulloch, April 10, 1756, and Jonathan Edwards to the Rev. Gideon Hawley, October 9, 1756, in *Letters and Personal Writings*, pp. 687, 691. Technically speaking, these "Canada Indians" were Schaghticokes, as was the earlier murder victim. See Sedgwick and Marquand, *Stockbridge*, pp. 73-75.

---

ever I had in my life." As he wrote to John Erskine when he recovered from this bout, he had been struck

with fits of the ague [fits of shivering from fever], which . . . were for a long time very severe and exceedingly wasted my flesh and strength, so that I became like a skeleton. I had several intermissions of the fits by the use of the Peruvian bark [taken from trees in South America, an early modern remedy for Malaria]; but they never wholly left me till about the middle of last January [1755]. In the meantime, I several times attempted to write letters to some of my friends about affairs of importance; but found that I could bear but little of such writing. Once, in attempting to write a letter, . . . a fit of the ague came upon me . . . so that I was obliged to lay by my pen. When my fits left me, they left me in a poor, weak state, all over bloated; so that I feared whether I was not going into a dropsy [a case of swelling from excess fluid in the tissue]. I am still something swelled, and much overrun with scorbutic maladies [symptoms tied to scurvy]. Nevertheless, I have of late gradually gained strength.[39]

No sooner had he recovered from this terrible disease, moreover, than Edwards had an accident while riding on his horse. In April of 1755, as he trotted south to Windsor for a visit with his family, he suffered a "great hurt" from what he described as "a dangerous fall from my horse, the horse pitching heels over head with his whole weight upon me."[40] Edwards survived the crash with little more than bumps and bruises. He could hardly help wondering, though, what God was doing with him.

Toward the Presidency of Princeton

In the midst of all this suffering, Edwards did manage to stay in touch with the larger world of Anglo-American Protestant Chris-

---

[39]Jonathan Edwards to the Rev. John Erskine, April 15, 1755, in *Letters and Personal Writings*, pp. 662-63. On this illness, see also Jonathan Edwards to Thomas Foxcroft, December 20, 1754, in *Letters and Personal Writings*, pp. 654-55.

[40]Jonathan Edwards to the Rev. Thomas Foxcroft, June 3, 1755, in *Letters and Personal Writings*, p. 668.

tianity. He traveled from time to time, preaching in pulpits far and wide. Most significantly, perhaps, he went to Newark in 1752 and stayed with daughter Esther and her husband Aaron Burr, who was serving as the president of the College of New Jersey. He addressed the students there. Then on September 28, he also addressed the Presbyterians of the Synod of New York (who were assembled then in Newark). Using a sermon he had written back in 1746, he stressed again the need for personal faith and spiritual rebirth. He spoke from James 2:19, "Thou believest that there is one God; thou doest well; the devils also believe, and tremble." His doctrine was as follows: "Nothing in the mind of man, that is of the same nature with what the devils experience, or are the subjects of, is any sure sign of saving grace." He went on to contend that mental assent is simply not enough. Unless we *relish* the gospel of Christ, we have no part in its salvation. Even the devil *believes* the truth. Indeed,

> The devil, before his fall, was among those bright and glorious angels
> of heaven, which are represented as morning stars, and flames of fire,
> that excel in strength and wisdom. . . . the devil has, undoubtedly a
> great degree of speculative knowledge in divinity; having been, as it
> were, educated in the best divinity school in the universe, viz. the
> heaven of heavens. . . . The devil is orthodox in his faith; he believes
> the true scheme of doctrine; he is no Deist, Socinian, Arian, Pela-
> gian, or Antinomian; the articles of his faith are all sound. . . . There-
> fore, for a person to believe the doctrines of Christianity, merely from
> the influence of things speculative, or from the force of arguments, as
> discerned only by speculation, is no evidence of grace.

If we can do no better than Satan, he concluded, we are doomed. The sermon was printed in New York the following year beneath the title *True Grace, Distinguished from the Experience of Devils.*[41]

Despite his relative isolation, Edwards became the best-known Christian in America at this time. During the later 1750s, he was

---

[41]Jonathan Edwards, "True Grace, Distinguished from the Experience of Devils," in *Sermons and Discourses, 1743–1758*, pp. 608-9, 613-17 (orig. New York: James Parker, 1753).

massively prolific (as discussed in chapter five). His works were read throughout the West. He stayed in touch with Princeton College through his ties with Aaron Burr. He sent his oldest son, Timothy, to study there with Burr beginning in 1753. And he journeyed there again in the fall of 1755, stayed with family, went to commencement and delivered a sermon in Newark. (The College did not move to Princeton until 1756.) Thus when Burr died unexpectedly at the age of forty-one—felled by fever from malaria on September 24, 1757— his trustees knew what to do. Five days later, still in mourning, they dispatched a letter to Stockbridge, asking Edwards to assume the Princeton presidency.

Edwards was honored by the offer. He was saddened by the death of his son-in-law and kindred spirit. He was worried about his daughter and her children, Sally and Aaron (who were toddlers at the time).[42] He was emotionally distraught, that is, and unprepared to entertain a prospect so momentous. What is more, he felt as though his life was finally coming together. Things at the mission had improved. He had found more time to write. His family had settled into Stockbridge and enjoyed their way of life. His daily affairs had stabilized and he was uneasy about the potential of another dislocation. He had tried to run a college once; it nearly ended his life. So in reply to Princeton's leaders, Edwards demurred. He outlined the obstacles impeding such a move. He spoke at length about the writing projects lying on his desk, which would probably not be finished if he took the job in Princeton (these are discussed in chapter three). And he whined about his chronically decrepit constitution in a manner so medieval, so thoroughly self-abasing, it is comical today. "I have a constitution in many respects peculiar unhappy," he wrote,

> attended with flaccid solids, vapid, sizy and scarce fluids, and a low
> tide of spirits; often occasioning a kind of childish weakness and con-

---

[42]Aaron Burr Jr. (1756–1836) would grow up to be the vice president of the United States under President Thomas Jefferson (1743–1826). A notorious infidel, he went down in infamy for killing his rival Alexander Hamilton (1755–1804) in a duel.

temptibleness of speech, presence, and demeanor; with a disagreeable dullness and stiffness, much unfitting me for conversation, but more especially for the government of a college. This poorness of constitution makes me shrink at the thoughts of taking upon me, in the decline of life, such a new and great business, attended with such a multiplicity of cares, and requiring such a degree of activity, alertness and spirit of government.

Edwards agreed to "ask advice" of friendly ministers in the region. He confessed, however, that "On the whole, I am much at a loss, with respect to the way of my duty in this important affair: I am in doubt, whether if I should engage in it, I should not do what both you and I should be sorry for afterwards."[43]

A regional council of clergymen convened to pray and seek the will of God for Edwards' life.[44] Meetings like this were often scary. They determined a person's future. They reminded him that he did not control his family's destiny. In Edwards' case, moreover, they usually made affairs more difficult. As he wrote to Gideon Hawley shortly after the council met, its members "unanimously determined" that he should move.[45] The Lord had spoken. Edwards obeyed, despite his genuine reluctance. His life was in God's hands. But it would never be easy again.

Edwards was flattered by the prestige attending a presidential post. But while submitting his will to that of his advisers in the matter, he would chafe beneath the burden they imposed. Samuel Hopkins noted later, in fact, that

> when they published their judgment and advice to Mr. Edwards and his people, he appear'd uncommonly mov'd and affected with it, and fell into tears on the occasion; . . . and soon after said to the gentle-

---

[43]Jonathan Edwards to the Trustees of the College of New Jersey, October 19, 1757, in *Letters and Personal Writings*, pp. 726, 729.

[44]Originally scheduled for December 21, this meeting was delayed by inclement weather, taking place despite "yet more difficult" conditions on January 4, 1758. See Jonathan Edwards to the Rev. Gideon Hawley, January 14, 1758, in *Letters and Personal Writings*, p. 737.

[45]Edwards to the Rev. Gideon Hawley, January 14, 1758, in *Letters and Personal Writings*, p. 737.

---

men, who had given their advice, that it was a matter of wonder to him, that they could so easily . . . get over the objections he had made against his removal, to be the head of a college; which appear'd great and weighty to him.[46]

Great and weighty indeed. Edwards had reason to lament.

---

[46]Hopkins, *The Life and Character of the Late Reverend Mr. Jonathan Edwards*, p. 79.

— Chapter 7 —

THE WORD OF THE LORD
ENDURETH FOR EVER

*Seeing ye have purified your souls in obeying the truth through the
Spirit unto unfeigned love of the brethren, see that ye love one another
with a pure heart fervently: Being born again, not of corruptible seed,
but of incorruptible, by the word of God, which liveth and abideth for
ever. For all flesh is as grass, and all the glory of man as the flower of
grass. The grass withereth, and the flower thereof falleth away: But
the word of the Lord endureth for ever. And this is the word which by
the gospel is preached unto you.*

1 PETER 1:22-25

Edwards' tenure at the College would be tragically short-lived—
two months long, to be exact. His feeble body finally failed shortly
after he moved to Princeton. His flower withered and fell. He died at
the age of fifty-four. Many have wondered how he might have blessed
us had he stayed in bloom.[1]

As soon as his colleagues had discerned that he should become
the third president of the College of New Jersey, "he girded up his

---

[1] I do a little more than wonder in my "Editor's Introduction" to The "Miscellanies," 1153-1360, WJE, vol. 23 (2003), pp. 9-33.

loins," as Hopkins stated, "and set off."[2] He left his wife and children behind, intending to move them in the spring after the weather had improved. Only Esther and her younger sister Lucy lived in Princeton.[3] Timothy lived nearby. He had graduated from Princeton in the fall of 1757 and moved to Elizabethtown to start a business.

After settling into his house (still in use on Princeton's campus),[4] Edwards met his students and tutors,[5] preached to them on several Sundays in the Princeton College chapel, wrote some questions in theology for Princeton's senior class, and was installed "in the president's chair" by the Princeton Corporation on the 16th of February, 1758.[6] Things seemed to be going smoothly. Hopkins noted, in fact, that

> during this time, Mr. Edwards seem'd to enjoy an uncommon degree of the presence of God. He told his daughters, he had had great exercise, concern and fear, relative to his engaging in that business [i.e., the Princeton presidency]; but since it now appeared . . . that he was call'd of God to that place and work, he did cheerfully devote himself to it, leaving himself and the event with God, to order what seemed to Him good.[7]

No sooner had he settled into a regular routine, however, than Edwards chose to set a good example for the locals and receive an inoculation. Smallpox threatened the region. Many feared that they would die. Before the rise of modern medicine, ministers usually had to take the lead in showing support for doctors (who were often fel-

---

[2]Samuel Hopkins, *The Life and Character of the Late Reverend Mr. Jonathan Edwards* (Boston: S. Kneeland, 1765), p. 79. As suggested above, the first two presidents of the College of New Jersey were the Revs. Jonathan Dickinson (1746–1747) and Aaron Burr Sr. (1748–1757).

[3]Lucy was twenty-one and single. She would marry six years later and return to settle in Stockbridge.

[4]Two buildings were constructed for the College of New Jersey when it moved to Princeton in 1756: Nassau Hall (the old main, named for the British King William III of the House of Orange-Nassau); and a residence named the Maclean House in 1968 (where the early presidents lived, and where President Edwards died). Both remain in use today.

[5]There were three tutors in Princeton at the time of Edwards' arrival.

[6]Hopkins, *Life and Character of the Late Reverend Mr. Jonathan Edwards*, p. 79.

[7]Ibid., p. 80.

low pastors) and their therapeutic methods, which had not yet been perfected.[8]

PRESIDENT EDWARDS FACES DEATH

He underwent the procedure on the 23rd of February with Esther and her children, Sally and Aaron. Their physician was a friend, William Shippen of Philadelphia, a brilliant Presbyterian who helped to found the College and design its first building (Nassau Hall, the old main). He would later serve for decades as a College trustee. Edwards seemed to respond well, at least at first, to his vaccine. However, several days later, while the others were recovering, he caught a terrible fever and began to feel some pustules emerging in his throat. The swelling grew severe. Soon he could swallow almost nothing—not the food his body needed to combat the new infection, not the liquids that were needed to subdue his raging fever, not the medicines that Shippen hoped would palliate his symptoms. His body shriveled away over the course of the next few weeks. As Hopkins summarized the process, "a secondary fever set in; and by reason of a number of pustles [*sic*] in his throat, the obstruction was such, that the medicines necessary to stanch the fever, could not be administer'd. It therefore raged till it put an end to his life."[9]

Edwards' soul was finally taken home to the world for which it longed, the wondrous heavenly "world of love," which he had described once in a sermon as "the Paradise of God, where everything has a cast of holy love, and everything conspires to promote and stir up love, and nothing to interrupt its exercises; where everything is fitted by an all-wise God for the enjoyment of love under the greatest

---

[8]See Patricia A. Watson, *The Angelical Conjunction: The Preacher-Physicians of Colonial New England* (Knoxville: University of Tennessee Press, 1991).

[9]Hopkins, *The Life and Character of the Late Reverend Mr. Jonathan Edwards*, p. 80. Cf. William Shippen to Sarah Pierpont Edwards, March 22, 1758, folder 1756-59C, #1-2, Franklin Trask Library, Andover-Newton Theological School. Shippen (1712–1801) was not a pastor. He came of age at the time when medical science in America was starting to develop on its own.

advantages." He continued in words that underline his reputation for artistry in describing spiritual things:

> And all this shall be without any fading of the beauty of the objects beloved, or any decaying of love in the lover, and any satiety in the faculty which enjoys love. O! what tranquility may we conclude there is in such a world as this! Who can express the sweetness of this peace? What a calm is this, what a heaven of rest is here to arrive at after persons have gone through a world of storms and tempests, a world of pride, and selfishness, and envy, and malice, and scorn, and contempt, and contention and war? What a Canaan of rest, a land flowing with milk and honey. . . . What joy may we conclude springs up in the hearts of the saints after they have passed their wearisome pilgrimage to be brought to such a paradise? Here is joy unspeakable indeed; here is humble, holy, divine joy in its perfection.[10]

Edwards entered this splendid place sometime between two and three o'clock p.m. on March 22, exhorting his loved ones to prepare themselves to follow him.[11]

In Edwards' early modern world, people usually died at home, spending their final days surrounded by friends and family. Evangelicals thought intently about the way that they should die. Deathbed scenes were public spectacles, remembered for posterity. They testified to the Christian faith and character of the deceased.[12] It should

---

[10]Jonathan Edwards, "Heaven Is a World of Love," in *Ethical Writings*, ed. Paul Ramsey, *WJE*, vol. 8 (1989), p. 385.

[11]As Shippen wrote to Sarah Edwards shortly after her husband expired, "this afternoon between two & three o'clock it pleased God to let him sleep in that dear Lord Jesus, whose Kingdom & Interest he has been faithfully & painfully Serving all his Life." Shippen to Sarah Pierpont Edwards, March 22, 1758, folder 1756-59C, #1-2, Franklin Trask Library, Andover-Newton Theological School. Jonathan and Sarah Edwards are buried near Aaron Burr Sr. (as well as Aaron Burr Jr.) in the presidential lot of the Princeton cemetery.

[12]For more on evangelical deathbeds in the early modern period, see Henry D. Rack, "Evangelical Endings: Death-Beds in Evangelical Biography," *Bulletin of the John Rylands University Library of Manchester* 74 (Spring 1992): 39-56; R. Cecil, "Holy Dying: Evangelical Attitudes to Death," *History Today* 32 (August 1982): 30-34; and Richard Bell, "'Our People Die Well': Deathbed Scenes in John Wesley's Arminian Magazine," *Mortality* 10 (August 2005): 210-23 (which treats the deaths of Christians after Edwards' time, 1778–1791). Cf. David E. Stannard, *The Puritan Way of Death: A Study in Religion, Culture, and Social Change* (New York: Oxford University Press, 1977); Ralph Houlbrooke, *Death, Religion, and the Family in England, 1480–1750*, Oxford Studies

come as no surprise, then, that Edwards died surrounded by a group of close companions, people hanging on the words he whispered painfully to them through his contagious, swollen throat. Shippen recorded them in a letter he sent to Sarah, still in Stockbridge. They were printed in Hopkins' *Life* of Edwards, published several years later. According to Shippen's account, "a very short time before he expired, he Spoke to Lucy" the following words:

> dear Lucy it seems to me to be the Will of God that I must shortly leave you[,] & therefore give my kindest Love to my dear Wife & tell her, that the uncommon Union that has so long subsisted between us has been of such a Nature as I trust is Spiritual and therefore will continue forever: and I hope she will be supported under so great a trial & submit chearfully to the Will of God; And as to my Children[,] you are now like to be left Fatherless which I hope will be an Inducement to you all to seek a Father who will never fail you; & as to my Funeral[,] I would have it to be like unto Mr. Burrs, and any additional Sum of Money that might be expected to be laid out that way, I would have it disposed of to charitable uses.[13]

Hopkins noted that Burr had "order'd . . . that his funeral should not be attended with that pomp and cost" so typical of the region's self-important. He asked that "nothing" be spent "but what was agreeable to the dictates of Christian decency. And that the sum" of "a *modish* funeral, over and above the necessary cost of a *decent* one, should be given to the poor, out of his estate."[14] Edwards ordered the same thing, preferring to aid the poor and needy rather than go to his grave in style.

As to the manner of his death, Shippen assured Mrs. Edwards of her husband's perseverance in the faith that he professed:

---

in Social History (Oxford: Clarendon, 1998); and John McManners, *Death and the Enlightenment: Changing Attitudes to Death among Christians and Unbelievers in Eighteenth-Century France* (Oxford: Clarendon, 1981).

[13]Shippen to Sarah Pierpont Edwards, March 22, 1758, folder 1756-59C, #1-2, Franklin Trask Library, Andover-Newton Theological School, Newton Centre, Massachusetts.

[14]Hopkins, *The Life and Character of the Late Reverend Mr. Jonathan Edwards*, pp. 80-81.

never did any Mortal Man more fully & clearly evidence the Sincerity of all his Profession, by one continued universal calm, chearful resignation & patient submission to the Divine Will through every Stage of his Disease than he[,] not so much as one discontented Expression nor the least appearance of murmuring thro [the] whole—and never did any Person expire with more perfect freedom from pain, not so much as one distorted hair[,] but in [the] most proper sense of the Words, he really fell asleep—for Death had certainly lost its Sting, as to him.[15]

Hopkins added the following note, recording Edwards' final words:

Just at the close of his life, as some persons, who stood by, and expected he would breath his last in a few minutes, were lamenting his death not only as a great frown on the college, but as having a dark aspect on the interest of religion in general; to their surprise, not imagining that he heard, or would ever speak another word, he said, "TRUST IN GOD, AND YE NEED NOT FEAR." These were his last words.[16]

Edwards did go out in style—the style of truly virtuous Protestants. These records of Shippen and Hopkins offer only the best-known of his encomiums.

Tragically, his death seemed to hasten the deaths of others, making 1758 a bitter year for the Edwards family. His daughter, Esther Burr, died of fever two weeks later at the age of twenty-six (April 7), though apparently not from smallpox. Sarah traveled to Princeton to retrieve her orphaned grandchildren, found them in Philadelphia where the Shippens had looked after them, but died of dysentery at the age of forty-eight (October 2) before she could take them back to Stockbridge.[17] Edwards' father, Timothy, had died in January.

---

[15]Shippen to Sarah Pierpont Edwards, March 22, 1758, folder 1756-59C, #1-2, Franklin Trask Library, Andover-Newton Theological School.

[16]Hopkins, *The Life and Character of the Late Reverend Mr. Jonathan Edwards*, p. 81.

[17]Sally and Aaron would remain in Philadelphia with the Shippens for another two years. After their Uncle Timothy married Rhoda Ogden on September 25, 1760, he took them in and raised them to adulthood (first in New Jersey, then in Stockbridge).

Mother Esther Stoddard Edwards lived another twelve years. But by the fall of 1758, her family had been decimated. Many mourned what seemed to be the end of a spiritual dynasty.

A Rich Spiritual Legacy

The dynasty lived on, however. Edwards' recognition that the Word endures forever and his faithfulness in ministering the Word to those around him yielded a harvest of spiritual fruit that God continues to bless today. In fact, Edwards has proven to be the most important Christian thinker in America since his death. Over the course of the nineteenth century, his descendants included hundreds of leading clergymen, professors, college presidents and lawyers in the new United States.[18] His theology gave birth to the first indigenous school of American Christian thought, the "New Divinity," which after 1800 came to be called "the New England Theology."[19] His students, led by the Revs. Samuel Hopkins (1721–1803) and Joseph Bellamy (1719–1790), spread his legacy far and wide by means of their storied "schools of the prophets" (ministerial training grounds that preceded modern seminaries), pure church polity, publications, concerts of prayer and frequent revivals. Edwards' distinction between a sinner's "natural ability" and "moral inability" to repent, and his related exhortations on the need for global evangelism, proved especially important after his death. By the end of the eighteenth century, his disciples, with these emphases, began to lead the modern, international missions movement—both from England and the United States—exporting Edwardsian evangelicalism to far-flung posts in Africa, south Asia and to the west of America's Appalachian Mountains.[20]

---

[18]See Albert E. Winship, *Jukes-Edwards: A Study in Education and Heredity* (Harrisburg, Penn.: R. L. Myers and Co., 1900), which compares Edwards' descendants to those of a man whose heirs included scores of criminals.

[19]Some in England would refer to it as "the American theology." For more on this tradition, see Douglas A. Sweeney and Allen C. Guelzo, eds., *The New England Theology: From Jonathan Edwards to Edwards Amasa Park* (Grand Rapids: Baker Academic, 2006).

[20]I have detailed these developments (and those discussed below) in Douglas A. Sweeney, "Evangelical Tradition in America," in *The Cambridge Companion to Jonathan Edwards*, ed. Stephen J.

During and after the revivals of the Second Great Awakening,[21] Edwards' views spread even further through the ministries of people like Nathaniel W. Taylor (1786–1858), a revivalistic pastor who became the founding theology teacher at Yale Divinity School (in 1822). They contributed to the life and work of Charles Grandison Finney (1792–1875);[22] they were contested during a rupture of Connecticut Congregationalists in the early 1830s; they shaped the doctrinal emphases of "New School" Presbyterians, north and south, yielding a schism beginning in 1837;[23] they informed the views of Baptists, both in England and the United States, from William Carey (1761–1834) and Andrew Fuller (1754–1815) to Isaac Backus (1724–1806), Jonathan Maxcy (1768–1820) and even William Bullein Johnson (1782–1862), the leading founder of the Southern Baptist Convention.[24]

Stein (New York: Cambridge University Press, 2007), pp. 217-38; and Douglas A. Sweeney, *Nathaniel Taylor, New Haven Theology, and the Legacy of Jonathan Edwards*, Religion in America Series (New York: Oxford University Press, 2003).

[21]America's Second Great Awakening, even bigger than the first, began in the late 1790s and continued through the early 1830s. See Douglas A. Sweeney, *The American Evangelical Story: A History of the Movement* (Grand Rapids: Baker Academic, 2005), pp. 66-78, which includes a bibliography of more important sources.

[22]See Allen C. Guelzo, "An Heir or a Rebel? Charles Grandison Finney and the New England Theology," *Journal of the Early Republic* 17 (Spring 1997): 61-94; and Allen C. Guelzo, "Oberlin Perfectionism and Its Edwardsian Origins, 1835–1870," in *Jonathan Edwards's Writings: Text, Context, Interpretation,* ed. Stephen J. Stein (Bloomington: Indiana University Press, 1996), pp. 159-74.

[23]For more on Edwards and American Presbyterianism, see Zebulon Crocker, *The Catastrophe of the Presbyterian Church, in 1837, Including a Full View of the Recent Theological Controversies in New England* (New Haven: B. and W. Noyes, 1838); Earl Pope, *New England Calvinism and the Disruption of the Presbyterian Church* (1962; New York: Garland, 1987); Sean Michael Lucas, "'He Cuts up Edwardsism by the Roots': Robert Lewis Dabney and the Edwardsian Legacy in the Nineteenth-Century South," in *The Legacy of Jonathan Edwards: American Religion and the Evangelical Tradition,* ed. D. G. Hart, Sean Michael Lucas and Stephen J. Nichols (Grand Rapids: Baker Academic, 2003), pp. 200-214; George M. Marsden, *The Evangelical Mind and the New School Presbyterian Experience: A Case Study of Thought and Theology in Nineteenth-Century America* (New Haven: Yale University Press, 1970); and Mark A. Noll, *America's God: From Jonathan Edwards to Abraham Lincoln* (New York: Oxford University Press, 2002).

[24]For more on Edwards and the Southern Baptist Convention, see Anthony L. Chute, *A Piety Above the Common Standard: Jesse Mercer and Evangelistic Calvinism* (Macon, Ga.: Mercer University Press, 2004); Robert Snyder, "William T. Brantly (1787–1845): A Southern Unionist and the Breakup of the Triennial Convention" (Ph.D. diss., Southern Baptist Theological Seminary, 2005); and Tom J. Nettles, "Edwards and His Impact on Baptists," *Founders Journal* 53 (Summer 2003): 1-18.

By the antebellum period (the time before the Civil War), Edwards' thought and reputation made their way into the leaves of American literary culture. His typology appeared in the work of Ralph Waldo Emerson (1803–1882). His doctrines shaped the "woman's fiction" of authors like Susan Warner (1819–1885). His persona, and the personae of his New Divinity followers, infused historical novels by writers like Harriet Beecher Stowe (1811–1896).[25]

The New England Theology proper died with Edwards Amasa Park (1808–1900), dubbed "the last of the consistent Calvinists," who defended Edwards' views for many years at Andover Seminary. But since the Civil War, Edwards' legacy has expanded through the lives of many who used his work selectively. Groups as diverse as the Old Princetonians (e.g., Charles Hodge and B. B. Warfield), the progressive New Theologians (e.g., Theodore Munger and Frank Hugh Foster), American Pragmatists (e.g., William James and John Dewey), neo-orthodox theologians (e.g., Joseph Haroutunian and Richard Niebuhr) and evangelical thinkers (e.g., R. C. Sproul and John Piper) have continued to make him known to modern audiences.[26]

During his lifetime, Edwards' writings appeared in several different countries. Today they are available in Arabic, Chinese, Choctaw, Dutch, English, French, Gaelic, German, Italian, Korean, Spanish, Swedish and Welsh. Henry Ward Beecher (1813–1887), a son of New

---

[25]Conrad Cherry, *Nature and Religious Imagination: From Edwards to Bushnell* (Philadelphia: Fortress, 1980); Sharon Y. Kim, "Beyond the Men in Black: Jonathan Edwards and Nineteenth-Century Woman's Fiction," in *Jonathan Edwards at Home and Abroad: Historical Memories, Cultural Movements, Global Horizons*, ed. David W. Kling and Douglas A. Sweeney (Columbia: University of South Carolina Press, 2003), pp. 137-53; Charles H. Foster, *The Rungless Ladder: Harriet Beecher Stowe and New England Puritanism* (Durham, N.C.: Duke University Press, 1954); Gayle Kimball, *The Religious Ideas of Harriet Beecher Stowe: Her Gospel of Womanhood* (Lewiston, N.Y.: Edwin Mellen, 1982); and Lawrence E. Buell, "Calvinism Romanticized: Harriet Beecher Stowe, Samuel Hopkins, and *The Minister's Wooing*," *Emerson Society Quarterly* 24 (1978): 119-32.

[26]Anthony C. Cecil Jr., *The Theological Development of Edwards Amasa Park: Last of the "Consistent Calvinists"* (Missoula, Mont.: Scholars Press, 1974); Sweeney, *Nathaniel Taylor, New England Theology*, pp. 144-53, 242-49; and Sweeney, "Evangelical Tradition in America," pp. 229-32, 236-38. On Edwards' vast popularity today among evangelicals, see Collin Hansen, *Young, Restless, Reformed: A Journalist's Journey with the New Calvinists* (Wheaton, Ill.: Crossway, 2008).

England often said to have been the most beloved preacher of his day, knew what it meant to be a celebrity, but also knew that Edwards' fame did not depend on charm, speaking ability or a gift for keeping pace with popular culture (as Beecher's own fame did).[27] It rested upon his faithfulness—and that of his many followers—in teaching Christian doctrine and theology. As Beecher noted in *Norwood: Or, Village Life in New England* (1867), a novel rich in historical detail on the region's social life:

> It may be that at any given time, a high doctrinal sermon is not so edifying as a simple practical one would be. But a community brought up, through a hundred years, to task their thought upon themes remote, difficult, and infinite, will be far nobler than if they had been fed upon easy thought. Something is always to be considered in such discussions, not only as to the effect of preaching on the immediate conduct, but also as to a slower, though even more important effect, upon that whole moral constitution and mental habit which is the grand fountain and source of conduct. . . . Look at the history of New England mind in a large way. I think we owe every thing to her theologians, and most to the most doctrinal. . . . Such men as Edwards [and his disciples] lifted up the New England mind into a range of speculation and conviction that ennobled and strengthened it as act never could have done.[28]

Edwards did ennoble and strengthen those he served throughout his life. His many writings—and his followers—have done so since his death, on every continent in the world. Perhaps we can learn about the challenges of Christian faith, life and even ministry from him. To be sure, he preached in a wig. He got himself fired by the

---

[27]For more on Beecher, see the Pulitzer Prize winning biography of Debby Applegate, *The Most Famous Man in America: The Biography of Henry Ward Beecher* (New York: Doubleday, 2006).

[28]Henry Ward Beecher, *Norwood: Or, Village Life in New England* (1867; New York: Fords, Howard, & Hulbert, 1887), pp. 133-34. Beecher spoke these words through the voice of Reuben Wentworth, one of the novel's leading characters. For more on the profound effect of Edwards' legacy upon the people of New England, read this novel in its entirety, especially chap. 18. Bear in mind that Beecher himself became a leading Protestant liberal; he was not a fan of Edwards.

people whom he led for most of his ministry. He seems old-fashioned today. Yet his love for God and his Word has never gone without a witness. He continues to inspire and instruct.

SEVEN THESES FOR DISCUSSION

I have chosen to end this book with seven theses for discussion, theses I hope will spark reflection about what we can learn from Edwards. As pointed out above, it is naïve to think that we should try to replicate his ministry. His world was different from ours. We face new challenges today. The question is *not* how we might clone him. Rather, the question is how to live in our own, twenty-first-century world, loving the people whom *we* serve, but using insights and examples gleaned from Edwards' life and ministry to enhance our Christian faith and fortify our gospel witness.

Thesis #1: Edwards shows us the importance of working to help people gain a vivid sense, an urgent impression, of God's activity in our world. As Christian witnesses in largely non- or post-Christian cultures, we should follow Edwards' lead in striving creatively to stem the tide of unbelief and apathy. Naturalism and materialism pervade our world today. They even pervade our best churches. God is calling us, like Edwards, to combat these powerful trends, to enhance the faith of others in the reality, centrality, beauty and practicality of God and divine things. Believe it or not, the Holy Spirit wants to use *you* in this way—in your culture and your church. Even in evangelical circles, Christian complacency is rampant. Edwards faced it more directly (as he worked in a state church). But all of us struggle with it daily. As his ministry makes clear, moreover, this problem is treated effectively with faithful, learned, responsive, heartfelt, biblical theology, spiritual conversation and "social religion."

Thesis #2: Edwards shows us that true religion is primarily a matter of holy affections. Christian doctrine is meant to be tasted, not just memorized, affirmed and then debated with those who differ. God communicates with us in order to draw us near to him. He helps us grow in spiritual knowledge so we can grow in divine love. Head and heart must work together. "There is a difference between having an opinion that God is holy and gracious, and having a sense of the loveliness and beauty of that holiness and grace." God reveals himself to us and dwells within us by his Spirit to inform, guide and fashion our love for him and those around us.

Thesis #3: Edwards shows us the advantages of keeping an eschatological perspective on our lives. The tyranny of the urgent and the pressure to "succeed" can thwart our Christian faith and practice. Keeping our minds on things eternal, though, can strengthen us for the day. As we remember God's call on our lives, his larger purposes for our work, as well as his promise to sustain us, we are emboldened to be the people he created us to be. Those who trust in Scripture truth—who really believe in God and his Word—have less debilitating fear than most conventional "believers." Conviction of the reality of heaven, hell and eternity provides the kind of perspective that can keep priorities straight. Those who truly fear the Lord are free to act with holy boldness, to do the right thing whatever the cost (including the loss of livelihood and public humiliation).

Thesis #4: Edwards shows us how God uses those who lose their lives for Christ. Those who live for themselves will lose themselves (Mt 10:39). But those who live for Christ, who die to themselves and cling to the cross, find themselves and their fulfillment in the One who loves them most. Edwards lived as a real martyr—a literal witness (Greek: *martys*) to his Lord—not a man with a martyr complex. He lived "with all his might" for "God's glory" while he lived. He shows us how to get over ourselves. He teaches us to see our lives as part of God's eternal plan to glorify himself through the redemption of the world. He certainly had his faults. He was tempted to self-pity. In the end, however, he tried to let the Scriptures set the agenda for his daily life and ministry, refusing to make decisions out of inordinate self-concern.

Thesis #5: Edwards shows us that theology can and should be done primarily in the church, by pastors, for the sake of the people of God. While this was easier to accomplish in his eighteenth-century world— before the professionalization of ministry and the specialization of disciplines—it remains a possibility today. In the early twenty-first century, when many pastors have abdicated their responsibilities as theologians, and many theologians do their work in a way that is lost on the people of God, we need to recover Edwards' model of Christian ministry. *Most* of the *best* theologians in the history of the church were parish pastors. Obviously, however, this is not the case today. Is it any wonder, then, that many struggle to think about their daily lives theologically, and often fail to understand the basics of the faith? I want to be realistic here. A certain amount of specialization is inevitable in complex, market-driven economies. And the specialization of roles within God's kingdom can enhance our Christian ministries. But when our pastors spend the bulk of their time on organizational matters, and professors spend their time on intramural academics, no one is left to do the crucial work of shaping God's people with the Word. Perhaps our pastors and professors, Christian activists and thinkers, need to collaborate more regularly in ministry. Perhaps the laity need to give their pastors time to think and write— for their local congregations and the larger kingdom of God.

Thesis #6: Edwards shows us that even the strongest Christians need support from others. Spiritual leaders need encouragement, advice, accountability. Edwards knew this well, as did many of the Puritans. New England Congregationalists had independent churches. But their pastors met together for prayer, study, counsel and fellowship. They were not lone rangers. They knew better than to strike out on their own.

Thesis #7: Edwards shows us the necessity of remaining in God's Word. Nearly everything discussed in the pages above confirms this thesis. Edwards spent the bulk of his time—nearly every day of his life—reading and meditating on Scripture. He believed his life and ministry depended on this practice. He understood the "importance and advantage" of theology. He taught that "every Christian should make a business of endeavoring to grow" in divine knowledge. He lived with the following truths emblazoned clearly on his life: "every one that useth milk is unskillful in the word of righteousness: for he is a babe. But strong meat belongeth to them that are of full age, even those who by reason of use have their senses exercised to discern both good and evil" (Heb 5:13-14). Would that all of us did the same, consuming a steady diet of "meat" and growing stronger in the Lord.

◦   ◦   ◦

It is only fitting to end a book like this with biblical reflection on the importance of Edwards' ministry. He would surely have shied away from any comparison of his life to that of the heroes of the Bible. But he probably would have condoned a brief comparison of his legacy to that of the ancient Corinthians, whose church was full of the sin and strife to which he was accustomed. As St. Paul addressed these Christians:

> Ye are our epistle written in our hearts, known and read of all men: Forasmuch as ye are manifestly declared to be the epistle of Christ ministered by us, written not with ink, but with the Spirit of the living God; not in tables of stone, but in fleshy tables of the heart. And such trust have we through Christ to God-ward: Not that we are sufficient of ourselves to think any thing as of ourselves; but our sufficiency is of God; Who also hath made us able ministers of the new testament; not of the letter, but of the spirit: for the letter killeth, but the spirit giveth life. . . . Now the Lord is that Spirit: and where the Spirit of the Lord is, there is liberty. But we all, with open face beholding as in a glass the glory of the Lord, are changed into the same image from glory to glory, even as by the Spirit of the Lord. (2 Cor 3:2-6, 17-18)

Edwards, too, is an epistle God has written on many hearts, commending the ministry of the gospel in the lives of countless readers. May his work continue to play a role in binding others to Christ, helping them shine the glory of God throughout the world.

Name and Subject Index

Scripture Index